Wireless Internet Access For Dummies®

D1579343

Choosing a Wireless Phone Provider

1. **Choose a provider first — not the phone.**

   Phones are programmed to work with certain providers, so you must choose the provider and then choose a supported Web-enabled phone.

2. **Check out the coverage maps.**

   All providers do not provide phone or Internet access in the same areas.

3. **Identify the home area.**

   Which areas can you call without being charged long-distance or roaming fees?

4. **Find a rate plan that is right for your needs and your wallet.**

   Take the time to shop around and get the deal that's right for you.

5. **Determine how you pay for the wireless Internet access.**

   Are you charged a flat rate or does Internet usage burn your airtime minutes?

6. **Buy yourself enough time.**

   If Internet usage burns airtime minutes, make sure you buy enough airtime minutes to meet both your Internet needs and your voice needs. On the other hand, do not purchase too many minutes, because you cannot transfer unused minutes from one month to the next.

7. **Find the freebies.**

   Watch for special plans and promotions that give you free weekend or night time usage.

8. **Don't be shy.**

   Ask your salesperson lots of questions!

Choosing a Web-Enabled Phone

1. **Choose a provider first.**

   You must purchase a phone that is compatible with your provider.

2. **Check the comfort of the phone.**

   How does the phone feel in your hand? Does it offer a comfortable fit when you hold it up to your ear and mouth? Are the keys easy to press? Can you hold the phone in one hand and press the keys with your thumb?

3. **Take a hard look at the screen.**

   Is the screen clear and easy to read? How many lines of text can the screen display? (Most can display three to five lines.)

4. **Check out the screen menus.**

   Are the menus easy to use and intuitive? Have a salesperson walk you through their usage and then decide whether you like the design.

5. **Take the keypad for a test drive.**

   The Yes/No, arrow, and Talk buttons should be easy to use and close to each other. Does the keypad have a clear, intuitive design so you can use the phone without staring at the keyboard?

6. **Explore model types.**

   Some phones are very small, some are larger, some use a flip-phone design, and some look more like a pager or personal digital assistant. Spend a few moments handling each one so you can determine which features you like — and which ones you don't.

7. **Take stock of the features the phone supports.**

   Wireless surfing and text messaging? What about voice recognition? Make sure the phone model offers all the features you want.

8. **Check the battery.**

   A typical charge should give you three to four hours of talk time and standby charge that lasts four to five days.

Wireless Internet Access For Dummies®

Cheat Sheet

Major Provider Web Sites Quick Reference

- **AT&T Wireless:** www.attwireless.com
- **Cingular Wireless:** www.cingular.com
- **Nextel Wireless:** www.nextel.com
- **Palm:** www.palm.com or www.palm.net
- **Research In Motion / Blackberry:** www.rim.net or www.blackberry.net
- **Sprint PCS:** www.sprintpcs.com
- **Verizon Wireless:** www.verizonwireless.com
- **VoiceStream Wireless:** www.voicestream.com

Wireless E-Mail Tips to Remember

- You cannot send or receive e-mail attachments with wireless devices.
- Wireless devices are intended for short, quick e-mail messages.
- Your provider establishes your e-mail account. Depending on your provider and your device, you may be able to access Internet e-mail, or even corporate e-mail.
- You can get all your mail by creating forwarding rules that send a copy of your mail from your wired ISP to your wireless ISP. (See Chapter 8 for details.)

Curt's Cool 10 WAP Sites

This book's Wireless Internet Access Online Directory includes a listing of WAP-enabled sites, but I've highlighted 10 of the cooler and more unusual sites you should visit on your wireless device:

- www.afterdawn.com: Get all your favorite MP3 and DVD news and info here. Very cool!
- www.atomica.com: Enter a word or topic and get all kinds of information — everything from news to translations.
- www.cheatsheets.net: Keep up with football projections and rankings here.
- www.funny.com: Come on, we all love jokes. Visit this site and give yourself a laugh or two.
- www.galaxies.com: Find out all kinds of cool information about our solar system here.
- www.mymotivator.com: Get motivated for the day by getting a "get going" quote! You can find all kinds of motivational quotes on this site.
- www.mysterynet.com: Love a good mystery? Then check out this WAP site and have fun solving mysteries and playing games.
- www.ngame.com: N Games provides multiplayer games for wireless devices. Check it out!
- www.peakadventures.net: Find information about cool trips and locations that you can visit.
- www.themeparkinsider.com: Get the lowdown on various theme parks and attractions.

Hungry Minds™

For Dummies: Bestselling Book Series for Beginners

™

References for the Rest of Us!®

BESTSELLING BOOK SERIES

Are you intimidated and confused by computers? Do you find that traditional manuals are overloaded with technical details you'll never use? Do your friends and family always call you to fix simple problems on their PCs? Then the For Dummies® computer book series from Hungry Minds, Inc. is for you.

For Dummies books are written for those frustrated computer users who know they aren't really dumb but find that PC hardware, software, and indeed the unique vocabulary of computing make them feel helpless. For Dummies books use a lighthearted approach, a down-to-earth style, and even cartoons and humorous icons to dispel computer novices' fears and build their confidence. Lighthearted but not lightweight, these books are a perfect survival guide for anyone forced to use a computer.

Already, millions of satisfied readers agree. They have made For Dummies books the #1 introductory level computer book series and have written asking for more. So, if you're looking for the most fun and easy way to learn about computers, look to For Dummies books to give you a helping hand.

Hungry Minds™

1/01

Wireless Internet Access

FOR

DUMMIES®

Wireless Internet Access

FOR

DUMMIES®

by Curt Simmons

Hungry Minds™

Best-Selling Books • Digital Downloads • e-Books • Answer Networks
e-Newsletters • Branded Web Sites • e-Learning

New York, NY ◆ Cleveland, OH ◆ Indianapolis, IN

Wireless Internet Access For Dummies®

Published by
Hungry Minds, Inc.
909 Third Avenue
New York, NY 10022
www.hungryminds.com
www.dummies.com

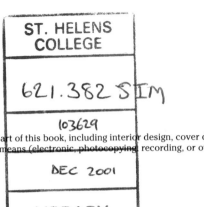
Library of Congress Control Number: 2001089276

ISBN: 0-7645-0853-9

Printed in the United States of America

10 9 8 7 6 5 4 3 2 1

1B/RV/QW/QR/IN

Distributed in the United States by Hungry Minds, Inc.

Distributed by CDG Books Canada Inc. for Canada; by Transworld Publishers Limited in the United Kingdom; by IDG Norge Books for Norway; by IDG Sweden Books for Sweden; by IDG Books Australia Publishing Corporation Pty. Ltd. for Australia and New Zealand; by TransQuest Publishers Pte Ltd. for Singapore, Malaysia, Thailand, Indonesia, and Hong Kong; by Gotop Information Inc. for Taiwan; by ICG Muse, Inc. for Japan; by Intersoft for South Africa; by Eyrolles for France; by International Thomson Publishing for Germany, Austria and Switzerland; by Distribuidora Cuspide for Argentina; by LR International for Brazil; by Galileo Libros for Chile; by Ediciones ZETA S.C.R. Ltda. for Peru; by WS Computer Publishing Corporation, Inc., for the Philippines; by Contemporanea de Ediciones for Venezuela; by Express Computer Distributors for the Caribbean and West Indies; by Micronesia Media Distributor, Inc. for Micronesia; by Chips Computadoras S.A. de C.V. for Mexico; by Editorial Norma de Panama S.A. for Panama; by American Bookshops for Finland.

For general information on Hungry Minds' products and services please contact our Customer Care Department within the U.S. at 800-762-2974, outside the U.S. at 317-572-3993 or fax 317-572-4002.

For sales inquiries and reseller information, including discounts, premium and bulk quantity sales, and foreign-language translations, please contact our Customer Care Department at 800-434-3422, fax 317-572-4002, or write to Hungry Minds, Inc., Attn: Customer Care Department, 10475 Crosspoint Boulevard, Indianapolis, IN 46256.

For information on licensing foreign or domestic rights, please contact our Sub-Rights Customer Care Department at 212-884-5000.

For information on using Hungry Minds' products and services in the classroom or for ordering examination copies, please contact our Educational Sales Department at 800-434-2086 or fax 317-572-4005.

For press review copies, author interviews, or other publicity information, please contact our Public Relations Department at 317-572-3168 or fax 317-572-4168.

For authorization to photocopy items for corporate, personal, or educational use, please contact Copyright Clearance Center, 222 Rosewood Drive, Danvers, MA 01923, or fax 978-750-4470.

Hungry Minds™ is a trademark of Hungry Minds, Inc.

About the Author

Curt Simmons is a technology author and trainer. Curt has written numerous computing books on Microsoft technologies as well as test-preparation books to help readers get ready for the Microsoft Certified Systems Engineer (MCSE) exams. He loves all new technology — especially anything to do with the Internet. Curt lives in a small town outside Dallas with his wife, Dawn, and their children. When he is not writing about technology and playing with new technology gadgets, he spends most of his time working on his 100-year-old historical home. You can visit Curt on the Internet at `http://curtsimmons.hypermart.net`.

Author's Acknowledgments

I would like to thank everyone at Hungry Minds for giving me the opportunity to write this book, particularly Carol Sheehan, for giving me the green light. As always, thanks to John Pont, one of the world's best editors, for making my words and sentences look and sound great. Thanks to my wife, Dawn, who helped craft several portions of this book and who helped research the wireless Internet. (Okay, next time, I'll give you the instructions before you start working!) Thanks to my agent, Margot Maley, at Waterside Productions, who helps manage my career. Thanks also to my technical reviewer, Gayle Ehrenman, for all her hard work on this book. Finally, thanks to all the companies and Web site owners who gave me permission to show you pictures of their products.

Publisher's Acknowledgments

We're proud of this book; please send us your comments through our Hungry Minds Online Registration Form located at www.dummies.com.

Some of the people who helped bring this book to market include the following:

Acquisitions, Editorial, and Media Development

Project Editor: John W. Pont

Acquisitions Editor: Carol Sheehan

Technical Editor: Gayle Ehrenman

Editorial Manager: Constance Carlisle

Editorial Assistants: Amanda Foxworth, Jean Rogers

Production

Project Coordinator: Regina Snyder

Layout and Graphics: Amy Adrian, Jackie Nicholas, Julie Trippetti, Jeremey Unger

Proofreaders: Andy Hollandbeck, Charles Spencer

Indexer: TECHBOOKS Production Services

General and Administrative

Hungry Minds, Inc.: John Kilcullen, CEO; Bill Barry, President and COO; John Ball, Executive VP, Operations & Administration; John Harris, CFO

Hungry Minds Technology Publishing Group: Richard Swadley, Senior Vice President and Publisher; Mary Bednarek, Vice President and Publisher, Networking and Certification; Walter R. Bruce III, Vice President and Publisher, General User and Design Professional; Joseph Wikert, Vice President and Publisher, Programming; Mary C. Corder, Editorial Director, Branded Technology Editorial; Andy Cummings, Publishing Director, General User and Design Professional; Barry Pruett, Publishing Director, Visual

Hungry Minds Manufacturing: Ivor Parker, Vice President, Manufacturing

Hungry Minds Marketing: John Helmus, Assistant Vice President, Director of Marketing

Hungry Minds Production for Branded Press: Debbie Stailey, Production Director

Hungry Minds Sales: Roland Elgey, Senior Vice President, Sales and Marketing; Michael Violano, Vice President, International Sales and Sub Rights

◆

The publisher would like to give special thanks to Patrick J. McGovern, without whom this book would not have been possible.

◆

Contents at a Glance

Introduction 1

Part I: Getting to Know the Wireless Internet 7
Chapter 1: The Wireless Internet and You 9
Chapter 2: Getting Connected to the Wireless Internet 25
Chapter 3: Putting the Wireless Internet to Work (and Play) 41

Part II: Choosing a Wireless Device 49
Chapter 4: Choosing a Wireless Internet Phone 51
Chapter 5: Choosing a Web-Enabled Pager 67
Chapter 6: Choosing a Wireless Personal Digital Assistant 77
Chapter 7: Wireless Devices of the Future 99

Part III: Communicating on the Wireless Internet 121
Chapter 8: Using Wireless E-Mail 123
Chapter 9: Having Fun with Instant Messaging 139
Chapter 10: Using a Wireless Calendar 145

Part IV: Working and Playing on the Wireless Internet 151
Chapter 11: Surfing the Wireless Internet 153
Chapter 12: Keeping Up With Your Money 167
Chapter 13: Shopping on the Wireless Internet 173
Chapter 14: Wireless and Your World 187

Part V: The Part of Tens 197
Chapter 15: Ten Common Questions and Answers
About the Wireless Internet 199
Chapter 16: Almost Ten Things You Can't Do with Wireless Internet Devices 205
Chapter 17: Ten Great Web-Enabled Phone Accessories 209
Chapter 18: Ten Great Wireless Internet Web Sites 213

The Wireless Internet Access Directory.......................D-1

Index 219

Book Registration Information....................Back of Book

Cartoons at a Glance

By Rich Tennant

page 151

page 49

page 197

page 7

page 121

Cartoon Information:
Fax: 978-546-7747
E-Mail: richtennant@the5thwave.com
World Wide Web: www.the5thwave.com

Table of Contents

Introduction **1**

About This Book 1
Foolish Assumptions 2
How to Use This Book 2
How This Book Is Organized 3
  Part I: Getting to Know the Wireless Internet 3
  Part II: Choosing a Wireless Device 3
  Part III: Communicating on the Wireless Internet 4
  Part IV: Working and Playing on the Wireless Internet 4
  Part V: The Part of Tens 4
  The Wireless Internet Access Directory 4
Conventions Used in This Book 5
Icons Used in This Book 5
Where to Go From Here 6

Part 1: Getting to Know the Wireless Internet **7**

Chapter 1: The Wireless Internet and You **9**

Exploring the Wireless Internet 9
  Defining the wireless Internet 10
  Living the wireless life 10
  Following your business 11
  Getting your information 11
Checking Out Wireless Internet Devices 12
  Dialing in to Web-enabled phones 13
  Calling all Web-enabled pagers 15
  Hiring your very own personal digital assistant (PDA) ...16
  What can these devices really do? 17
Taking Care of Business with the Wireless Internet 18
  Breaking free from the wired world 18
  Getting information 19
Managing Your Life with the Wireless Internet 20
  Getting information your way 20
  Keeping track of your money 20
  Shopping online 20
  Finding your way 20
  Having fun 21
Defining Your Needs 21
  Defining your business needs 21
  Defining your personal needs 22
Spending a Day in My Wireless World 22

Chapter 2: Getting Connected to the Wireless Internet 25

Understanding the Basics of Internet Connections 26
Hey, Where's the Plug? 27
    Hooking up with a PDA 28
    Getting connected with a Web-enabled phone 28
Sizing Up the Major Wireless Service Providers 34
    AT&T Digital PocketNet: National coverage and flexible plans 35
    Sprint PCS: Great rates, great coverage .37
    Verizon Wireless: Easy plan 37
    Cingular Wireless: Single, simple plans .38
    Nextel Online: Services for business 38
    VoiceStream: E-mail and alerts 39

Chapter 3: Putting the Wireless Internet to Work (and Play) 41

Working with the Wireless Internet 42
    Information on the go 42
    Portable e-mail 43
    Calendars to keep track of appointments 44
    Wireless messaging 45
    News at your fingertips 46
    Travel information that travels with you .46
Living with the Wireless Internet 47
    Bringing information to you 48
    Having fun 48

Part II: Choosing a Wireless Device *49*

Chapter 4: Choosing a Wireless Internet Phone 51

Understanding Wireless Phone Technology 52
Considering Internet Phone Features 54
    Holding the phone 54
    Feeling comfy? 54
    Casing the joint 55
    Checking out the antenna 55
    Getting in touch with the keypad 56
    Putting the screen on display 57
    Double-checking features 59
    Getting a charge out of the battery 59
Choosing the Phone That's Right for You 59
Quick Directory of Wireless Internet Phone Manufacturers 60
    Alcatel 61
    Audiovox 61
    Casio 61
    Denso 61
    Ericsson 62
    Kyocera 63

Mitsubishi 63
Motorola 64
NeoPoint 64
Nokia 65
Philips 65
Samsung 65
Sanyo 65
Siemens 65

Chapter 5: Choosing a Web-Enabled Pager 67

Getting to Know Web-Enabled Pagers 67
Checking Out Web-Enabled Pager Features 68
Examining Web-Enabled Pager Service Plans 69
    Finding a service provider 69
    Purchasing the desired plan 70
    Choosing a pager 71
Quick Catalog of Web-Enabled Pagers 72
    RIM BlackBerry 950 72
    Motorola Personal Interactive Communicators 73

Chapter 6: Choosing a Wireless Personal Digital Assistant 77

Understanding How PDAs Work 78
    Checking out two primary types of PDAs 78
    Scoping out PDA operating systems 79
    Using applications with PDAs 81
    Synching up with the desktop computer 81
Understanding What a PDA Does 82
    Making a date 83
    Keeping up with people 83
    Taking care of business 85
    Managing your memos 85
    Tracking your expenses 85
    Securing your information 86
Accessing the Wireless Internet with a PDA 86
    Getting connected 87
    Surfing the Internet with a PDA 88
    Using e-mail with a wireless PDA 89
Quick Catalog of Web-Enabled PDAs 91
    Palm: Wireless Internet and e-mail 91
    RIM BlackBerry: Access to corporate e-mail 93
    Compaq iPAQ: Versatile and powerful 95
    HP Jornada 540 Series: Complete computing in your hand 96

Chapter 7: Wireless Devices of the Future 99

Where Have We Been? 99
    Remembering the Internet 100
    Remembering the computer . . . from surfing to crawling 103

What Do Wireless Internet Users Want? 104
    Freedom from desktop PCs 104
    Quick, easy searches for Internet information 104
    Real content, pictures, and files 105
    Small devices that can do everything 105
    One simple interface — not a bunch of applications 106
    Control over the content that enters our homes 106
    An Internet that knows who we are 106
Where Is the Internet Headed? 107
    Automatic recognition 107
    Universal data manipulation 108
    Customizable user experience 108
    More interactivity 109
Where Are Wireless Devices Headed? 109
    Space savers 110
    Multiple-function products 110
    Appliance-based computing 110
    Human interface 111
What Can We Expect from Wireless Internet Devices of Tomorrow? ...112
    Combination devices 113
    Information on the move 115
    Natural communication 117

Part III: Communicating on the Wireless Internet 121

Chapter 8: Using Wireless E-Mail 123

E-Mail 101: Reviewing the Basics 123
    Understanding how e-mail works 124
    Growing attached to e-mail attachments 125
    Reviewing the basics of e-mail accounts 126
Wireless E-Mail 101: Understanding the Differences 127
Getting Connected to Your Wireless E-Mail 128
Using Your Wireless E-Mail 129
    Creating and sending an e-mail message 129
    Receiving e-mail 130
Managing Contacts 132
    Storing contact data on your PDA 132
    Storing contact data with a Web-enabled phone 133
Getting Other Internet Mail on Your Wireless Device 134

Chapter 9: Having Fun with Instant Messaging 139

Getting to Know Instant Messaging 139
Why Use Instant Messaging? 140
    Saving money 141
    Communicating on the run 141
    Making work easy 141

Talking to people who can't talk 142
Having fun 142
Understanding How Instant Messaging Works 142
Sending Messages via the Wired Internet 143
Quick Tips for Instant Messaging 144

Chapter 10: Using a Wireless Calendar **145**

Getting to Know Electronic Calendars 145
Making Dates with Your PDA 147
Calling up a Calendar on Your Web-Enabled Phone 148
Considering Web Calendar Options 149
Curt's Calendar Quick Tips 149

Part IV: Working and Playing
on the Wireless Internet *151*

Chapter 11: Surfing the Wireless Internet **153**

Surfing in the Wired World 153
Understanding Web addressing 154
Hyperlinking around the world 155
Surfing in the Wireless World 157
Surfing on a PDA 158
Deleting wireless Web applications 160
Surfing on a Web-enabled phone 162

Chapter 12: Keeping Up With Your Money **167**

E-Money and You! 167
Managing Your Money with the Wireless Internet 169
Banking at the lake 169
Finding an ATM 170
Managing cards and accounts 170
Exploring other money management tools 171
Investing Online via the Wireless Internet 171

Chapter 13: Shopping on the Wireless Internet **173**

Shopping at the World's Biggest Mall 173
You can find anything and everything 174
You can shop anytime, anywhere 174
The Internet is not grouchy 175
The Internet remembers you 175
It never rains, snows, or hails on the Internet 175
Products are always where they are "supposed" to be ...176
Prices are usually lower 176
You can comparison shop in one place 177
You can shop at stores in distant locations 177
You can shop in your underwear 177

Practicing Safe Shopping 177
Understanding Internet Shipping and Returns 179
Managing Internet shipping 180
Returning items purchased online 181
Shopping the Wireless Internet 182
Finding shopping sites 182
Searching for products on wireless Internet shopping sites 183
Purchasing an item 184
Checking the status of your order 184
Having even more shopping-related fun
on the wireless Internet 185

Chapter 14: Wireless and Your World **187**
Getting the News 187
Following Sports 188
Watching the Weather 190
Getting Travel Help 191
Planning an Evening Out 193
Getting Information 193
Having Fun 195

Part V: The Part of Tens *197*

Chapter 15 : Ten Common Questions and Answers
About the Wireless Internet **199**
Can I Access Corporate E-Mail via the Wireless Internet? 199
Can I Send and Receive E-Mail Attachments? 200
How Am I Billed for My Wireless Internet Access? 200
What Kind of Internet Access Plans Are Available? 201
Why Doesn't My Wireless Internet Device Work in All Locations? 201
Can I Access Any Web Site on the Internet? 202
Do Wireless Devices Provide Any Security? 202
Which Wireless Internet Service Is Best? 202
What Is the Coolest New Wireless Device Coming onto the Market? ...203
Where Can I Get Current Information about Wireless Devices? 203

Chapter 16: Almost Ten Things You Can't Do
with Wireless Internet Devices **205**
Welcome to a Barren Graphics Landscape 205
No Web Surfing 206
No Favorites or Bookmarks 206
May I Have a Cookie? 206
No File Downloads Allowed 207
No E-Mail Attachments 207
No E-Mail Formatting 207
Little to No Support for Internet Multimedia 208
Black Holes Abound 208

Chapter 17: Ten Great Web-Enabled Phone Accessories 209

Getting a Cool Removable Faceplate 209
Talking Freely with a Headset 210
Going Hands-Free in Your Car 210
Keeping Charged and Ready 210
Getting a Charge from Your Car 211
Living Longer with a Lithium Battery 211
Displaying Your Phone on a Belt Clip 211
Keeping Your Phone Secure with a Case 211
Using a Replacement Antenna 212
Working at Your Desk 212

Chapter 18: Ten Great Wireless Internet Web Sites 213

Unstrung 213
ZDNet 214
WirelessAdvisor.com 214
Internet Wireless Access 215
Cellular Telecommunications & Internet Association 215
Wireless Week 216
The W@P Forum 216
The Gadgeteer 216
MSN Computing Central 216
Wireless.com 217

The Wireless Internet Access Directory *D-1*

About This Directory D-3
Entertainment D-3
Financial Sites D-12
News and Sports Sites D-18
Reference and Directories D-28
Shopping D-38
Travel Information and Assistance D-40

Index *219*

Book Registration Information ....*Back of Book*

Introduction

. . . .

*I*magine a world where you are free to roam. A world where you can access your e-mail, cruise the Internet, and get all the information you need — anytime and anywhere — without being stuck in front of a PC. Thanks to the wireless devices I describe in this book, this world is reality, not a dreamland. The world of wireless Internet access is here, and you can break free from the wired PC world.

For example, if you're stuck in a traffic jam, you don't have to sit mindlessly listening to the radio and tapping your fingers on the steering wheel. While you wait on the traffic, why not catch up on some business e-mail, or go online and buy that book you want? The wireless Internet has burst on the scene with Web-enabled phones, pagers, and wireless handheld devices. It's all there for the taking, and believe it or not, the wireless Internet is easy to use and reasonably priced. The future is now — and the future is wireless!

About This Book

I wrote this book to help you make the most of the wireless Internet. I understand that you have to sift through lots of choices and lots of advertisements, and choosing a wireless device can get a little confusing. And after you find the wireless device that meets your needs, you have to figure out how to put it to work for you. Don't worry about getting lost, though; this book serves as your roadmap to wireless Internet access — a place where you can get information quickly and easily.

No matter why you are interested in wireless Internet access, this book can help you find your way in the wireless world. The wireless Internet gives you the freedom you need while giving you the information you need. It's fun, helpful, convenient, and I must say, very cool. This book will help you choose the right device and service plan for your needs, as well as show you how to use the wireless Internet easily and effectively.

Foolish Assumptions

As I write, I try to picture my audience, and in doing so, I have made the following assumptions about you, the reader:

✔ You are naturally curious. You want to know what technology is available and how you can use it to make your life easier and better.

✔ You are familiar with the Internet and e-mail. Because you are thinking about joining the wireless world, I assume that you already know a thing or two about e-mail and the Internet. You probably own a PC, or least have access to one.

✔ You use e-mail and the Internet for either personal or business communications — or both.

✔ Although you use e-mail and the Internet frequently, you would rather not spend your entire day staring at a computer.

✔ You are on the go. During your daily routine, you move from one location to the next, which is why wireless Internet is so intriguing to you.

✔ You want fast and easy information about the wireless Internet. After all, your life is on the move and you want a book that moves with you!

✔ You are an intelligent, attractive person with exceptionally high standards in all facets of your life. After all, you bought this book.

How to Use This Book

My goal in writing this book is to deliver the information you need in an easy-to-read, no-nonsense manner. I understand that you do not want to wade through hundreds of pages of background information, nerdy technical details, and lengthy descriptions of obscure features that you probably will not use. I designed this book so you can quickly get the information you need and then get on with your life.

Like all the *For Dummies* books, *Wireless Internet Access For Dummies* is a reference, not a book that you should read from cover to cover. Feel free to skip around. And when you are done skipping, use the book's table of contents or index to locate the information you need. Then, turn directly to the appropriate pages, find the answers to your questions, and get back to work (or play) with your wireless device.

How This Book Is Organized

To make information in this book as accessible as possible, I've organized the book into five parts, with each part exploring a specific facet of wireless Internet access. In addition to the five parts, the book also includes a handy directory of wireless Internet sites.

Here's a brief overview of what you'll find in each part of the book.

Part 1: Getting to Know the Wireless Internet

So, you want to use the wireless Internet, do you? Part I gets your feet on solid ground by helping you understand what the wireless Internet is all about and what it can do for you. In Chapter 1, you gain a perspective of how the wireless Internet can help you in your personal life and in your business, and how you can define your wireless Internet needs. In Chapter 2, you find out about getting connected to the wireless Web with the service provider that best meets your needs. You explore common service contracts and the nitty-gritty of what the wireless Internet will cost you. And in Chapter 3, you discover how to put the wireless Internet to work for you, as well as how you can have some fun on the wireless Internet.

Part 11: Choosing a Wireless Device

Okay, you're hooked and you can't wait to get connected to the wireless Internet. Turn to the chapters in Part II when you need to decide on a service plan and the type of wireless device that you want to use.

Chapter 4 examines the most popular type of device, the Web-enabled phone. Web-enabled phones look and act like regular cell phones, but they also enable you to use the Internet. As I explain in Chapter 5, you also can access the wireless Internet via Web-enabled pagers. These devices look and act just like regular two-way pagers, but also enable you to get your e-mail, send e-mail, access the Internet, and even send two-way messages. Chapter 6 explores wireless personal digital assistants (PDAs), or *handhelds* — small computers that can do all sorts of things, including access the Internet. And in Chapter 7, I take a little artistic license, describing some wireless devices that you may see in the near future.

Part III: Communicating on the Wireless Internet

The wireless Internet enables you to keep up with your e-mail and even use instant messaging, no matter where you are. In Part III, I explain how you can communicate with friends, family, and business partners using the wireless Internet. Chapter 8 explores wireless e-mail and shows you how it works. In Chapter 9, I show you how to communicate directly with someone using instant messaging, a very cool feature of the wireless Internet. Chapter 10 explains how you can make the most of the calendar functions in your wireless device.

Part IV: Working and Playing on the Wireless Internet

You can access a vast array of specialized Web sites that cater to users of wireless Internet devices. In Part IV, you explore various ways in which you can work and have fun on the wireless Internet. Chapter 11 explains how to surf the wireless Internet using each type of wireless device. In Chapter 12, you explore resources that the wireless Internet offers to help you manage your money. Chapter 13 explains what you need to know about shopping in a wireless world. And in Chapter 14, you find out how to access news, travel information, weather reports, and all manner of fun, all from your handy wireless device.

Part V: The Part of Tens

Like all *For Dummies* books, *Wireless Internet Access For Dummies* includes a Part of Tens — a group of chapters in which I give you concise, top ten-style lists of useful information. In this part, you find ten common questions and answers about the wireless Internet, ten limitations of wireless devices, ten great accessories for your wireless device, and ten great wireless Web sites.

The Wireless Internet Access Directory

So, exactly which Web sites support wireless devices? I tell you which sites you can visit and what those sites are all about in this book's Wireless Internet Access Directory.

Conventions Used in This Book

To help you get the information you need quickly and painlessly, I employ several features throughout the pages of this book:

- ✔ Tables compare information. I use tables only for really important information, so pay close attention to any tables you see.

- ✔ Bulleted lists give you a quick snapshot of information. In many cases, I use bulleted lists to highlight important features or even potential problems, so always skim through a bulleted list when you see one.

- ✔ A special `monotype font` points out Internet sites. When you see an Internet site, such as `www.hungryminds.com`, you know you are looking at an exact address you can access on the Internet.

- ✔ Numbered lists describe step-by-step processes, showing you how to use wireless e-mail and the Internet. However, this book does not focus on a particular wireless Internet device, and the actual steps you need to follow will vary from device to device. Use this book as a guide, but remember to check your wireless Internet device's instructions as well.

- ✔ The general term *wireless device* refers to any Web-enabled phone, pager, or PDA (handheld). I clearly identify those instances in which I refer to a specific wireless device, such as a Web-enabled phone.

Wireless devices all work a little differently, so I give you various instructions along the way. For example, if I say press a button, use your fingers to press that particular button one time. If I'm talking about a wireless handheld device that uses a stylus, I may say tap the screen. This instruction means that you should touch the screen one time with your stylus.

Icons Used in This Book

Throughout the book, I use icons to point out important information that you should note. Pay attention when you come across any of the following icons in the margins of this book:

The Cross-Reference icon points the way to related information in another part of the book.

The Remember icon points out some really important piece of information that you should not forget.

The Technical Stuff icon points out technical details that you can read if you like, but also safely skip.

A Tip icon identifies a piece of friendly advice that may save you time or give you one of those "Ah-ha" moments.

A Warning icon alerts you to a potential problem or pitfall. Be sure to check these out!

Where to Go From Here

Are you ready? The wireless Internet is waiting for you, and it's all there for the taking. Dive into this book, get the information you need, make a purchase decision, and join the millions of other people who are flying without wires. If you're still trying to figure out the wireless Internet, jump right into Part I, and I'll show you what it's all about. If you're familiar with the wireless Internet and already have a good idea of what you need, move on to Part II.

Part I
Getting to Know the Wireless Internet

The 5th Wave   By Rich Tennant

EXPERIMENTING WITH THE WIRELESS LASER BEAM NETWORK

"Okay—did you get that?"

In this part . . .

The wireless Internet is a cool and fun place to work and play, and the chapters in this part of the book help you discover what the wireless Internet is all about. In Chapter 1, you explore what you can do on the wireless Internet. In Chapter 2, you find out how you can get connected to the wireless Internet. Chapter 3 describes how you can put the wireless Internet to work for you — and how you can have fun in the wireless world.

Chapter 1

The Wireless Internet and You

In This Chapter

▶ Breaking free from the wired world

▶ Examining wireless Internet devices

▶ Getting down to business on the wireless Internet

▶ Managing your life in an unwired world

▶ Defining your business and personal needs

▶ Taking a walk in my wireless shoes

A s you think about the wireless Internet, you may feel a bit confused. After all, you see too many ads, too many devices, and yes, too much conflicting information. Fortunately, you have this book to help you make sense of all this wireless stuff.

To get you started on the right track, this chapter introduces you to the wireless Internet and explains how it can help you — both in your business and in other facets of your life. I introduce you to the various types of wireless devices you can choose, provide guidelines for defining your wireless Internet needs, and then invite you to spend a day with me in my wireless world.

Exploring the Wireless Internet

The wireless Internet gives you the freedom to access your e-mail and surf the Internet anytime, anywhere. For example, you can catch up on your e-mail messages while you wait for a connecting flight or do a little online shopping while you're stuck in a traffic jam.

This freedom represents an important change in Internet access. With wireless Internet access, you have almost complete control over when and where you access the Internet. In contrast, old-fashioned, wired connections sometimes seem to control their users.

Defining the wireless Internet

Before you jump into the details of the wireless Internet and see how the wireless Internet can help you, the phrase *wireless Internet* needs a quick definition. Is the wireless Internet the Internet that lives in the sky, or is it a separate part of the wired Internet, or is it . . . ?

The wireless Internet is the same thing as the wired Internet; you just access it differently. Using special communication protocols, wireless devices can access Web sites that support wireless technology and get the information you want. Web pages, e-mail, stock quotes, the news — they're all available from Internet sites that support wireless communication.

Living the wireless life

Before the advent of the wireless Internet, Internet access made puppets of many users. The wired Internet plays the role of puppeteer, controlling what the wired users can and can't do. To understand what I mean, consider an average workday: I sit at a PC and send and receive e-mail for the day. I answer all my mail, grab my laptop, and then dash off to a meeting. During a break from the meeting, I need to check my e-mail again, so I have to find a phone jack where I can connect. After the meeting, I rush back to my PC, answer more e-mail, and then order a birthday present for my wife from an online merchant. On my way home, while sitting in rush-hour traffic, I realize that I ordered the wrong size. If I could only get to the Internet, I could change the order, but now I'm stuck in traffic. . . .

Sound familiar? Like a puppeteer, the wired Internet constantly pulls you one way or the other. You're not in control of information; instead, it controls you because of the wired restrictions you face. As the Internet has become more and more important to us all, those wired restrictions have become more and more pervasive. "I use the Internet for work and play, but being stuck in front of a PC all the time is a real drag." Does this sound like you? If so, you're not alone.

Fortunately, you can join the millions of people who are breaking free from the wired world's puppet strings by entering the wireless world. Instead of running to a computer and a wired connection whenever you need to access the Internet, you can take the Internet with you — with no strings . . . er, I mean wires . . . attached.

Don't take this to mean that you'll never need the wired Internet again. The wireless Internet and wireless Internet devices probably will not meet every Internet need you have. In fact, wireless Internet access has some important restrictions, which I explore in this book. So, don't throw out your computer just yet!

Following your business

In the olden days, you arrived at the office, did your work, and then went home. On the digital scene in the 21st century, workers are more mobile and need access to information all the time. When the Internet first came onto the scene, many people thought it would solve all of our information problems. Electronic business would flourish, and life would never be the same.

In a sense, that has happened. But despite all that the Internet can offer business, and all the ways that businesses can leverage the power of the Internet, the technology still falls short of expectations. *Bandwidth* — the speed of the Internet — presents a problem; finding information you need continues to be a major issue; and obtaining quick, easy access to the Internet is no small task.

The restrictions of the wired Internet tend to slow business down, but the wireless Internet can help solve these kinds of problems. With handheld wireless devices and Web-enabled phones, your e-mail and data are only a few key presses away — wherever you may be. You can access news, pull up financial sites and see what is happening on the stock market, access your datebook — all of this while you are away from the office.

So, what can the wireless Internet do for your business? Just about anything you need it to do, and this book shows you all that is available.

Getting your information

You may be thinking, "Okay, this all sounds great, but what can I really do with the wireless Internet?" Allow me to subdue your excitement for a moment. You can't get everything on the Internet via wireless devices — not yet anyway. In most cases, however, you can get what you need. For example, you can use the wireless Internet to

- ✔ **Send and receive e-mail:** As I've already mentioned, you can send and receive e-mail using wireless Internet devices.
- ✔ **Manage your time:** You can use Web calendars to keep track of your schedule and appointments while you're away from your home or office.
- ✔ **Buy items online:** The wireless Internet supports many popular online merchants where you can buy products, such as Buy.com, Amazon.com, BN.com, and many more.
- ✔ **Get information:** You can gather all kinds of information from *Web portals* — Web sites that give you access to personalized information, such as weather, news, shopping, games, and much more. Common examples of Web portals include AOL, MSN, Yahoo!, and Go.

✔ **Find yourself:** Feeling lost in a new city? You can access map information to help you find your way. Pull up travel information from Web sites, such as `Travelocity.com` and `Mapquest.com`, and even check the local weather.

✔ **Send instant messages:** Need to send an instant message to Uncle Bob's Web phone? No problem! Instant messaging (also known as direct messaging or short text messaging) enables you to send brief messages directly to other wireless devices. It's like a pager with no phone numbers to remember.

✔ **Keep informed:** You can access popular news sites to see what's going on in the world.

✔ **Check out sports results:** Missing the big game because you are stuck on the freeway? Use the wireless Internet to get the latest scores. You can access news and sports sites like `CNN.com`, `ESPN.com`, `Footballguys.com`, and many more.

✔ **Make money:** You can keep up with the stock market and other financial news. Visit `CharlesSchwab.com`, `CBSMarketWatch.com`, and many other popular financial sites.

And that's only a sampling of what you can do via the wireless Internet. The wireless Internet can provide all kinds of information while you're away from your home computer or your office.

Checking Out Wireless Internet Devices

So, you don't want to be stuck sitting in front of a computer every time you need information. You know the wireless Internet frees you from the computer, but what kind of device can you use to access the wireless Internet? It must be small enough to carry, yet powerful enough to access the Internet. At this time, you can choose from three types of devices:

✔ Web-enabled phones

✔ Web-enabled pagers

✔ Wireless PDAs

The following sections give you an overview of these devices.

You can find much, much more about these devices in Part II of this book. Chapter 4 offers details about Web-enabled phones. I describe Web-enabled pagers in Chapter 5. Chapter 6 takes a closer look at PDAs.

Wanna get WAPed?

If you've spent any time recently wandering through a mall or an electronics store, you've probably seen the ads for Web-enabled phones, pagers, and PDAs. You may be wondering, "How in the world does this stuff work?" I won't go into the gory details, but I can say that wireless Internet does not turn your phone, pager, or PDA into a computer. These devices do not use the same kind of Internet communication methods as a computer. Instead, these devices use the Web Application Protocol (WAP) to retrieve information from the Internet. Portable devices use WAP to retrieve Web site information that can be displayed on small screens, such as the one on your phone or pager. WAP is a protocol, or communications standard, that wireless Internet devices use so that they can function on the Internet. Of course, you don't need to know anything about WAP to use a WAP device, and for the most part, you can simply remain oblivious to WAP's existence. However, as you prowl around the Internet looking for wireless Internet Web sites, you'll see some references here and there to WAP, and I thought you might like to know what it means. If you're very curious about it, visit www.wapforum.org, the Web site of the official WAP industry association.

Dialing in to Web-enabled phones

When cellular phones first came onto the scene, I didn't get one because I couldn't image why I would need it. But now that I have one, I can't even make a quick trip to a gas station without taking my phone along with me. Cellular phones have quickly become a way of life. They give us the freedom to be on the move and still communicate with people as needed. They also give travelers a great feeling of safety. After all, you definitely want a phone in your hand if you're stranded on the side of the road.

A Web-enabled phone is simply a phone that supports WAP. It provides all the functions and features of a typical cell phone, as well as the ability to access the Internet and send and receive e-mail.

You accomplish all this through the standard phone keypad interface, and Web-enabled phones can be quite effective — depending on your needs. You can talk to someone one moment and then check your e-mail the next. The phones are small, easy to carry, and most importantly, serve your voice and Internet needs. For this reason, the Web-enabled phone is the most popular type of wireless device at the moment, with several million of them in service and millions more to be added in the coming months. Figure 1-1 gives you a look at a typical Web-enabled phone.

Welcome to the
Wireless
Internet

Figure 1-1:
A typical
Web-
enabled
phone.

For you skeptics out there, allow me to support, yet alleviate, one of your concerns. You may have heard that Web-enabled phones are slow in terms of transmission time. That is true. A typical Web-enabled phone (or pager) can only send or receive data at around 8 Kbps to 14.4 Kbps, while a typical dial-up account on a computer gets somewhere around 56 Kbps. However, keep in mind that the Web-enabled phone provides you with text only — not all the graphics and pictures you see when surfing the Internet from a computer. Because you download and upload only text, the slower speed works just fine. You can expect this speed, as well as the capabilities of Web-enabled phones, to increase and improve in the future.

So, if you can surf the Internet with a Web-enabled phone, does the phone use a browser? Computers use a Web browser, such Netscape or Internet Explorer, to access and surf the Web. These browsers retrieve information from the Internet, read it, and display it to you. Web-enabled phones use a microbrowser, which enables your phone to read Internet data. Most

Web-enabled phones use the same browser, the UP.Browser produced by the Openwave Company. You can find the UP.Browser in more than 200 models of Web-enabled phones and other devices, making it the most popular type of browser for wireless handheld devices.

Calling all Web-enabled pagers

For the most part, Web-enabled pagers act just like Web-enabled phones. You can surf the Internet and send and receive e-mail using a small keypad. As with the Web-enabled phones, you can also send and receive instant messages to other pagers and phones. Of course, you can't place a call to someone using a pager as you can with a phone. However, that does not make Web-enabled pagers inferior devices. They can do everything on the Internet that a Web-enabled phone can do, and they are easier to carry.

Some pagers stick to the basics, providing Internet access and standard pager features. However, some new models blur the lines between the pager and the PDA. Of course, the choice is yours, and you can find more information in Part II of the book to help you make a purchase decision. Figure 1-2 shows a typical Web-enabled pager.

Figure 1-2:
A typical Web-enabled pager.

Hiring your very own personal digital assistant (PDA)

Personal digital assistants (PDAs) exploded on the scene a few years ago and have become extremely popular. Many people now depend on devices, such as the Palm organizers, the Handspring, and the RIM BlackBerry.

So, what exactly is a PDA? A PDA is an electronic device that stores information and enables you to manage data. Sound like a computer? Well, in reality, a PDA is a type of computer. Like a computer, a PDA has a processor and memory and it can store information. Also like computers, PDAs have applications that enable you to do all kinds of things. For example, you can create and manage calendars, address books, and to-do lists, as well as create memos. However, the PDA is more than a simple electronic organizer. You can load applications that do all kinds of work and you can synchronize your PDA with your PC. Because it has no keyboard or mouse, however, a PDA has a different interface from the computer's. PDAs often use a touch-sensitive screen so you can run the system, and some now have a mini-keyboard where you can enter information.

As you might guess, new models of PDAs offer wireless Internet access so they can do all the things that a regular PDA can do, as well as get on the Internet, send and receive e-mail, and do all those other great things the Internet has to offer. Most PDAs use the UP.Browser, which I introduce in the section, "Dialing in to Web-enabled phones," earlier in this chapter. If the PDA has enough memory and a hard drive, you can store information and manage your e-mail from the PDA in the same way you would on a computer.

I explore all these options in more detail in Part II of the book, but Figure 1-3 gives you a glance at a typical PDA.

Decisions, decisions, decisions

Whether you're thinking about buying a PDA, a cell phone, or a Web pager, you'll quickly find that sorting through the many available options is difficult. Part II of this book helps you make sense of all the choices, but as you start thinking about getting a wireless device, create a checklist of the features you want. Especially with the PDAs, finding the right device presents a big challenge because you can get all kinds of different features and prices. Think about all the tasks you can perform with the wireless device and decide which features and functions are must-haves and which are negotiable. This short list will help keep you on the right track as you face the onslaught of options and marketing campaigns.

Welcome to the
Wireless Internet

Figure 1-3:
A typical
wireless
PDA.

What can these devices really do?

If I come across like a used-car salesman so far in this book, please forgive me — it's just that I really like the wireless Internet! However, I don't live in wireless dreamland, and I'll be the first to tell you that the wireless Internet isn't without its problems or restrictions. Although I believe the wireless Internet has a lot to offer, don't be fooled by all the hoopla. I point out the wireless Internet's shortcomings and problems throughout the book, but for now, I just want to give you the top five questions people ask me about wireless devices and wireless access and the true answers to those questions:

> ✔ **Can I really get on the Internet anywhere?** No, you can't. When you purchase a wireless device, you purchase a plan that gives you access to the Internet. That plan will show you what areas of the country provide wireless connectivity. In most major cities, you'll find good connectivity and not too many "dead zones." However, if you live in the middle of

nowhere (like me), you don't have as many options and you may even be out of luck. Fortunately, you can find this information before you buy, and the wireless coverage area is constantly growing.

- ✔ **Can I send and receive e-mail files?** You can send and receive text-based e-mail, but you cannot receive attachments, such as pictures and documents. Current phones, pagers, and PDAs do not support these attachment items.

- ✔ **Can I get corporate e-mail?** Maybe — depending on the device. Some PDAs can sync up with corporate e-mail, but the most practical solution involves using two different e-mail accounts or Internet mail. I show you how in Chapter 8.

- ✔ **Can I visit any site on the Internet?** No. WAP devices can only access a limited number of Internet sites that support WAP. Fortunately, many major sites already support WAP, and the list is always growing. For a listing and explanation of supported Web sites, see this book's Wireless Internet Access Directory.

- ✔ **Can I manage my electronic calendar?** Yes. Different devices offer differing levels of calendar functionality, but as a general rule, you can use a wireless device to manage your electronic calendar.

Check out Chapter 16 for more information about wireless device limitations.

Taking Care of Business with the Wireless Internet

The wireless Internet offers many interesting options for businesspeople. Because the Internet has become so important to business in so many different ways, the wireless Internet has the potential to, once again, change the way you do business.

Breaking free from the wired world

I already mentioned the benefits of the wireless world a few times in this chapter — and rightfully so. After all, the wired world of the Internet is very restrictive. You're forced to sit at a computer, or at least drag one with you wherever you go. In the past, this wasn't too bad because most businesspeople simply sat at their desks and did their work.

The need to break free from the wired world is a foregone conclusion. We did this with cellular phones, and the reception to this idea was more than popular. Wireless digital access is widely popular and businesspeople can make better use of their time and resources by having a communication device with them at all times. The natural next step is the Internet.

By breaking from the wired world, you gain the following business advantages:

- **E-mail on the fly:** Depending on your device, you can get and even synchronize with corporate e-mail and corporate network calendars.

- **Synchronization with your PC:** The information you generate on your wireless device can be synchronized with your PC. For example, if you attend a convention and gather a bunch of new contacts, you can store those contacts on your wireless device and then synchronize that contact info with your PC's address book. It's easy!

- **Up-to-the-minute news:** Your wireless device can help you get up-to-the minute business and financial news. In fact, you can even have this news e-mailed to your wireless device.

- **More effective time management:** Use the wireless Internet to make the most of your time and resources while you are in transit.

- **Help when you need it:** If your business requires travel, the wireless Internet can keep you on track. Get flight information, maps, local city information — your wireless device can even help you find a gas station.

Freedom from the wired world gives you freedom in your business. You save time and energy. And most importantly, possible opportunities do not slip by while you're stuck in rush hour. Wireless is the way of the future, and the business implications are incredible.

Getting information

Cell phones enable businesspeople to talk to one another anywhere. That is good news because no one has to stay tied to a desk permanently. The wireless Internet gives you a way to access information when you're on the move, just as you can talk to people on the move with your cell phone.

The most important Internet access items available to you are e-mail and calendar data. You cannot use wireless devices to access FTP sites where you can download corporate files and the like. However, wireless Internet access provides an easy way to keep track of e-mail contacts and surf the Web for work or pleasure when you're away from your desk.

Managing Your Life with the Wireless Internet

In addition to managing your business, you can also use the wireless Internet to manage your life. The Internet includes numerous WAP-compliant sites where you can get the latest news, manage your money, shop, find travel information, and have lots of fun — all using your wireless device.

Getting information your way

Depending on the device you purchase, you can subscribe to information and have that information downloaded to your device. Want to know what's going in the news headlines? You can get that information on your wireless device by surfing for it, or you can have it downloaded automatically. Gotta find out what's happening at the game? WAP-enabled sports sites can easily keep you up-to-date without your radio or TV. In general, you can get the information you want and need at your fingertips — no matter where you may be at the moment. Check out Chapter 14 for details.

Keeping track of your money

Do you play the stock market? Your wireless device can take you straight to Wall Street via WAP-enabled financial sites, such as etrade.com, fidelity.com, and ameritrade.com. Manage your money on your own time using wireless Internet access — it's effective and easy. See Chapter 12 to find out more.

Shopping online

Can you shop online using a wireless device? You bet! WAP-enabled sites, such as amazon.com, ecompare.com, and ftd.com work with your wireless device. You can locate and buy products with your wireless device — just as you would when sitting at a computer. Read Chapter 13 to find out more.

Finding your way

Can't figure out where you are or what to do? The wireless Internet includes sites, such as getthere.com and citysearch.com, so you can figure out where you are and where you need to go. You won't get lost in a strange city again as long as you have wireless Internet by your side.

Having fun

The wireless Internet provides many entertainment Web sites so you can pass the time using your wireless device when you're not at home. You find joke and cartoon sites, discussion sites, popular culture sites, and many, many more. For example, check out Funny.com, Ngame.com, or VH1.com.

Web sites and WAP functionality are always changing and growing. What you can do now on the wireless Internet is only the tip of iceberg in terms of what's to come.

Defining Your Needs

By now, you are probably hooked on the idea of the wireless Internet. The rest of this book shows you how to get the kind of device and access you need, and then use the wireless Internet to your best advantage. However, while you still have your money tucked safely in your pocket, you should carefully consider if you need the wireless Internet. To get you started on that path, the following sections help you define your need for Internet access.

Defining your business needs

If you are primarily interested in wireless Internet access for your business, you should stop and take a look at your average, daily business activities and then determine whether the wireless Internet can help you. After all, from a business perspective, wireless Internet represents a business expense for which you have to spend some hard-earned money. So, make sure you can justify the expense before you jump on the wireless Internet bandwagon.

Of course, no rules are carved in stone and the final decision is up to you, but consider the following checklist. If at least three of these items apply to you, you should consider getting wireless Internet access for your business needs:

- ✔ E-mail is an important part of my daily business.
- ✔ I travel a lot.
- ✔ I have a desk, but I am in several other areas of the building(s) during the day.
- ✔ I spend a significant amount of time commuting that I could use to do work.
- ✔ I often receive important e-mail that requires quick responses.
- ✔ My business depends on keeping up with current events.

✔ I watch and analyze financial markets as a part of my business.

✔ I often need travel assistance and map help when I travel for business.

After you decide whether the wireless Internet suits your business, you need to determine whether the wireless Internet can be of personal assistance to you as well.

Defining your personal needs

If your business needs warrant the purchase of a wireless Internet device, you will probably use the wireless Internet for your personal needs as well. However, if your business needs do not include the wireless Internet, you must then take a look at your personal needs to determine whether the wireless Internet can be helpful to you. As with all things in life, you need to balance nice-to-have and need-to-have items, and you need to consider your budget. However, if at least three of the following items sound like you, I think that you will find the wireless Internet useful and enjoyable:

✔ I send and receive e-mail every day and often several times a day.

✔ I use a Web site personal calendar to keep up with my life.

✔ I shop and buy products online.

✔ I like to keep up with news and sports.

✔ I use financial Web sites regularly.

✔ I travel frequently.

✔ When I travel to another town, I like to find interesting things to do.

✔ I am a frequent air traveler.

✔ I like to keep up with the weather when I'm not home.

✔ When I'm not home, I would like to be able to use the Internet to pass the time.

You can use the wireless Internet for any of the items in this list and much, much more. And now that you have decided the wireless Internet is right for you, use this book as your handy reference to make all the right decisions.

Spending a Day in My Wireless World

In previous sections of this chapter, you take a look at the wireless world and your own wireless needs. To ensure that you understand the benefits of wireless Internet access, this section gives you a brief look into a wireless day.

Not all days are this busy, of course, but this example shows you not only how useful the wireless Internet can be, but also the freedom it can bring to your life.

It's 8:05 on a Tuesday morning. I'm sitting in a terminal at the Dallas-Fort Worth airport, waiting for a flight to Atlanta, where I'll have a few meetings with some colleagues. While I wait for my flight to be called, I pull out my Palm VIIx, a wireless PDA, and check my e-mail. I find a few business e-mail messages and couple of personal messages. I answer those e-mail messages with my PDA and then board the plane.

I land in Atlanta at 10:20 A.M. After checking voice mail on my Web-enabled phone, I pull up my e-mail account and check for messages. Because I have both a PDA and a Web-enabled phone, I can switch from a voice call to the Internet easily and quickly. I find an important e-mail from a colleague and I answer it just before my cab arrives.

After I arrive at my hotel, I use my wireless PDA to access the Weather Channel on the Internet so I can see what's coming up in today's weather in Atlanta before I leave my hotel room. I hop into a cab and get on my way to a lunch meeting. While I'm in the cab, I use my wireless device to access a flower store. I surf the site and purchase some flowers for my mother's birthday just before arriving at the meeting.

After the meeting, I have a short break so I once again check and answer e-mail. Then, I spend a little time reviewing the stock market. I notice that a few stocks are not doing so well, so I decide to sell them. After I complete those stock transactions, I rummage through my briefcase for my afternoon schedule. Of course, I can't find the piece of paper that lists some contacts and meeting times. No problem. I store all my calendar information on a Web server, so I just use my PDA to access my mail site to see what my calendar says.

After a few more hours of meetings, I have a break before a dinner meeting, so I spend a little time checking out Internet news sites and a few entertainment sites, such as `funny.com` and `hollywood.com`. After my business dinner, I check and answer e-mail. I know I have a few hours before my flight leaves in the morning, so I access the Internet to find information about Atlanta so I can see a few sites before I leave town.

I get all this done using the wireless Internet. It's all easy, and best of all, the wireless Internet puts me in charge of my business and my life while I'm away from home.

Chapter 2

Getting Connected to the Wireless Internet

In This Chapter

▶ Understanding the basics of Internet connections

▶ Choosing a service plan

▶ Examining standard plan options

▶ Considering service areas

▶ Checking out the major service providers

*U*sing the wireless Internet is not terribly complicated, but before you can get started, you have to find a service provider and then decide which wireless device will meet your needs — both fairly daunting tasks. In fact, getting connected to the wireless Internet poses some of the same challenges you face when buying a new car. Just as you do when buying a new car, you must contend with advertising hoopla, confusing, often contradictory information, and lots of fine print.

Perhaps you have wandered innocently to a Web phone booth at the mall and started asking questions, only to find yourself falling into a black hole of information that leaves you even more confused. You're not alone. Making the right wireless decision can be difficult, and you have to do some homework to make sure you purchase the right service plan and wireless device for your needs.

Don't worry, though; this chapter cuts through all the confusion and helps you make decisions that fit your needs and your budget. In this chapter, you explore wireless Internet service provider options, how they work, and what you should know (as well as what they don't want you to know). Then, you examine the service plans offered by leading national service providers.

Understanding the Basics of Internet Connections

In many respects, a connection to the wireless Internet is just like an Internet connection for a computer. Although this book focuses on the wireless Internet, I make comparisons to the wired world throughout the book in order to help you see the differences, advantages, and disadvantages.

Perhaps you're connected to the Internet using a computer at home or through a computer at work. No matter where you connect in the wired world, your connection to the wired Internet requires three components:

- A computer, of course
- A modem or other connection hardware
- An account with an Internet Service Provider (ISP)

As shown in Figure 2-1, your computer must have a piece of hardware — typically, a modem — that enables the computer to connect with an ISP. Other types of connection hardware include DSL modems and cable modems. Or, you may have an Internet satellite connection, which uses a mini-satellite dish. All these different types of hardware serve the same purpose: enabling your computer to connect with an *Internet service provider (ISP)* — a company that maintains Internet servers.

Figure 2-1:
A wired Internet connection consists of your computer, connection hardware, and an ISP account.

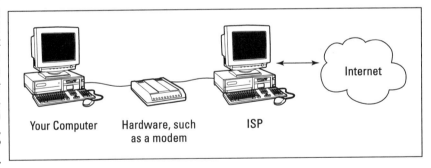

Your Computer   Hardware, such   ISP   Internet
                 as a modem

Your computer connects with the ISP, which gets the items you want from the Internet and returns them to your computer. Without the ISP, you can't connect to the Internet. You can think of the ISP as an entry ramp to a busy freeway.

In the wireless world, connectivity works in almost the same way. However, your connection to the wireless Internet requires only two items:

 ✔ A wireless device, such as a Web-enabled phone, pager, or PDA

 ✔ An ISP account

The wireless device has a built-in wireless "modem" — technically, a transmitter — that enables the device to connect to the Internet. So, when you buy a device, you don't have to worry about buying any connection hardware. You only have to worry about two things: getting an ISP account that will enable you to connect to the Internet, and then getting the right device for your needs. Your wireless device connects to the ISP, which then communicates with the wired Internet to retrieve the information you want and need, as shown in Figure 2-2.

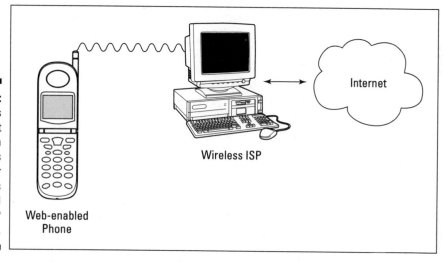

Figure 2-2: A wireless Internet connection consists of your wireless device and an ISP account.

Internet

Wireless ISP

Web-enabled Phone

Phone companies do not refer to themselves as ISPs. For example, you can sign up for Sprint wireless service and get the Web service with your phone plan. Sprint doesn't call itself an ISP, even though the company is providing wireless Internet access. So, the lines between an ISP and a simple service provider are kinda fuzzy, and that's okay as long you don't let these terms confuse you. In short, any plans or companies that can provide access to the wireless Internet are ISPs — even if they don't refer to themselves as such.

Hey, Where's the Plug?

In order to connect to the wireless Internet, you need a wireless Internet device and an account with an ISP or service provider. At this time, that device is going to be either a PDA, a phone, or a pager, although the lines between these three items are starting to blur and will continue to do so in the coming months (see Chapter 7).

For the time being, however, you need to decide whether you want a PDA or a phone/pager, because your approach to getting connected differs depending on the type of device you choose. If you're not sure which type of device you want just yet, check out the chapters in Part II of this book.

Hooking up with a PDA

Getting connected to the wireless Internet with a PDA is rather easy because you don't have many options, which means less confusion for you.

To get connected to the Internet with a PDA

1. **Buy the PDA you want.**

2. **Follow the PDA's instructions for connecting to the Internet.**

It's that simple, because you must use the ISP you get with your PDA. With a desktop computer, you can choose from any number of ISPs, but not so with a PDA. You are limited to one or two ISPs that support your wireless device. For example, if you buy one of the wireless Internet Palm models, you have to use the Palm.net service for connectivity — you can't choose another provider.

So, before you buy, do your homework by exploring what the PDA can do and what connectivity will cost you. ISP accounts typically cost anywhere from $10 to $50 a month, depending on what you want. After you buy your PDA, follow the instructions to connect to the Internet and choose a service plan. The process is quick and painless, and you can find out more about PDAs and service plans in Chapter 6.

Before buying any wireless PDA, make sure the wireless service is available where you live and work. Check out the PDA's Web site for details.

Getting connected with a Web-enabled phone

If you decide that you want to connect to the wireless Internet with a Web-enabled phone, you have to make some decisions. In order to connect to the Internet with a Web-enabled phone, you complete these steps:

1. **Choose a service provider.**

2. **Select the desired, supported phone.**

Now, if you just read the preceding section about connecting with a PDA, you'll see that the process for connecting to the wireless Internet with a phone is exactly the opposite. First, you must pick a service provider that provides wireless service for your area and then you choose a phone that will work with that provider.

For example, assume that you're surfing the Internet and you find a really cool Web-enabled phone that you just can't live without. You pay your hard-earned money and buy the phone. When you get the phone, you call your wireless provider, who says, "Sorry, that phone does not work with our service." Basically, you're out of luck.

The wireless phone industry is a confusing maze of service providers and phone manufacturers. One service provider may work only with a certain group of manufacturers, while another service provider may work with another group. The U.S. Congress has not passed legislation requiring the wireless networks to standardize on a certain set of technologies, so the various networks are incompatible with one another, and the phone you buy must be programmed to work with the network you use. The bottom line: You must decide which company will provide your service before you can choose the phone you want. This way is not as much fun as picking out a cool device first, but these are the cold, hard facts.

Choose a provider before you ever shell out your money for a phone. Otherwise, you may end up with a cool Web-enabled phone that you can't use.

Exploring coverage maps

As you think about finding a wireless service provider, you will probably consider going with a major provider, such as Sprint, AT&T, Verizon, or Cingular. Which service you choose will depend on many factors, starting with the service provider's coverage map.

Depending on where you live, you may have several wireless providers from which you can choose. On the other hand, you may have only one or two. Or, sadly, your area may not have any wireless providers at all. For this reason, you must do your homework first.

If you live in an area that can get wireless phone service, you can probably get wireless Internet service, too. However, the keyword here is *probably*. Quiz the sales representatives about this issue.

Consider my example. My wife and I escaped the Dallas suburbs a few years ago and now live in a small town about 60 miles from the Dallas/Ft. Worth metro area. I had a digital cell phone that works fine out here in the sticks. However, when I wanted to move to a Web-enabled phone, I discovered that my provider did not reach out to my area. So, in order to use the wireless Web, I had to change to a provider that has coverage in my area.

Fortunately, you can easily come by this information. While you're shopping for a provider, ask for the coverage map first, or just look on the provider's

Web site and in any provider literature, such as brochures. After you know which providers offer wireless Web service for your area, you can begin looking at the providers' service plans.

Evaluating service plans: Have they got a plan for you!

Okay, now the fun begins. After you figure out which providers are available for your area, you can begin comparing service plans in order to find one that is right for your budget and your needs. The plans all work in essentially the same as any wireless voice plan. To choose the right wireless phone plan, you have to consider both voice and wireless Internet needs. Usually, you decide which voice plan meets your cell-phone needs and then you look at the wireless Internet option and fees available with that plan. Then, you decide which combination of voice and wireless Internet options best meets your needs and your budget.

First, consider the basics of the wireless voice plan. When you purchase a wireless voice plan from a provider, you typically buy a certain number of minutes per month, and agree to pay an additional charge per minute after you exceed your plan minutes. Many wired long-distance companies work in the same way. Typically, the following basic rules apply to all wireless phone service plans:

- ✔ Fewer phone minutes equal a lower monthly fee, but you may be charged upwards of 35 cents per minute if you run out of plan minutes. For example, you may have a phone plan that costs $30 per month for 180 minutes, with additional charges of 35 cents per minute after you use your 180 minutes. Under this plan, if you use 300 minutes, your bill totals $72 (not to mention taxes, government fees, and all the other surcharges that no one really understands).

- ✔ A greater number of phone minutes costs more for the monthly fee, but is a better deal if you use your phone a lot. For example, if you purchase 1,000 minutes per month for $100, your calls cost only 10 cents a minute.

- ✔ Package options may be available that give you free usage on weekends or at night.

Finally, make sure the coverage area included in your plan is large enough to meet your calling needs. After all, you don't want to pay long-distance charges every time you call Aunt Ruth.

To figure out which plan offers the right options for your needs, consider the following important points when choosing a service plan:

- ✔ **If you have a phone for incidental calls and emergencies, go with a low minute plan.** These plans charge a low monthly fee, but charge you more if you run out of minutes. Still, if you don't use your phone that often, you don't want to pay a monthly fee for a bunch of minutes that you don't use. Providers do not give refunds for minutes that you do not use. Use them or lose them, but you still have to pay for them each month.

✔ **If you use your phone a lot, get a higher monthly minute package.** Although 1,000 minutes a month may seem excessive, and the $100 monthly fee may give you the chills, these plans ensure that you do not run out of minutes and begin racking up 25- to 35-cent per minute charges. So, be realistic, yet honest with yourself about your phone usage when making a decision.

✔ **Look for and ask about promotion plans.** The wireless market is competitive, and you may be able to get a certain number of free minutes per month or free usage times during the week. Remember, those who ask will receive, so always quiz your salesperson about options and bonuses.

✔ **If a provider has lots of sticky rules about long-distance coverage and calling plan areas, shop elsewhere, if you can.** You should be able to call most places within your home state at no additional charge, so make sure you know exactly what the plan provides before you sign on the dotted line.

After you look at the provider's calling plan minutes and any other features, turn your attention to the wireless Internet and e-mail. Charges for wireless Internet usage and e-mail vary from provider to provider, as I explain in the section, "Sizing Up the Major Wireless Service Providers," later in the chapter. For now, consider the basics of how providers usually charge you for Internet usage with your phone plan:

✔ **Plan minutes:** This option enables you to use the wireless Internet on a time basis, using your plan minutes. In other words, surfing the Internet is just like placing a call. You are charged per minute according to your plan. If you run out of plan minutes, you can continue to use the Internet, but you will be charged a per-minute rate, which may be higher than your voice per-minute rate (upwards of 40 cents per minute).

✔ **Free usage:** Some providers give you free usage of the Internet without using any of your plan minutes. In other words, you can surf all you want at no additional charge. That sounds great, but you typically can't use wireless e-mail under the free plan.

✔ **Flat rate:** Some providers charge you a flat rate for Internet usage and e-mail. Typically, you pay between $5 and $20 per month on top of your voice plan for Internet access and e-mail usage. These plans offer unlimited Internet access time, but they often limit you to sending only a certain number of e-mail messages per month; exceed that limit, and they charge you extra.

So, now that you know what you are likely to see in terms of wireless Internet plans on your wireless phone, I can give you my humble recommendations:

✔ **The best plan gives you a flat rate for Internet access and e-mail.** Make sure you get the e-mail option because you are likely to regret it later if you don't. Saving a few bucks is good, but don't do so at the cost of e-mail.

✔ **If no provider for your area offers a flat-rate plan, make sure you have enough minutes to meet both your surfing needs and your voice needs.** Think carefully about how much you are likely to use your phone in a given day, both for voice and the Web, and then try to buy plan minutes that exceed that minimum amount so you'll have room to grow.

Checking out additional services

As you examine the phone contract and service, focus on the network coverage, monthly minutes and rate, and the Internet access options. However, don't get so wrapped up in wireless Internet that you neglect the additional calling features that you may need. As you examine plans and grill salespeople, remember that most wireless phone plans can also provide

✔ **Call waiting:** Tells you that an incoming call is trying to reach you when you're talking to someone else. This feature ensures that you never miss a call.

✔ **Call forwarding:** Enables you to send calls to another number when you're unavailable.

✔ **Caller ID:** Identifies the caller before you answer by displaying the caller's name and phone number on your phone's screen.

✔ **Voicemail:** Provides an "answering machine" so you can receive messages from callers when you're not available.

✔ **Paging and text messages:** Enable you to receive text messages, much like pages, directly on your phone.

Remembering the not-so-good old days

Exploring wireless Internet phone plans reminds me of the not-so-good old days of wired Internet service. If you were on the Internet a few years ago, you may remember that most ISPs gave you the option of buying so many minutes per month, with a per-minute charge thereafter, or you could buy an unlimited plan. For example, my first ISP connection on my Macintosh computer with a 21Kbps modem cost me $5.95 per month for five hours of monthly access. I thought that was great — until I realized that five hours a month wasn't much and I was spending far more than $5.95. I upgraded to the unlimited plan so I didn't have to worry about time while using the Internet.

Various wireless providers currently use this model, or a variation of it, but — you heard it here first — that will change because consumers are going to get sick of it. Just like they complained about the ISP fees in the olden days, users will say, "Give us one low, flat access rate." And that's what the wireless phone companies will do — and probably very soon.

Be sure to check out these options. Does your plan provide them? Can you buy a bundle of them inexpensively? Does your provider offer any special rates that include these services? Ask all these questions before you decide to buy a particular plan.

Magnifying the fine print

Ah, the fine print. Those lines and lines of little words that accompany just about every agreement you enter into these days. Make sure you read the fine print, because ignoring it can get you into big trouble!

Any wireless phone service plan includes some restrictions and fine print that apply to your account. Of course, you should read and digest all this boring information, but I understand that most people don't.

This section summarizes all that fine print for you, quickly, easily, and painlessly. I gathered the fine print from the major wireless providers and sat down to study it so I could report my findings back to you, and I must say, I started to read and felt like I was sinking to the bottom of the ocean. The fine print is boring and dull, but I did discover some important things you should know.

When you purchase a wireless phone plan, you agree to stay with that phone plan for a specified period of time. This feature enables you to get a Web-enabled phone rather inexpensively and locks in a certain rate. Being invited to a party is always fun; not being able to leave is not much fun, but those are the typical game rules for wireless phone accounts.

So, exactly what does the fine print say? The following list highlights the important points I found in the fine print provided by several carriers. Depending on your carrier, some of these restrictions may apply to you, or perhaps even all of them. Read this list as a warning list for things you should aware of, and again, read the fine print yourself for your particular provider's plan so you know exactly what you are getting into.

- ✔ Service plans typically round usage to the nearest full minute. For example, if you use the wireless Internet for 20 seconds, you are charged for 60 seconds. If you use the wireless Internet for 2 minutes and 30 seconds, you are charged for 3 minutes. The same is true for voice usage.

- ✔ You sign an agreement for a specified period of time — typically for one year. If you cancel the agreement before it expires, you are charged a steep termination fee — often between $150 and $200.

- ✔ Your voice and Internet usage cost more if you roam — often up to 60 cents per minute, depending on your location.

- ✔ Within your area, you have no long-distance charges for Internet usage, but you are charged for calling numbers outside your local area.

- Promotional services give you the service and promotional rate for a specific period of time — after that time, you pay the full rate.

- You lose any unused plan minutes — they are not carried forward to the next month.

- Your e-mail messages may not be guaranteed. In other words, if delivery fails, you may not get a failure notice, depending on your plan.

- If you access URLs outside your plan's core sites (for example, through a menu or homepage), your wireless phone number may be exposed to the Internet. That's probably not a big deal, but it could be a privacy issue. A wireless phone thief could manage to get your phone number and use it for crime and mischief. Again, this risk is minimal, but it is something to keep in mind.

- With most phones and plans, you cannot receive calls while you are using the Internet, or vice versa. In other words, you can make calls or use the Internet, but not both at the same time.

- Your e-mail account on the server will accept a limited number of messages. If you do not check your e-mail regularly, your inbox may reach capacity and you may stop receiving messages.

- With most providers, you have 60 days to retrieve your e-mail from the server; after that time, the provider deletes those old messages that you have not read.

- You may be able to get Hotmail, Yahoo! mail, and other types of Internet mail on your phone, but the wireless provider typically does not provide support if you experience problems with those types of e-mail.

- You can connect your wireless phone to a computer or PDA so the phone acts like a wireless modem. However, you are typically charged extra if you use the phone in this way — possibly as much as 5 cents per kilobyte, which is very expensive! A typical text e-mail message could cost you 50 cents to $1.

- Your Internet connectivity may experience delays from time to time, and your plan does not guarantee you uninterrupted access.

Sizing Up the Major Wireless Service Providers

As I explain in the previous sections of this chapter, you must choose a wireless provider before you get to choose a Web-enabled phone. Not all phones are compatible with all services, so your job begins with finding the right service. Finding the right service may not be as much fun as picking out a really cool Web-enabled phone, but choosing the right provider is an essential first step.

So, who should you choose? That depends on many factors, and depending on where you live, you may have only a couple of choices. In order to help you make a decision, this section offers an overview of the more popular service provider plans, with a focus on wireless Internet, of course.

I must also make a big disclaimer here: Service providers are in constant competition with each other, so the prices and promotional deals are constantly changing. The prices and plans I list in this chapter reflect the market at the time of this book's writing, but technology is always on the move, so you'll need to do some homework of your own before you make a decision.

This section helps you figure out which providers are available, the basics of their plans, and where to go for more information. Get their current pricing information before you make a decision, and use the following sections as a guide while you study your wireless Internet access options.

Throughout the following sections, I tell you where to go on the Web to get more information about these plans. These Web sites include coverage maps so you can find out whether a carrier provides service in your area.

AT&T Digital PocketNet: National coverage and flexible plans

AT&T has, without question, the largest wireless network in the world. Depending on where you live or the areas to which you travel, AT&T may be your only wireless option if it is the only provider that can give you coverage. Because of AT&T's wide coverage, its plans may be more expensive in certain markets, especially if it has little or no competition. However, if you live in a metropolitan area, AT&T's rates and plans are competitive with other carriers.

AT&T provides various package minutes to meet your needs and your budget. For example, you can pay about $30 a month for 250 minutes, with charges of 30 cents per minute if you exceed 250 minutes. Another package charges about $200 per month for 3,000 minutes, with an additional 15 cents for each minute over that limit. These prices vary depending on where you live, and AT&T has all kinds of plans between these two that may work for you.

The standard plan includes caller ID, call waiting, and detailed billing. For additional fees, you can get call forwarding, three-way calling, voicemail, and text messaging.

In terms of Internet service, AT&T offers three plan options via its PocketNet service. With PocketNet, you do not use your monthly minutes to access the Internet. I like this service because you can use the Internet without spending your time worrying about how many plan minutes you are burning. Table 2-1 outlines the three AT&T PocketNet plan options available at the time of this writing.

Table 2-1	AT&T Digital PocketNet Service	
Wireless Plan	*What It Offers*	*Monthly Fee*
Basic	Browse Web sites, bookmark favorite Web sites, and use a provided personal Web site to organize your wireless Internet.	Free with the purchase of a digital PCS calling plan and the purchase of an Internet phone.
Plus	Get all the features of the Basic plan, plus a PocketNet e-mail account and service. You can also access AT&T WorldNet e-mail if you use WorldNet as your wired ISP. You can manage e-mail from your phone and from a PC using your personal Web site and even send Word, Acrobat, and text attachments from the site. You can also access e-mail from other selected providers such as EarthLink, MindSpring, RCN, and other national ISPs.	$6.99
Premium	Get all the features of the Basic and Plus plans, as well as address book, calendar, and to-do lists. Manage everything from your phone or at your personal Web site via the PC and set up personal portals and site filters.	$14.99

You may see certain advantages from using AT&T as your long-distance carrier, wireless carrier, and wired ISP. If you use all these services, you should get really good rates. Make sure you ask about advantages and specials for customers using all these services.

Also, when checking out the service area, make sure you pointedly ask about wireless Internet. Just because the AT&T wireless phone network reaches to your area does not necessarily mean the wireless Internet reaches your area.

You can find out more about AT&T wireless by visiting www.attwireless.com, and you can learn the specifics and up-to-the-minute deals for the PocketNet service at www.att.com/pocketnet. That site also has a demonstration of the PocketNet service.

Sprint PCS: Great rates, great coverage

Sprint is a popular long-distance and wireless carrier. Sprint has monthly airtime minute plans, ranging from $20 per month for 20 minutes and 40 cents per extra minute up to $200 per month for 2,000 minutes and 35 cents per extra minute. (Prices vary depending on where you live.) All plans include voicemail with numeric paging, caller ID, call waiting, and three-way calling. Call forwarding costs you an extra 10 cents per minute.

The Sprint PCS network is available in many metropolitan areas, and the PCS Wireless Web is available everywhere that the Sprint PCS network is available. That's good news, and another piece of good news is that every Sprint PCS phone is Web-enabled — so you have lots of model options from which you can choose.

The not-so-good news is that Sprint does not give you a flat-rate Internet plan. Your Internet usage is deducted from your airtime minutes, so you have to determine how many minutes you will need for voice, Internet, and e-mail, and then come up with a total so you can buy the correct plan. Whew!

Your Sprint PCS plan probably includes e-mail, but it will cost a little extra. Under most Sprint plans, you pay $10 per month for 50 updates or messages, but each additional update or message will cost you 10 cents. That can get expensive if you send and receive lots of e-mail.

You may get a really good deal on your long distance if you move to Sprint, so ask about this option and keep it in mind as you're closing the deal.

You can find out more about Sprint Wireless Internet at www.sprintpcs.com.

Verizon Wireless: Easy plan

Verizon Wireless is a national wireless phone and wireless Internet carrier that provides service in most major metropolitan markets. Verizon Wireless offers competitive wireless phone packages and rates. Depending on your area, you can purchase 75 minutes for about $25 and up to 1,500 minutes for about $150. Verizon also offers different plans depending on your roaming needs, as well as caller ID, call waiting, and other typical services.

Verizon typically charges a flat rate of about $6.95 for access to the Internet and e-mail and then charges against your plan minutes for Web usage. In other words, you pay a fee to use the Internet and then you burn your plan minutes while using the Internet. This option enables you to use a personalized Web site, found at www.myvzw.com, which you can customize via your phone or from your PC. This plan gives you about 100 alerts and messages per month.

For more information about Verizon Wireless, visit `www.verizonwireless.com`. Be sure to check out the FAQ section to see the details of Verizon's plans.

Cingular Wireless: Single, simple plans

Cingular Wireless, formerly Bell South Wireless Data, provides competitive, national rates along with wireless Internet service. Cingular offers national calling plans that enable you to travel to any state in the US and make calls without paying any roaming charges. Typical call plans cost about $30 for 100 minutes up to $150 for 1,500 minutes. Additional airtime minutes are 35 cents each. All plans include call waiting, caller ID, call forwarding, three-way calling, voice mail, and detailed billing.

Cingular Wireless Internet provides all the surfing features and e-mail features you might need, including your own Web site, found at `www.mywirelesswindow.com`. However, Cingular's wireless Internet market is rather limited. Table 2-2 reviews Cingular's wireless Internet access coverage and pricing.

Table 2-2	Cingular Wireless Internet Plans
Coverage	**Fee**
California and Nevada	$6.99 per month for 100 minutes for wireless Internet access, and 15 cents for each additional minute.
Boston, Central Illinois, Chicago, Dallas, Detroit, Kansas City, New York, Philadelphia, St. Louis, San Antonio, Tulsa	$6.99 access fee and used minutes are deducted from your regular phone plan rate.

As you can see, the market is rather limited, but if you live in California or Nevada, the provided plan is not a bad deal. You can learn more about Cingular's offerings at `www.cingular.com`.

Nextel Online: Services for business

Nextel provides digital wireless services and some very good wireless Internet features and options. Nextel tends to be geared more to businesses, and its services reflect that business orientation. Depending on your area, you can get around 300 minutes for about $60 per month as well as higher rate plans that give you 2,000 minutes for around $200 per month. Overage charges cost 25 cents per minute.

Nextel Online provides a wide range of Internet services for your cellular phone, such as browsing, MSN Mobile, two-way text messaging, e-mail that can function with Microsoft Exchange or Lotus Domino, and all other typical Web options you would expect to see.

Nextel Online is included with any typical wireless access plan free of charge. With Nextel Online, you get MSN Mobile, which enables MSN customers to access e-mail and information remotely, as well as shopping, Nextel Services, which give you a combination of Internet access portals and sites, and 300 pages of text. In other words, for the online plan, you can view 300 individual phone pages before being charged extra. If you want more, you can go with Nextel's Online Plus option for $10 per month. This option gives you all the basic features, plus the option for dial-up service, 300 text pages, and Web browsing. The dial-up service enables you to use your phone as a modem when working with a PDA (with a Nextel Online connectivity kit). However, the dial-up service does burn your plan minutes. Also, if you want to use two-way messaging, you pay an additional $5 charge per month.

Nextel gives you lots of wireless Internet options. You can read more about Nextel Online at www.nextel.com.

VoiceStream: E-mail and alerts

VoiceStream provides cellular phone service in various markets, but its Internet offerings are limited. VoiceStream offers plans ranging from around 300 minutes per month for about $40 up to 1,500 minutes for about $140 a month. Overage charges will cost you around 30 cents for the $40 plan and 25 cents for the $140 plan.

All plans give you voicemail, caller ID, paging, call waiting, and detailed billing. However, VoiceStream offers only wireless e-mail and limited Internet access in a service package called *InfoStream*. The e-mail service is called *Wireless Enotes,* and text messaging is also available. You can't browse the Internet through VoiceStream's services, however.

You can see more information about VoiceStream by visiting www.voicestream.com.

Chapter 3

Putting the Wireless Internet to Work (and Play)

. . . .

In This Chapter

▶ Doing business with the wireless Internet

▶ Living your life with the wireless Internet

▶ Managing information

▶ Managing travel

▶ Having fun

. . . .

I tend to be somewhat skeptical about almost everything — especially technology. And that's not necessarily a bad thing. Despite claims that technology will revolutionize our lives and simplify our work, it often does just the opposite. Don't get me wrong — I love technology. After all, I write about it for a living. But I am also very skeptical about technology and rather critical of new devices and gadgets. If technology doesn't help us, we don't need it!

The wireless Internet is a technology that gets my seal of approval. That's why I decided to write this book. Now, the marketing claims and salespeople might tell you that the wireless Internet is taking over the world. That's not true because the wireless Internet is still in its infancy and needs time to mature. However, I do think wireless is the wave of the future, and I'm glad you're considering getting on that wave early.

I wrote this chapter for my fellow critics and cynics who know a little about the wireless Internet, but want to know what it can really provide before they part with their hard-earned money. I hear you and I agree, so I've written this chapter to give you an overview of how the wireless Internet can affect both your business and your life. Subsequent chapters in this book explore all the ideas in this chapter in more detail and in a hands-on way. So join with me, fellow critics: This chapter is for you!

Working with the Wireless Internet

First things first: How can the wireless Internet affect your business? Maybe you are considering getting on the wireless Internet because you need the connectivity for your job. Perhaps you travel a lot and you need to stay in touch with the world via the Internet. Maybe you own a business, and you wonder how the wireless Internet can help you.

The wireless Internet has the potential to help businesspeople do their jobs more efficiently and effectively. You can always have needed information at your fingertips, no matter where you are. You can manage and watch business without being stuck in front of a PC.

So, how can the wireless Internet help you in your business? The following sections give you a quick overview of some of the more important business uses of the wireless Internet.

Information on the go

For business users, the phrase *portable information* represents the most important benefit that the wireless Internet offers. Business has changed a lot during the past several years, becoming more distributed and relying more on information technology. Businesspeople who were previously tied to a particular location — an office, a desk, or at least one building — now find themselves on the move. You may travel to other cities frequently, or you may travel to different sites within the same city on a regular basis. Perhaps you work at home some days, at an office on other days, at a client's site on yet other days — the possibilities are endless.

Portable people need portable information. In other words, because people are on the move, information must be on the move, as well. Laptop computers, handheld devices, and cellular phones all help to meet that need, but they do not fully address one important element: Internet access. In the business world, you often hear people say, "If I could just get to my e-mail . . ." or "If I could see the Web site . . . ." Increasingly, businesspeople rely on the Internet, and our ability to use e-mail and the Internet affects business — that is the bottom line. Consequently, the next step in the evolution of the Internet involves accessing the Internet everywhere. Being stuck in front of a computer is no good because the computer and all those wires do not travel easily. The solution is to bring the Internet to us — wirelessly and on small devices that can fit in our pockets or purses.

Information on the go is the driving force behind the wireless Internet, and it represents a real, important business need. This is the primary reason why the wireless Internet is growing so quickly, and you can only expect this trend to continue.

Portable e-mail

One of the more important business uses of the wireless Internet is portable e-mail. Businesses of all sizes have grown increasingly dependent on e-mail during the past several years. In fact, many larger companies maintain their own internal mail servers and often have several technical administrators hired just to manage e-mail. That tells you how important e-mail is to business.

As shown in Figure 3-1, today's business communication includes both *internal e-mail* — that is, e-mail communication among colleagues within the company — and *external e-mail* — communication with customers and other businesses via the Internet. The Internet provides the means for connecting these people together and meeting the business needs of a global economy.

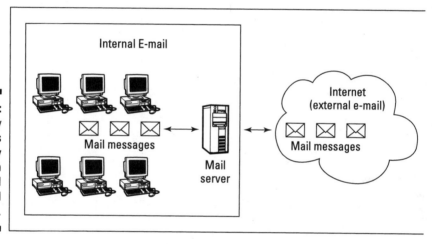

Figure 3-1:
Many businesses rely heavily on both internal and external e-mail.

As business has become more mobile, and our dependence on e-mail has grown, many businesspeople have struggled with the need for portable e-mail. Sure, you can drag your laptop along and plug into a phone jack to get your e-mail — if you can find an available phone jack. For example, while trapped in the Denver airport one fine summer morning on a business trip, I saw a horde of harried businesspeople waiting in long lines at a bank of phones that contained additional jacks for laptop computers. As I watched those desperate businesspeople trying to get connected, trying to get their e-mail, and trying to work in a wired world, I couldn't help but think, "There must be a better way." And as you know, there certainly is, thanks to the wireless Internet.

The wireless Internet gives you the power to access your business e-mail. Depending on the type of device and the service that your company's network supports, you can even get your corporate e-mail right on your wireless device. Consider these points:

- ✔ The RIM BlackBerry PDA and pager can sync up with Microsoft Exchange and Lotus Domino mail systems. That means your corporate e-mail follows you everywhere! See Chapter 6 for more information.

- ✔ The Palm VIIx, m500, and m505 model PDAs contain numerous e-mail options, including access to Palm.net mail, mail from various major ISPs, such as AOL and MSN, and Web e-mail, such as Yahoo! and Hotmail. See Chapter 6 for more information.

- ✔ Nextel Online wireless services and Web-enabled phones can get e-mail from all kinds of Internet servers — even your corporate e-mail (if your corporate network uses the POP3 mail protocol). See Chapter 2 for more information.

- ✔ You can connect PDAs and some phone models to your PC so you can synchronize your e-mail.

- ✔ You can set up e-mail forwarding rules to forward any mail to your wireless e-mail account, ensuring that you always get your mail from any source. Chapter 8 shows you how.

As you can see, you can choose various wireless e-mail options, ranging from the simple to the complex, depending on your business needs. By doing your homework, you can find the right solution for you and your business, ensuring that you can always access your e-mail from a simple PDA or Web-enabled phone — no matter where you are.

Calendars to keep track of appointments

Electronic calendars have become very popular during the past several years, and most major e-mail programs provide built-in calendars that can help you manage your time. In corporate environments, other users can even send you meeting requests, which the system can automatically add to your calendar. You also can allow other users to manage your calendar as needed.

The wireless Internet would not be complete without wireless calendars, and they are available to you in various ways. PDAs, such as the Palm or the BlackBerry, have built-in calendars that synchronize with the calendar on your desktop computer. Virtually all Web-enabled phone plans also give you the option to use calendars, and you may get a private Web site where all calendar data is saved so you can manage that data from your phone.

Many wireless devices include features that enable you to keep your wireless calendar in sync with the calendar program on your desktop computer. For example, assume that you use Microsoft Outlook for your corporate e-mail software. You keep track of all your appointments by using Outlook's calendar. You go on a business trip for a few days and take your PDA along so you can get your e-mail and manage your schedule. During the business trip, you make several calendar entries and changes. When you return to your office, do you have to manually reenter all that calendar information? No way! Simply use the PDA's synchronization capabilities and synchronize your wireless calendar with your Outlook calendar. It's simple, quick, and very easy. See Chapters 4 and 6 for more information about synchronization with a desktop computer for phones and PDAs.

Chapter 10 explores all your wireless calendar options in more detail.

Wireless messaging

Wireless messaging enables you to send short text messages to another person using a wireless device. For example, maybe you need to let a co-worker know about a sudden price change in a product. You know the co-worker has his phone, but you also know that he is in the middle of a meeting talking about that very same product. How can you get the message to him without disturbing the meeting? Use wireless instant messaging.

Instant messaging has become popular in the past few months, and major ISPs, such as MSN and AOL even provide utilities so you can communicate with people directly and easily. For example, the MSN Messenger service shown in Figure 3-2 enables you to communicate with another MSN member in a live, chat format. You can immediately send and receive instant messages with other businesspeople and even friends and family who are connected at the moment. Instant messaging via your wireless device works in the same way, just without wires.

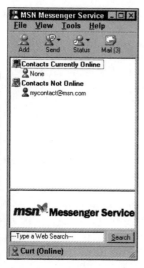

Figure 3-2: Most ISPs and mail services now include instant messaging utilities, such as the MSN Messenger.

The instant messaging utilities also enable you to get your e-mail or search the Internet for items you want to find. They're fun and very useful in various situations.

Wireless phones, pagers, and PDAs all have the capability of receiving instant messages. These messages appear on the screen so you do not have to physically retrieve the message, as you would have to do when using e-mail. You can find out more about instant messaging in Chapter 9.

News at your fingertips

Depending on your business, keeping up with current events may be of paramount importance. With the wireless Internet, you can keep up with the latest developments by accessing all kinds of popular news sites. For example, you can keep up with local and world events by making a wireless visit to cnn.com or abcnews.com.

You can also access business and financial sites to see up-to-the-minute stock market information and reports from industry analysts. Check out CBSMarketWatch.com to get industry news. You can even wirelessly buy and sell stocks at a site, such as CharlesSchwab.com. See Chapters 12 and 14 for more information.

Travel information that travels with you

Another important aspect of the wireless Internet is travel. Consider this scenario: You've landed in an unfamiliar city, and you want recommendations for a nice restaurant. You can rely on the cab driver's advice, or you can find out all kinds of information about that city on the wireless Internet.

Are you lost? You can also access popular travel sites, such as MapQuest.com, and get driving directions while you're in the car.

Looking for entertainment? You can use the wireless Internet to find out about current events in the city you are visiting.

What about your flight? Is it on time or late? You can easily find out by using the wireless Internet.

As you can imagine, the wireless Internet has all kinds of travel-related information. See Chapter 14 for more information and be sure to check out this book's Wireless Internet Access Directory.

Living with the Wireless Internet

In Chapter 1 of this book, I explore some of the ways the wireless Internet can affect your life. Indeed, the wireless Internet is not just for business users. The wireless Internet keeps you connected to the Internet and to the information you are looking for — no matter what kind of information you need.

I will not repeat the information from Chapter 1 here, but if you're still standing on the edge of the wireless Internet world not sure if you should make the jump, consider just a few of the many important things you can do with wireless Internet access:

- ✔ Get your e-mail no matter where you are.
- ✔ Keep up with breaking news.
- ✔ Manage your money and keep track of financial news.
- ✔ Follow your favorite sports teams.
- ✔ Get driving directions.
- ✔ Find out what is happening with the weather.
- ✔ Send instant messages.
- ✔ Shop online.
- ✔ Get concert tickets.
- ✔ Plan a night on the town.
- ✔ Check on the status of your flight.
- ✔ Make a reservation.
- ✔ Read restaurant reviews.
- ✔ Check the price of a car.
- ✔ Call a cab.
- ✔ Have fun — anytime and anywhere.

And if you're still not convinced, let me give you another tidbit of information.

If you go the Web-enabled phone route, you may be able to pick up the wireless Internet service for free or for a nominal fee. In fact, the wireless Internet may add almost nothing in terms of expense to your current wireless phone plan. You may need to upgrade to a different phone, but the upgrade prices are often nominal. Check out Chapter 2 for more information.

Bringing information to you

I think the Internet should give me the information I want, and I don't want to have to look for information. I understand that those are lofty expectations, but in many ways, available technology can meet them. Using the wireless Internet, you can find all kinds of information on just about any subject, but can you bring that information to you?

Consider an example. I want to keep up with technology reports. Every time a new technology report comes out, I want to know about it, and I don't want to have to check Web sites for those reports. What can I do? I can configure various wireless Internet sites, such as abcnews.com, to deliver the content I want directly to my phone or PDA's mailbox. I simply check my mail, and the latest information I want is waiting for me to read it! That's very cool, and very helpful to both businesses and individuals.

In fact, all kinds of services are available that can send the information you want directly to you. For example, you can get headline information, stock quotes, and even e-mail newsletters. What about packages I have shipped? No problem: Services, such as FedEx and UPS, can provide you with up-to-the-minute tracking reports.

Having fun

The wireless Internet is a great tool for your business and your personal life, and I must admit that the wireless Internet is a lot of fun, too. If you travel frequently and need a distraction, the wireless Internet can help you pass the time, get information, and keep up with the world while you're in transit. Just consider some of the fun things you can do:

- ✔ Check up on your favorite stars at Hollywood.com.
- ✔ Scope out movie news and reviews at MovieFone.com.
- ✔ Never miss a play at ESPN.com.
- ✔ Meet and hang out with people at sites, such as Bolt.com.
- ✔ Get down with your bad self at music sites, such as VH1.com.
- ✔ Try to beat the house in online casinos, such as Dorcino.com.
- ✔ Tickle your funny bone at Funny.com.
- ✔ Play games and solve puzzles at Boxerjam.com.

You name it; it's out there. The wireless Internet provides the content you want or need. See this book's Wireless Internet Access Directory to browse the content available to you on the wireless Internet.

Part II
Choosing a Wireless Device

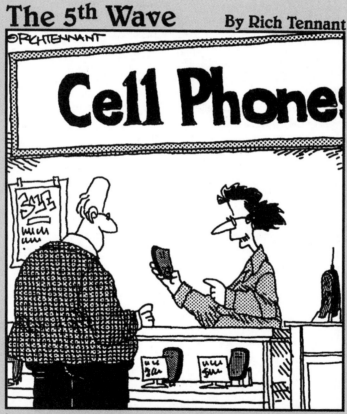

The 5th Wave   By Rich Tennant

Cell Phones

"This model comes with a particularly useful function — the simulated static button for breaking out of long-winded meaningless conversations."

In this part . . .

In order to use the wireless Internet and wireless e-mail, you must have a wireless device and a service plan that gives you access. The chapters in this part of the book help you figure out what is available so you can make the decision that is right for you. In this part, you can check out Web-enabled phones, pagers, and wireless personal digital assistants (PDAs), and you get a glimpse into the future of wireless devices.

Chapter 4

Choosing a Wireless Internet Phone

• •

In This Chapter

▶ Understanding wireless technology

▶ Considering phone features

▶ Making a decision that is right for you

▶ Quick directory of Internet phone manufacturers

• •

*T*he fun part of getting on the wireless Internet with a Web-enabled, or Internet, phone is choosing the phone you want. The not-so-fun part is choosing a service agreement with a provider, such as AT&T, Sprint, or Verizon. Before you wade into this chapter and start shopping for a Web-enabled phone, I strongly recommend that you read Chapter 2, which shows you how to choose a service plan that is right for you. Also, make sure you understand this important concept: You must buy a service plan before you buy an Internet phone!

Each wireless provider has its own wireless infrastructure, and only compatible phones will work on that particular infrastructure. If you are cruising the Internet, and you find an Internet phone that you can't live without, don't buy it! First, make sure the phone is compatible with your provider. And if you don't have a provider yet, take care of that step before you buy the phone. Not as much fun, certainly, but absolutely necessary.

Now that I'm done ranting and raving, you can turn your attention to choosing an Internet phone. After all, you have lots of options, and determining what you need and what is best for you can be a little tricky. So, in this chapter, I explain what you need to know so you can purchase the best Internet phone for your needs.

Understanding Wireless Phone Technology

Wireless phone technology is a maze of confusing information and strange acronyms. But don't worry; I'm not going to jump off the wireless deep end and drag you along with me. In fact, you don't need to know much at all about the technology behind wireless phones to use them. However, as you're surfing the Internet and doing your own research, you will run into several acronyms and concepts that you should understand. So, this section gives you a quick and painless overview of wireless phone technology.

Each wireless carrier uses its own wireless infrastructure technology and communications protocols. In other words, no wireless standard exists, and each network is not compatible with the next. That's why you must choose a service provider before you choose a phone. AT&T phones are not compatible with Sprint phones, which may not be compatible with Verizon's phones. You get the picture.

Why all the madness? To get the full picture, you have to back up a bit and look at computer and communications technology. In particular, you need to understand two important terms: analog and digital. A regular, old telephone uses _analog transmission_ (sending data over the phone lines in the form of sound waves). In contrast, your computer — and all computers on the Internet — speak in a _digital format_ (transmitting data in numerical form). To transfer data to and from the Internet via the phone lines, your computer uses a _modem_ — a device that translates data from the digital format used by computers to the analog format used by the phone lines, and vice versa.

The first cellular phones all used an analog network called the Advanced Mobile Phone Service (AMPS). Analog wireless networks still use this service.

However, analog networks often do not have the quality of digital networks. More importantly, the wireless Internet works only on digital networks, because Internet data, which is all computer-based, is digital.

To further complicate matters, no standard digital wireless network exists. Instead, the various service providers use several different types of networks. Phones that sport the world phone logo work with Global System for Mobile Communications (GSM), which is the most widely used wireless network around the world. AT&T and Cingular use Time Division Multiple Access (TDMA). Sprint PCS and Verizon support Code Division Multiple Access (CDMA). Each of these networks processes and transmits wireless data differently. To us, they all sound the same, but they are actually very different.

WAPing our way into the future

If you think that WAP is here to stay, then you are right. Although the wireless Internet is somewhat limited at the moment, it will not stay that way. Wireless networking is getting faster and better all the time. A revision of GSM called *General Packet Radio Service (GPRS)* is currently being tested in Europe, and it provides wireless transfer rates of up to 128 Kbps. GPRS is slated for release in the United States in late 2001. Other technologies currently being developed include Enhanced Data Rates for Global Evolution (EDGE), which can theoretically provide transfer rates of up to 473 Kbps, and the Wideband Code Division Multiple Access (WCDMA) technology, which theoretically have transfer rates of about 384 Kbps. That may not sound like much, but these numbers are about 30 times faster than what wireless networks can do now. The end result will be a wireless network that can handle the power of the Internet. Want full graphics, color, sound, and all the other bells and whistles of the wired Internet on a portable device? Don't worry — it's coming, and it won't take long!

You must purchase a phone that is compatible with the network you are using. A TDMA Internet phone will not work on a Sprint PCS network, and a CDMA phone won't work on AT&T, and so on.

However, some higher-end phone models can support both digital and analog networks. These phones, often called *dual-band phones,* work on one of the digital networks as well as the analog network. On the other hand, a single-band phone works only on one of the digital networks or on the analog network.

So, now that you know how the different wireless networks come into play in all this madness, how does Wireless Access Protocol (WAP) fit into this scheme? WAP is the standard protocol that all wireless devices use to access the Internet and retrieve Internet data. All Web-enabled phones — regardless of whether they are TDMA, CDMA, or GSM — use WAP to access the Internet.

Most phones use the UP.Browser produced by Phone.com, and you can read more about some of the phone manufacturers who use the UP.Browser in the section "Quick Directory of Wireless Internet Phone Manufacturers," later in this chapter. The UP.Browser uses the Handheld Devices Markup Language (HDML) or Wireless Markup Language (WML) in the same manner that a computer uses the Hypertext Markup Language (HTML).

The Internet works basically the same way for a wireless device as it does for a computer. Your computer uses the Hypertext Transfer Protocol (HTTP) in order to get HTML documents from the Internet, and your wireless device uses WAP in order to get HDML or WML documents from the Internet. The end result is the same; wireless and wired devices just use different tools to get there.

Considering Internet Phone Features

So, how do you pick an Internet phone that's right for you? After all, you'll have your pick of various different brands and models, regardless of which wireless carrier you choose. Picking the right model is not easy. (I almost drove the salesperson crazy because I chose a service plan and then couldn't decide which phone I wanted.) Take your time and make sure you're happy with your decision. To help you make that decision, read the following sections for tips and advice.

Holding the phone

You can buy a compatible Internet phone directly from your service provider, or you can buy one somewhere else — for example, from online stores, such as www.buy.com or www.amazon.com. However, I strongly recommend that you physically hold the phone before you buy it. You can't do that on the Internet, of course, but if you are curious about a certain model, visit a store so you can play with that phone. After you check out the phone, you can shop for bargains on the Internet.

Why should you hold the phone? Although you certainly want strong, clear reception, using an Internet phone is as much a tactile experience as it is an auditory experience. You'll hold your phone a lot and use the keypad a lot in order to use the Internet. So, you need to find a phone that feels right to you. Consider the following questions when checking out the feel of your phone:

✔ Does the phone fit comfortably in the palm of your hand? When you hold the phone in the palm of your hand and let your fingers relax, does the phone fit easily in your hand, or is it a little bulky and cumbersome?

✔ Can you easily hold the phone in the palm of your hand and press numbers with your thumb at the same time? If not, the model is probably too big for your hand.

✔ Does the phone feel lightweight resting in the palm of your hand? Could you comfortably hold the phone in that position for a long time?

✔ Is the phone too small? Several models of phones barely reach four inches. Those tiny, compact models are very cool, but they may not be the best for you. Choose a size that feels comfortable to you.

Feeling comfy?

In addition to checking the comfort of the phone in your hand, decide whether you feel comfortable when you put it to your ear and mouth. Each phone's design differs from the others, and a phone that feels okay in your hand may feel strange when you put it next to your face. Some phones have a more con-toured design and may be more comfortable than others. You should feel com-fortable with the phone pressed against your ear and the side of your face.

Put the phone to your ear and pretend you are talking. Now imagine that you have to keep talking for an hour. Could you comfortably use the phone for an hour?

Of course, you probably won't want to hold a phone that long. If you often have long conversations or need to use the phone in your car, consider pur-chasing a headset and other devices to make using your phone easier. See Chapter 17 for my top-ten list of accessories.

Casing the joint

Internet phones come in all shapes and sizes, and you should examine the case (or the outer shell of the phone). Many phones have a single oval-type case, with the screen, keypad, and antenna all in one unit. This design is very popular and can easily fit into your pocket or purse.

Another popular design, used by Motorola's StarTAC phones, is the flip phone or clamshell. The flip phone has a bottom piece containing the micro-phone that folds out away from the keypad when you need to use it. Or, the top of the phone may flip up, revealing the earpiece. Either way, the phone folds together to make it more compact. Some people love this design and some find it aggravating.

Carefully consider the phone's durability. Does the phone look as if it could survive being dropped on a concrete floor, or does it seem a little too deli-cate? Remember that you will carry the phone with you, so it probably will get dropped, bumped, hit, and so on, during your normal daily routine. Pick a phone that looks as though it can keep up with you.

Checking out the antenna

Although it will not be a major decision-making factor, be sure to check the antenna. Most phones use a fixed antenna that you do not have to move, and some models completely hide the antenna on the inside. However, some phones provide a retractable antenna that you can raise or lower, as needed. There's no good or bad here, but think about what you like and don't like. If you have no preference, don't worry about it — you'll get the same quality no matter what kind you choose.

Getting in touch with the keypad

Carefully consider the keypad when you are choosing an Internet phone. After all, the keypad is your interface with the phone, and thus, your interface with the Internet and your e-mail. So, you want a phone keypad that is easy to use and intuitive. Figure 4-1 shows an example of a keypad from a Web-enabled phone.

Most Internet phones provide a typical alphanumeric keypad with control buttons at the top of the keypad. These control buttons enable you to maneuver through menus and select what you want to view. As you decide which keypad you like best, keep these points in mind:

✔ Run your fingers over the buttons. Are the buttons comfortable and smooth?

✔ Play with the menu selection (scroll) button. Is the button comfortable?

✔ Examine all the buttons you would use for the Internet. Are the buttons easy to access? In other words, are the buttons close enough to each other, but not too close?

✔ Overall, does the keypad design make sense to you? Is the design easy to memorize?

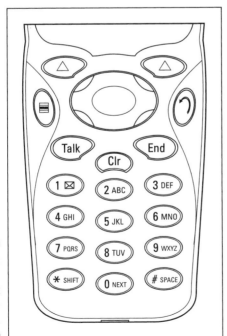

Figure 4-1:
A typical
Internet
phone
keyboard.

Don't be afraid to ask a salesperson to give you a demonstration and then let you hold and use the phone. If the store can't (or won't) provide this demonstration for you, shop elsewhere.

Putting the screen on display

Screen size and display represent significant factors in your search for the right Internet phone. With a typical cellular phone, the screen is not that important, but with an Internet phone, the screen is very important. Most Internet phone screens are easy to read, but a smaller screen means smaller type. Also, smaller screens cannot display as much information at one time.

Typically, the screen should be able to display three to five lines of text — if not, you should probably find one that can. The more lines of text the phone can display, the easier it will be to use.

Internet phone screens come in two primary flavors. The first is the basic text screen, like the one shown in Figure 4-2.

Figure 4-2:
A typical
Internet
phone
screen
display.

The screen displays lines of text but very limited graphics due to its size. Using your keypad, you scroll through the menus.

Another type of interface that is not as popular yet, but will be during the next few months, is the icon-based interface. Figure 4-3 shows an example.

Figure 4-3:
An icon-
based
screen
display.

With the icon-based interface, you use the selection key to select the icon you want and then open it — a lot like you would do using a computer. You can see an example of this kind of interface with the NeoPoint NP1000 shown in the Quick Directory at the end of this chapter.

So, what features should you look for in your screen display? Here's my list of tips:

✔ The larger the screen, the better your viewing ability for Internet sites. Balance screen size with the overall phone size so you arrive at an all-around size that is right for you.

✔ The screen graphics and icons should be smooth and easy to read.

✔ Ask the salesperson how many lines of text the screen can display. Get a phone that can display at least five lines of text at one time.

Again, you should be able to see the screen in action before you make a decision. Ask the salesperson to show you how the phone model works before you buy.

Double-checking features

As you explore your phone options, ask about other services that you may want. Not all phones support all services, so make sure you know which features you can't live without before making a decision. Some common questions you may ask are

- ✔ Does the phone support text messaging?
- ✔ How does the phone support e-mail?
- ✔ Are call-forwarding and related services available?
- ✔ Does the phone support voice recognition? In other words, if you say, "Call Uncle Norman," does the phone automatically dial the correct number for you?
- ✔ Does the phone support multiple ring options, programmable features, ring vibration, and related features?
- ✔ What accessories are available for the phone?

Getting a charge out of the battery

Under most circumstances, you do not need to worry about the phone battery. You can probably get a good battery that can support your phone usage needs. However, it never hurts to ask so you can be sure of what you are getting. As a general rule, a good battery should provide three hours of talk time and remain on standby charge for at least five days. Anything less tells you that the battery is under par. Also, check out the lifespan of the battery — it should last a few years. Finally, some batteries must be fully discharged before you can recharge them, which is a real pain. Be sure to ask the sales rep about this issue, too.

Choosing the Phone That's Right for You

After you consider all the phone's options and its design, you can decide which Internet phone you want. If you have lots of options available to you, that final decision can be a little difficult. So, here are some last-minute questions to help you decide which phone you really want and need:

- ✔ How important is phone size? Does the phone need to fit in your pocket or purse?
- ✔ How often do you plan on using the phone?
- ✔ What is the largest screen size you can get that is still comfortable and practical?

✔ Which case design do you like best?

✔ Does the phone have all the features you want and need?

✔ Does the phone fit comfortably in your hand?

✔ Are you comfortable when you hold the phone to your ear and face?

✔ What are your favorite features?

✔ Which feature is most important to you?

Quick Directory of Wireless Internet Phone Manufacturers

I've probably said it a hundred times, but I'll say it again: You must choose a wireless service provider before you can choose a Web-enabled phone. It's that simple. Each wireless network, such as AT&T, Sprint, and Verizon, has its own network infrastructure, and your Web-enabled phone, or Internet phone, must function on that infrastructure. If you buy the phone first, you may end up with an Internet phone that you can't use.

Now that I have that little speech out of the way, you can turn your attention to finding an Internet phone. This section gives you a listing of the more common phone manufacturers who produce WAP phones. In other words, these phones conform to the common WAP standards, and they all use the same type of UP.Browser for Web access.

Before you wade into this brief directory, I have to mention a few disclaimers:

✔ Phone models are always changing; so check each manufacturer's Web site for new items.

✔ I've included Web site information with each listing so you can see the phones on the Web. Some of these Web sites include interactive demos, and I encourage you to check them out.

✔ This section offers a brief overview of major manufacturers, not a comprehensive directory. I encourage you to use this section as a guide to help you know what is available. However, you may find the perfect phone from another manufacturer that I do not include in this section.

✔ If you want to see reviews of many of these manufacturer's phones, visit www.zdnet.com, look in the Wireless section, and check out Internet Phone Reviews.

✔ Try to get your hands on a model phone before you make a decision, and make sure you read the sections earlier in this chapter about choosing a phone that is right for you.

> ✔ I do not provide a price guide in this section because the prices of the phones vary depending on your service provider. The best advice I can give is to choose a service provider, examine its prices, and then shop around for a compatible phone that has a price you like.

So, with all of that said, the following sections point out some of the major manufacturers, a few phone models, and Web site information so you can find out more.

Alcatel

Alcatel produces telecommunications equipment and provides services. Alcatel also provides a line of very effective Web-enabled phones, called the One Touch Pocket. The One Touch Pocket models are geared toward business users and provide an integrated Web browser. The phones feature easy navigation around the Internet and through your e-mail. Alcatel also offers vibrating models and support for more than forty international languages. You can read more about Alcatel's wireless Internet phones at www.alcatel.com.

Audiovox

You may recognize the Audiovox name for car stereos. This company also operates in the wireless phone market, featuring the CDM 4500 and 9000 series phones. Audiovox phones feature smooth interfaces and easy-to-use scroll and select buttons. Audiovox is gaining in national popularity, and its models are available under Verizon agreements. Some models provide vibration features and voice-activated calling. You can find out more about Audiovox phones at www.audiovox.com.

Casio

Casio produces various home electronics products, and you may recognize the name from electronic keyboards and calculators. However, Casio also produces an impressive line of Web-enabled phones, such as the C303CA model. Casio also produces the Cassiopeia PDA, and you should watch for some interesting new phone/PDA combo devices in the near future. Find out more about Casio products at www.shopwireless.com.

Denso

Denso produces automotive parts and a line of wireless phones for Sprint PCS. Its phone products are very popular in the Japanese market, and Denso provides the TouchPoint Dual Band wireless Internet phone to the U.S. market. You can read more about Denso at www.1-800cellularphone.com.

Ericsson

Ericsson is a very large company (more than 100,000 employees) that produces all kinds of products and technical services. Ericsson provides some of the more popular Web-enabled phones that fit both your needs and your budget. You can choose Ericsson phones from several different service providers, and Figures 4-4 and 4-5 show the popular R520 and R380 models. You can find out more about Ericsson phones at www.ericsson.com.

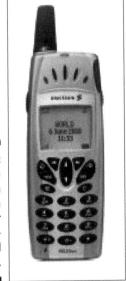

Figure 4-4:
The Ericsson R520 is a very popular Web-enabled phone.

© *Telefonaktiebolaget LM Ericsson.*
Photo used by permission.

Figure 4-5:
The Ericsson R380 combines the features of a phone and a PDA.

© *Telefonaktiebolaget LM Ericsson. Photo used by permission.*

Kyocera

Kyocera produces numerous telecommunications products worldwide and is a leader in wireless technology. Kyocera offers several stylish and attractive Web-enabled phones in its QCP series. Kyocera also has received lots of attention for its new pdQ SmartPhone series, which combines the Palm operating system with a wireless phone. You can see a picture of the SmartPhone in Chapter 7, and you can find out more about Kyocera's phones at `www.kyocera-wireless.com`.

Mitsubishi

Mitsubishi is an international company that produces all kinds of electronic goods. The company has a very popular line of Web-enabled phones, including the MobileAccess T250 and 255 models. All Mitsubishi phones feature large screens and easy-to-use function keys. Figure 4-6 shows the T250 model, which is provided by major carriers, such as AT&T. You can see more information about Mitsubishi's phones at `www.mitsubishiwireless.com`.

Figure 4-6:
Major carriers, such as AT&T, offer Mitsubishi's very popular T250 model Web-enabled phone.

© Mitsubishi Wireless. Photo used by permission.

Motorola

Motorola produces numerous electronic products, with a strong market presence in phones and pagers. In fact, Motorola produces several Web-enabled phones and pager products, including the i1000plus. Most major carriers offer Motorola phones, and you can pick from numerous options, including flip phones. Visit Motorola on the Internet at www.mot.com.

NeoPoint

NeoPoint appeared on the scene a few years ago and now produces some of the hottest Web-enabled phones on the market. As shown in Figure 4-7, NeoPoint phones, such as the NP1000, give you a sleek interface with a very large screen, making your wireless Internet usage a snap. You'll find NeoPoint products available from several major carriers, and you can read more about NeoPoint's phones at www.neopoint.com.

Figure 4-7:
The
NeoPoint
NP1000
gives you
plenty of
surfing
room.

© NeoPoint, Inc. Photo used by permission.

Nokia

Nokia phones are everywhere, made popular by carriers, such as AT&T. Nokia phones provide a smooth, easy-to-use interface and standard wireless phone features. Nokia produces several different models and series in order to meet your needs. The 7100 series provides very nice screens and Internet capabilities. Read more about Nokia phones at www.nokia.com.

Philips

Philips is an international company that produces all kinds of electronics for home users and businesses. The Philips Xenium wireless Internet phone models are becoming very popular. Philips research is also producing some very interesting and cool phone/clothing products. (See Chapter 7.) You can find out more about Philips products at www.pcc.philips.com.

Samsung

Samsung produces numerous electronics devices, including wireless Internet phones. Samsung recently released the first MP3 wireless Internet phone, the Samsung Uproar, so you can listen to MP3 on the Internet. (MP3 is an Internet technology that enables you to download and listen to songs.) You can expect other phone models to follow suit. Find out more about the Samsung Uproar and other models at www.samsungelectronics.com.

Sanyo

Sanyo produces consumer electronics products. The Sanyo SCP-4000 model provides Internet surfing and usage through easy menus, and some newer models support voice activation. You can find out more about Sanyo phones at www.sanyousa.com.

Siemens

Siemens is a large international company that produces all kinds of technology products. The Siemens S40 phone is a popular model that is fully Web-enabled. Find out more about the Siemens phones and features at www.ic.siemens.com/mySiemens.

Chapter 5

Choosing a Web-Enabled Pager

In This Chapter

▶ Understanding what Web-enabled pagers can do

▶ Checking out Web pager features

▶ Considering pager service plans

▶ Taking a look at popular Web-enabled pagers

I remember the days when I hated my pager. After all, it almost always signaled more work for me or a problem that I had to solve. However, the little gadgets known as pagers have changed dramatically during the past few years. Pagers can store all kinds of information and enable you to send pages as well as receive them.

The wireless Internet brings even more changes to pagers, and a few models available today give you many more options than those found on traditional pagers. These devices, often called *communicators,* go beyond simple paging, giving you the power of the Internet and e-mail — and all on a small device that fits in your pocket.

Intrigued? I thought you might be. This chapter gives you the skinny on Web-enabled pagers. I explore what they can do, describe what the service plans cover, and then give you a look at a few popular models.

Getting to Know Web-Enabled Pagers

Web-enabled pagers, or personal communicators, are basically tiny computers that provide all the typical pager functions, and much, much more. About the size of a small wallet, a Web-enabled pager gives you a small QWERTY keyboard, which you operate with your thumbs, scroll buttons, and a high-resolution screen.

So, what's the difference between a Web-enabled pager and an Internet phone? Well, the Web-enabled pager doesn't have all the features of an Internet phone. You can't have voice conversations via a pager, and you typically cannot access as many Internet sites. However, the pager does support instant-messaging features, Web usage, and wireless e-mail. So, the choice between Web-enabled phones and pagers really comes down to a matter of preference. Personally, I prefer an Internet phone to a Web-enabled pager, but a phone is more practical for me to own. Depending on your needs, a Web-enabled pager may be just the ticket.

Checking Out Web-Enabled Pager Features

You can choose from two basic flavors of pagers: one-way and two-way. One-way pagers are the devices that people typically think of when they hear the word *pager*. These small devices can receive pages from other people. With most service plans, you can record a voicemail message that people hear when they call the access number to send you a page. If someone sends you a page, you see a phone number displayed on your pager so you can call the person back. Depending on your service and your pager, you also may be able to receive short messages.

A two-way pager does everything the one-way pager does, and a lot more. With a two-way pager, you can send pages and messages to other pagers, cellular phones, or PDAs that support the feature. You can also access the wireless Internet and send and receive e-mail as well as view some Web pages.

In fact, you can do quite a few things with a two-way pager, and the lines between pagers, cell phones, and PDAs continue to blur as these devices perform more and more tasks. Here are some of the important functions that you can perform with a Web-enabled pager:

- ✔ Receive pages and messages.

- ✔ Send pages and messages.

- ✔ Send e-mail to any e-mail address. However, you cannot attach files to your e-mail messages, and pagers typically limit your e-mail messages to 500 characters.

- ✔ Receive e-mail from anyone on the Internet. However, you cannot receive file attachments, and your pager will probably limit message lengths to 500 characters.

- ✔ Use instant messaging. (Depending on the pager model, this feature may be called *chat.*)

- ✔ Access some Web sites via applications or updates. Many plans give you a certain number of updates per month (for example, news, sports, or entertainment updates), which arrive directly on your pager.

- ✔ Maintain an address book.

✔ Synchronize with your PC.

✔ Use calendar and To Do lists.

Your ability to perform all the tasks in this list depends on your service plan and the pager you buy. Before you buy, make sure the pager offers the features you want.

E-mail and instant messaging work in the same manner on Web-enabled pagers as they do on any other wireless device. Check out Chapter 8 for more information about wireless e-mail, and see Chapter 9 to read more about instant messaging.

Examining Web-Enabled Pager Service Plans

As with all wireless Internet products, you must purchase some kind of service plan for your pager to work. Otherwise, you end up with a really cool-looking gadget that doesn't do anything. The service plan enables your pager to connect with the service provider so you can send and receive pages as well as use the wireless Internet.

Service plans for pagers are a lot like phone service plans. You pay a monthly rate that covers the plan's basic features and any add-on features you choose. Fortunately, however, pager plans usually are less complicated than cellular phone plans.

To get the right Web-enabled pager plan for your needs, you must complete three basic steps:

1. **Find a provider that services your area.**

2. **Purchase the desired plan.**

3. **Purchase the desired pager.**

The following sections explore these three steps in more detail.

Finding a service provider

To use a pager, you must work with a service provider that services your area. The service provider has a wireless tower with which your pager communicates. Typically, the service provider shows you a map of all the local or even national locations with which your pager can communicate. Regardless of whether you are sending or receiving pages, Internet e-mail, or instant messages, your pager operates by exchanging data with the wireless tower, which then communicates with the Internet, as needed. Figure 5-1 shows these connections.

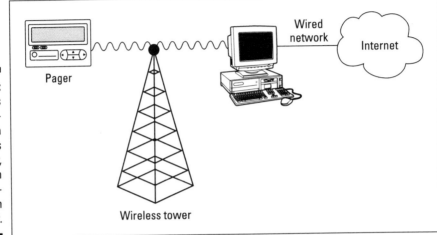

Figure 5-1:
Pagers communicate with a wireless tower, which communicates with the Internet.

To use your pager, you must be in an area that your service provider covers. You can find out about a service provider for your area by visiting a local electronics store or checking the telephone directory for your city.

If you travel a lot, check out the other areas in which your pager will function. Try to find a provider that gives you the most versatile service and covers the greatest possible area.

Purchasing the desired plan

After you find a service provider that can meet your needs in the areas where you live and work, you choose a plan. As with phone plans, you have numerous options. Fortunately, however, service providers typically offer the basic service for a flat rate instead of charging for a specific number of minutes per month.

One-way paging, which doesn't give you any Internet, e-mail, or instant messaging capabilities, typically costs about $10 per month for your service area and between $20 and $50 per month for statewide to national coverage.

Of course, depending on your provider, you can find various rates for two-way paging that includes all the bells and whistles of the Internet. Generally, however, these services cost anywhere from $15 to $20 per month for your

---

Do I get guaranteed message delivery?

Yes, most two-way pager plans offer guaranteed delivery of your e-mail and instant messages. For example, assume that you are traveling and you type an e-mail message. When you press Send, you are notified that you are outside your pager's coverage area. What happens? Your e-mail is stored on the pager and is sent as soon as you return to your service area. This way, your pager can help ensure that all e-mail messages you type are sent to the desired recipients.

---

local area and around $30 to $50 per month for national coverage. These plans include wireless e-mail and a limited number of messages (usually around 200).

You can also purchase additional usage plans if you expect to send and receive lots of e-mail and instant messages. These services typically give you an additional 500 messages per month for around $15, or as many as 2,000 messages per month for $30. As you can see, considering the number of messages available, these services are relatively inexpensive.

So, what kind of plan should you purchase? Fortunately, you can easily sort through most pager plans, but keep these points in mind as you are choosing a plan:

 ✔ **Choose a plan based on your usage.** If you typically stay in one area, don't buy a national plan. Otherwise, you'll spend too much and you will not use the plan enough to justify the cost.

 ✔ **If you expect to send and receive lots of e-mail or instant messages, upgrade your plan to cover this additional usage.** With most plans, you incur additional charges (5 to 10 cents per message) if you exceed your plan's message limit, and those additional charges can get expensive.

 ✔ **Try to balance cost and features — that is, buy the best plan you afford, but be realistic about your usage.** After all, you don't want to pay for something you don't use.

Choosing a pager

After you select a service plan, you get the fun of choosing the pager you want. Typically, you choose a pager with your service provider's help to ensure that the pager you buy is compatible with the service provider.

What is a message, exactly?

In terms of pager use, the word *message* typically refers to an instant message or e-mail message that you send or receive. However, many plans define a single message as a fixed number of characters (including spaces). For example, many plans consider 100 characters as a single message. If you type an e-mail message that consists of 125 characters, that e-mail represents two messages in terms of your plan usage. So, you have to be careful. Your plan may treat a longer e-mail and instant message as three to five messages. Carefully read the fine print in your service plan so you know exactly what constitutes a message and exactly what you pay if you exceed your message limit during a given month.

You may find a cool pager on the Internet for sale, but you have no guarantee that the pager will work with your service provider. At a minimum, make sure you get a list of compatible products from your service provider before buying your pager.

When you get ready to choose a pager, check out the next section in this chapter, which examines some of the more popular Web-enabled pagers.

Quick Catalog of Web-Enabled Pagers

The bad news is that you do not have many Web-enabled pager choices at this time. The good news is that the choices you have are very cool! As I write this book, you have two basic choices: the RIM BlackBerry 950 and several Motorola Personal Interactive Communicators (PICs). But frankly, these products are so good that you will not feel confined.

The following sections tell you a little about each of these products.

RIM BlackBerry 950

Research In Motion (RIM) makes two different BlackBerry handheld products: the 957 and the 950. The 957 functions more like a PDA, and I describe it in more detail in Chapter 6. However, most of the 957 functions are also available on the 950. The 950 is the size of a pager, but it packs a lot of power into one small device. Figure 5-2 shows the BlackBerry 950.

The BlackBerry 950 gives you an easy-to-use keyboard and a very intuitive interface. The BlackBerry 950 is always connected to the wireless network, so you simply send and receive e-mail as needed — no need to connect because you're always connected.

Figure 5-2:
The RIM
BlackBerry
950
handheld.

The 950 can do everything a traditional two-way pager can do, and it also contains the power of a PDA. The BlackBerry comes with a docking cradle so you can connect it to your PC to synchronize with various applications, such as Microsoft Outlook, Lotus Notes, and GroupWise. The BlackBerry 950 contains 4MB of memory. It also has a built-in calendar, task list, address book, Web browser, and other applications that you typically see on a PDA. Like the 957 model, the 950 can seamlessly synchronize with corporate e-mail applications, such as Microsoft Exchange and Lotus Domino. For this reason, this product is quickly becoming very popular in the corporate sector. It has an easy-to-read LCD screen that can display six to eight lines of text at a time.

At this time, the BlackBerry runs only via a wireless account with Aether Systems, which will cost you about $40 per month. However, the fee provides unlimited access to e-mail and Web-based updates. Of course, you should check out coverage areas to make sure the BlackBerry is the right product for you. You can find coverage maps at www.myaetherbb.com, and you can see more about the BlackBerry, including an interactive demonstration, at www. blackberry.net. The 950 model costs approximately $400.

Motorola Personal Interactive Communicators

Motorola Personal Interactive Communicators (PICs) give you four product options (at the moment) that provide all the services of two-way pagers and much more. The Motorola products are very popular, and most service providers support Motorola pagers. The following sections give you an overview of the four PIC products, and you can also find out more about them and see interactive demos at www.motorola.com.

Talkabout T900 2way

The Talkabout T900 2way gives you all the features of a two-way pager plus the power of the wireless Internet. Send and receive e-mail and check out information on the Internet, such as news, sports, and entertainment. The T900 also supports two-way messaging.

The T900 gives you a sleek, cool design that can display four lines of text at a time. You can create folders to organize and manage your e-mail, and you get an address book that can store as many as 250 entries. The T900 costs approximately $180, but I should note here that you cannot synchronize this one with your PC. Figure 5-3 shows the T900.

Timeport P935 2way

The Timeport P935 2way does everything the T900 model can do, but the P935 works more like a pager/PDA combination rather than just a simple pager. You can use calendar, tasks, memos, and other related tools. Also, the P935 can synchronize with your PC and gives you 4.5MB of memory. It can display as many as nine lines of text. Figure 5-4 shows the Timeport P935, which costs about $400.

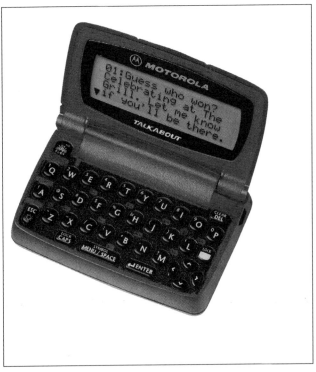

Figure 5-3:
The
Motorola
T900 pager.

© 2001, Motorola, Inc. Reproduced with Permission from Motorola, Inc.

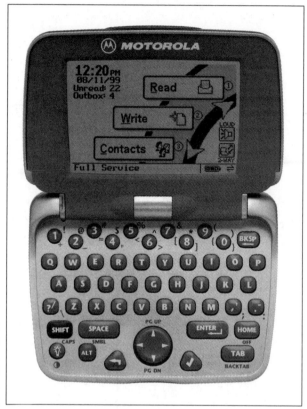

Figure 5-4:
The
Motorola
Timeport
P935 pager.

PageWriter 2000X

The PageWriter 2000X is like the P935, but it doesn't have all the PDA-type features of the P935, such as the calendar and address book. In other words, the PageWriter model is designed primarily as a pager while the Timeport functions more like a PDA. However, you can upgrade current 2000X software to the P935 to get all the additional calendar and software features for about $50. The PageWriter 2000X can also synchronize with the PC and gives you 4.5MB of memory.

This model can display as many as nine lines of text and will cost you around $320.

Timeport P930

The Timeport P930 model offers the same features as the PageWriter 2000X. The only difference is the case design, which is silver. You can also upgrade this model so that you get all the features of the P935, which costs about $50. The Timeport P930 costs around $320.

Chapter 6

Choosing a Wireless Personal Digital Assistant

. . . .

In This Chapter

▶ Getting to know personal digital assistants (PDAs)

▶ Discovering what you can do with a PDA

▶ Checking out the wireless Internet features of PDAs

▶ Exploring a quick catalog of PDAs

. . . .

The Personal Digital Assistant (PDA), also called a *handheld,* has become very popular during the past few years, primarily due to the Palm Pilot, which exploded onto the scene a few years back. In a nutshell, the PDA is a small computer that you can hold in your hand. It is no larger than a typical calculator and can easily fit into your pocket or purse. Despite their small size, however, PDAs offer truly amazing power and usefulness. As a technology author, I own many computers, gadgets, and other electronic devices. But I have to say, my PDA is one of the niftier and more useful items I own — next to my small fleet of PCs, of course.

So, what's the big deal about PDAs? Well, consider this scenario. You're heading to a meeting across town. You need calendar data, contact information, e-mail addresses, various memos, and other piles of paperwork. You can stuff all those items into a briefcase and go to the meeting, or you can store everything in a palm-sized PDA, with which you can dynamically change your data wherever you go. Add wireless e-mail and Internet access no matter where you are, and you have a winner!

In this chapter, I give you the inside scoop on what wireless Internet PDAs can do, how you can use them, and what they may cost you. I also introduce you to several popular PDAs.

Understanding How PDAs Work

You may have heard of PDAs or even seen one here or there, but maybe you're not sure whether a PDA would be useful to you. Don't worry; in this chapter I give you the complete lowdown on PDAs so you can decide whether you could use one for your work and your daily life. In the following sections, I introduce you to the two major types of PDAs, tell you a little about the software that makes PDAs work, and then explain how you can keep your PDA and your computer in sync with one another. Subsequent sections in this chapter explore the basic functions of PDAs, the wireless Internet and e-mail capabilities that these devices offer, and some of the popular models that you may want to consider.

Checking out two primary types of PDAs

As I mention at the beginning of this chapter, the PDA is a handheld device, about the size of a typical calculator. The PDA has control buttons and a screen that presents the information you want to see. You can choose from two basic types of PDA: the keypad PDA and the stylus PDA.

As shown in Figure 6-1, a keypad PDA contains a miniature keyboard, usually called the QWERTY keyboard. This miniature keyboard looks a little tricky, but you'll quickly become a pro. Although the keyboard is small, it enables you to interact with the PDA in the same way as you use a desktop PC. The RIM BlackBerry is an example of a PDA that uses a QWERTY keyboard.

The other type of PDA uses a stylus instead of a keyboard. A *stylus* is a plastic device that looks like a pen. The PDA has a touch-sensitive screen, and you use the stylus to touch areas of the screen in order to interact with the PDA, as shown in Figure 6-2. The Palm PDA uses a stylus.

The stylus PDA typically contains an area in which you can write numbers and symbols that the PDA can interpret for you, as shown in Figure 6-3. If you are using the writing feature of a stylus, you must also learn a shorthand-type language for the PDA. For example, the Palm uses the Palm Graffiti character set so you can easily input words and numbers. The character set you must learn for stylus PDAs may seem a little daunting, but you can learn it easily.

Most PDAs that use a stylus also provide an onscreen keyboard. You use the onscreen keyboard by typing with the stylus. This process is typically slower and more difficult than using a built-in mini keyboard, but if you're sitting on a crowded bus, the stylus approach can be easier.

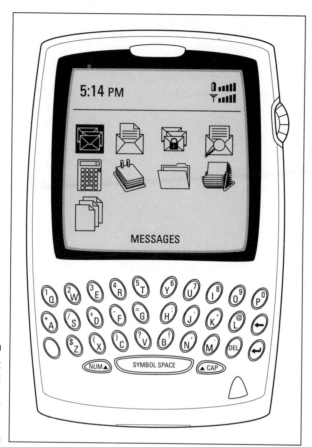

Figure 6-1:
A typical
PDA with a
QWERTY
keyboard.

Of course, some PDAs blur the lines between the two types by providing both a QWERTY keyboard and a stylus. You can use the keyboard or the stylus — the choice is up to you.

Scoping out PDA operating systems

A PDA uses an operating system, just as a desktop computer does. The operating system enables you to interact with the PDA and make the PDA do things that are helpful to you. PDAs generally use two basic operating systems or operating system variations: the Palm OS or Windows CE.

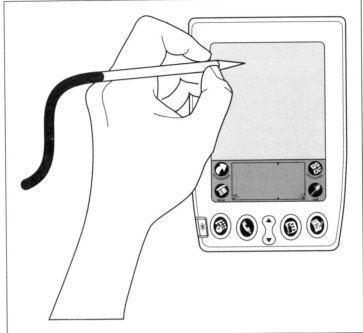

Figure 6-2:
A stylus-
based PDA.

Figure 6-3:
A typical
onscreen
PDA
keyboard.

The Palm OS is available on all Palm products. The Palm OS provides an easy-
to-use, intuitive PDA interface that you can learn in just a few hours. Unlike
computer operating systems, which can be very complicated and frustrating,
the Palm OS gives you easy access to all the functions and features offered in
the Palm with a minimal learning curve. The Palm OS uses icons and menus
so you can move around within the operating system and access items that
you need. Other PDAs, like the BlackBerry, also use this same type of icon
and menu approach.

The second type of operating system commonly available on PDAs is Windows CE. Windows CE is a miniature version of Microsoft Windows. It has the same look and feel as Windows, but of course, does not provide all of the functionality of the desktop version. Some people love Windows CE, while others feel that it is too much for such a small space.

You can find a lot of information on the Internet about PDAs, but if you're new to these devices, just march into an electronics store and play around with a few of them to get a feel for how they work and look, and how the various operating systems function. Information is great, but a hands-on test drive will help you make a final decision about which PDA is right for you.

Using applications with PDAs

When you stop and think about it, a desktop computer operating system doesn't do a whole lot without a bunch of applications that are preinstalled or that you install yourself. Applications — for example, word processing, databases, and even games — enable you to do what you want with your computer so that the computer is something useful to you. PDAs are no exception to this rule. All PDAs use a variety of applications that make them usable. Like most PCs, PDAs come with various built-in applications that are already available on the PDA when you buy it. For example, both the Palm and the BlackBerry include built-in calendars, To Do lists, address books, and other related applications that help you organize and manage information.

In addition, most PDA Web sites have additional applications and tools that you can install on your PDA as needed. For example, the Palm Web site regularly provides updates to the Palm OS so you can download the new tools and applications as they become available. Windows CE PDAs even have miniature versions of Microsoft Word, Excel, and related programs that you can use on the PDA. Of course, the PDA applications are not made of entire CD-ROMs full of stuff — they're simpler, but you'll still find vast functionality and tons of things you can do while you're on the go.

Synching up with the desktop computer

PDAs can synchronize with various programs installed on a desktop computer. When you buy a PDA, you get software that you can install on your desktop computer so you can transfer information from your PDA to your desktop PC, and vice-versa. For example, if you add several names to your PDA's address book while you're away on a business trip, you can synchronize the PDA's address book with the address book on your desktop computer, ensuring that those new contacts get added to both address books. This is a very cool and very useful feature of PDAs.

When you purchase a PDA, you get a small cradle similar to the example shown in Figure 6-4. The cradle connects to your computer, usually via a serial or USB port. The software you install on your computer then works with the PDA so that the two can synchronize various types of information — for example, ensuring that e-mail received on your PDA also appears on your desktop computer.

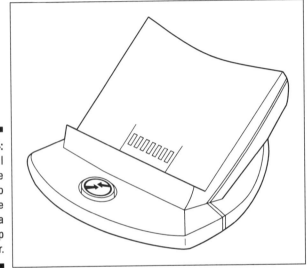

Figure 6-4:
A typical
PDA cradle
used to
synchronize
with a
desktop
computer.

Many PDAs also synchronize with specific e-mail programs, such as Microsoft Outlook. Using a wireless Internet PDA, you can create and send e-mail messages, receive new ones, and then synchronize with your desktop Outlook program when convenient. This way, you do not have some e-mail messages here, some e-mail messages there, and some e-mail messages everywhere.

Of course, each PDA offers somewhat different synchronization capabilities. In other words, you may need to buy extra software to synchronize with the mail client you use, such as Outlook. As always, shop carefully to find the PDA that is just right for you and your needs. And when you are ready to start shopping, see the section, "Quick Catalog of Web-Enabled PDAs," later in this chapter, for a look at some great models that you may want to consider.

Understanding What a PDA Does

PDAs provide lots of great functions to help you keep up with your business and other aspects of your life. Like your desktop computer, a PDA uses applications to provide the different types of functionality. Some applications come built-in when you purchase the PDA, some can be purchased and installed, and for some PDA models, you can download additional applications to your desktop PC and then add them to the PDA via the PDA/computer synchronization feature. Each brand and model works a little differently, so carefully read the manufacturer's instructions to find out how you get all the functionality you need for your PDA.

In the following sections, I review the basic functions that PDAs typically provide and show you some examples from the Palm VIIx. Depending on the brand and model, your PDA may look different from the examples you see here, but if you're thinking about buying a PDA, this section can help you get a handle on the basic functionality that's available.

Making a date

Wouldn't life be nice if we could all float along with no worries at all, completely unaware of the day and time? Okay, I admit that some people actually live that way, but I've never been so lucky. Unfortunately, most of us live on a schedule — often a very crowded and busy one. Thanks to your PDA's datebook functions, however, your calendar information can travel with you.

A PDA's datebook typically functions like any other type of desktop calendar program, especially those found in e-mail programs. As you can see in Figure 6-5, you can use the PDA to make entries into a calendar and then use that calendar to keep up with appointments. The great advantage of the electronic datebook is that you can make changes on the fly without having to cross out previous dates. The simple, compact PDA datebook can give you a daily and hourly look as well as weekly and monthly views. You can add notes to remind yourself of the details regarding your appointments, and most PDAs enable you to set alarms so you can make sure you don't miss any appointments.

Keeping up with people

Electronic address books have become very popular, and many people use an e-mail address book. A desktop computer's address book enables you to store information about people and quickly find that information when needed. Unfortunately, that desktop address book doesn't follow you around, and you often make great contacts when you're away from your computer. For example, you may go to convention in another city. At that convention, you meet ten excellent new contacts for your business. You could scribble all that contact information on pieces of scrap paper and hope those notes survive the trip home. Then, you would have to decipher your own handwriting and enter all that information into your desktop computer.

Figure 6-5:
Stay on
schedule
with a
handy PDA
datebook.

Or, you can simply enter the information into your PDA as you make contacts. And when you arrive back at your home or office, just synchronize the PDA's address book with the one on your computer — not a bad solution!

PDA address books, like the one shown in Figure 6-6, enable you to enter typical contact information about people and then store that information in the PDA. You can then search your address book to find people as needed, and most address books provide different categories, such as business, personal, and so on. Overall, PDA address books are fast, efficient, and very productive.

Figure 6-6:
PDA
address
books help
you keep
track of
people.

Most PDA address books have numerous fields in which you can enter all kinds of information, and most of them include a notes category in which you can type a whole paragraph about that person. Use this feature to record helpful reminders about business contacts, or just to vent against people you really don't like.

Taking care of business

Perhaps this scenario sounds familiar: Before you head out to face another busy day, you jot down a list of things you need to do, items you need to pick up at the grocery store, and so on. Of course, you soon forget where you put the list, but at least you remember to go to the grocery store. You think you remember everything you wanted to buy, but if you're like me, you end up with lots of stuff you don't need — mainly ice cream.

Most people keep To Do lists, whether they scribble the list on paper or try to keep it mentally organized and arranged. For most of us, neither of these options works very well. Fortunately, the PDA can solve these problems by keeping all your To Do lists in one central location where you can create, edit, and manage them as needed. As shown in Figure 6-7, a typical To Do list enables you to create and manage items, and even check them off when you complete them. Now, armed with your PDA, you can always find your To Do lists, unless you manage to lose the entire PDA. Incidentally, many PDAs offer warranty coverage in case of loss or theft.

Managing your memos

In the business world, memos are a must. Unfortunately, I usually compose my best memos while I'm stuck in a taxi or on an airplane. No problem. You can create memos on your PDA and then synchronize the PDA with your desktop computer, where you can further use, edit, or distribute the memos.

Most PDAs include a memo option that provides a screen on which you can type your memo, save it, and then manage an entire list of memos, as needed. The best thing about the memo feature is that you only have to enter the information once. You can type the memo while riding in a cab, synch up with the desktop computer, and go from there. Most importantly, you can keep track of ideas when they come to you — no matter where you are.

Tracking your expenses

During your business trips, do you need to track of all your expenses? Or, do you want to keep closer tabs on how much money leaves your wallet or purse during your next mall shopping spree? Several PDAs include expense applications that can help you keep track of your expenses. Of course, you have to enter the correct information into your PDA, but these programs definitely can help you keep your expenses organized and tallied. Most PDA expense applications enable you to export data to a desktop computer's spreadsheet application so you can quickly generate an expense report (and get your money back).

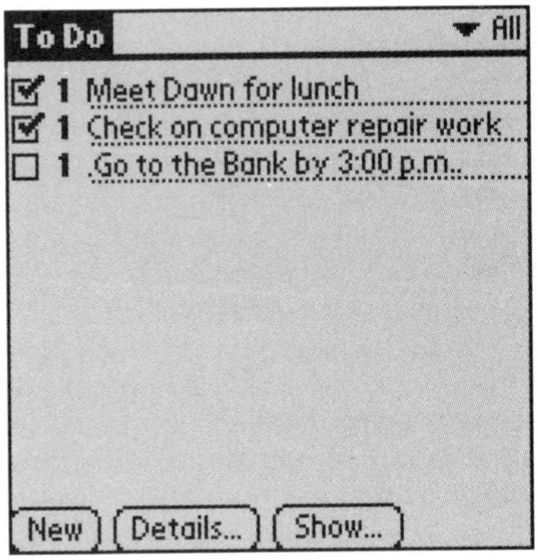

```
To Do                    ▼ All
☑ 1  Meet Dawn for lunch
☑ 1  Check on computer repair work
☐ 1  Go to the Bank by 3:00 p.m.




[ New ] [ Details... ] [ Show... ]
```

Figure 6-7:
Get things
done with
a PDA's
To Do list.

Securing your information

Most PDAs can secure information that you do not want anyone else to see. You can specify which records you want to hide and set a password that must be entered in order to view those records. This simple feature is very useful if you have private information stored in your PDA, and you are worried about theft or prying eyes. With most PDAs, you can even password-protect the entire PDA so that no one can use it if it is stolen or left unattended.

Accessing the Wireless Internet with a PDA

Wireless Internet PDAs contain all the standard PDA features you might expect to find, as well as wireless Internet and e-mail capabilities. Wireless Internet access and e-mail functionality are relatively new features for PDAs, and you will not find many brands and models available to choose from, at least at the moment. Within a year, however, I expect that you'll see more and more PDAs joining the wireless Internet access world. Eventually, wireless Internet access will be a standard PDA feature — much like all computers today ship with a 56Kb modem.

In the meantime, the brands and models available for wireless Internet access are super cool, but quite different from each other. I explore them in the "Quick Catalog of Web-Enabled PDAs," later in this chapter. In the following sections, I describe how PDAs handle wireless Internet access and e-mail.

Getting connected

Without going into the boring, gory details, I want to spend a moment telling you about wireless connectivity and the PDA. Wireless connectivity with a PDA works basically like it does with your cellular phone. The PDA has a built-in transmitter, or it may have a wireless modem. The transmitter or modem connects with a wireless tower so that Internet and e-mail communications can take place. It's easy, painless, and very effective.

Wireless connectivity does not work everywhere. The more heavily populated areas usually have wireless connectivity, but if you are traveling in a rural area, you may lose connectivity. Before you purchase any wireless Internet device, study the coverage maps freely available on different vendor Web sites, or ask a salesperson to make sure your wireless device will operate in the area where you live and work.

The good news about wireless Internet connectivity via a PDA is that you usually do not pay roaming charges. After you're connected, you can use it anywhere, as long as a tower is within reach. In other words, you do not have to contend with any out-of-area charges and related issues.

After you purchase a PDA and a wireless service plan, review the instructions that ship with your PDA to find out how to set up your Internet account. After you purchase the PDA, you usually activate your Internet account in one of the following ways:

- **Automatic activation:** Simply turn on the PDA or raise the antenna, and the device walks you through a series of steps to complete activation. These steps gather information about you, your credit card number, and your setup. It's quick and easy.

- **Web site activation:** After you choose a service provider (with some PDAs, you have a choice), visit the service provider's Web site, sign up online, and then you can connect and activate your PDA.

Carefully follow the manufacturer's guide for complete instructions on how to activate your wireless PDA. And if your PDA provides several different service options, study them carefully to find the one that is right for you. Some PDAs charge on a kilobyte basis — in other words, you are given so many kilobytes you can use on the Internet before more charges apply. Basic plans sometimes allow you 50 KB, which gives you enough data for simple e-mail messages, while others give you larger blocks of data. Some plans, on the other hand, simply charge you a flat fee, which I prefer.

Surfing the Internet with a PDA

In some respects, surfing the wireless Internet with a PDA is easier than using a Web-enabled phone. A PDA offers a larger screen, and you can quickly input information using a stylus or the PDA's keyboard. However, like Web-enabled phones, PDAs have some display limitations so you cannot freely visit any Web site you want to see. Because most PDAs cannot support all the color and graphics files that typical Web sites use, PDAs use scaled-down versions of Web sites so you can still get the information you need.

Although PDAs differ from one another in their approach to Internet usage and Web surfing, they all use *launch pages* as a means to access the Web sites that they support. For example, the Palm VIIx, which is a wireless Internet PDA, calls these launch pages *Web clippings*.

Some Web clippings are installed when you purchase the device, and you can download many other Web clippings and install them on the PDA so you can access the sites you want. As shown in Figures 6-8 and 6-9, the typical Web site you see with a computer browser is scaled down to basic text compatible with the PDA. As you can see, the MyMotivator.com Web clipping contains a basic interface, but no graphics. This clipping enables you to enter search information or click on category links. Then, through the wireless Internet connectivity, you can interact with the Web site. Although some wireless Web sites do provide graphics, they are usually very basic and simple.

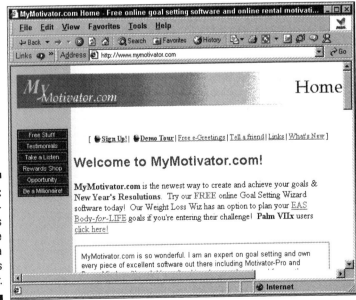

Figure 6-8: MyMotivator.com's home page seen on a computer's browser.

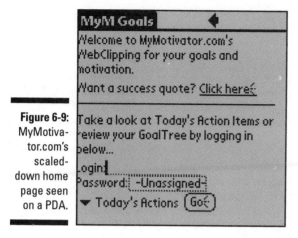

Figure 6-9:
MyMotiva-
tor.com's
scaled-
down home
page seen
on a PDA.

As you can see, these Web clippings maintain the basic functionality of the Web site without all the graphics and pictures. Some PDAs, such as Compaq's iPAQ, provide more graphic and color support, and you can even manage the level of colors and graphics that are downloaded on those models.

At this time, wireless PDAs and phones do not offer very fast connectivity speed — usually around 9 Kbps. So, even if you could download all the pictures and graphics Web sites have to offer, you probably would not want to do so because of the lengthy download times.

So, you don't really surf the Internet using PDAs. With a computer browser, you can hop from site to site and visit any Web site you want to see. The PDA is more restrictive because not all Web sites support interactive functionality with the PDA. However, you can still access many, many sites, and the list continues to grow every day.

See this book's "Wireless Internet Access Directory" for information about Web sites that support mobile access from devices, such as PDAs and Web-enabled phones.

Using e-mail with a wireless PDA

You can send and receive wireless e-mail using a PDA in much the same way you do when using a desktop computer. As with the Internet access feature, each PDA takes a slightly different approach to its e-mail features and operations. For example, some wireless PDAs provide access to a certain e-mail account that you sign up for when you activate the PDA. Others provide complex synchronization features with corporate e-mail. I explain which PDAs offer these options in the "Quick Catalog of Web-Enabled PDAs," later in this chapter. In this section, I consider the basics of wireless e-mail.

Like the e-mail application or Web browser in your desktop PC, the PDA contains an application that sends, receives, and stores e-mail. As shown in Figure 6-10, the PDA's e-mail application is designed to send short e-mail messages and enable you to receive and read your e-mail when you are away from your desktop computer.

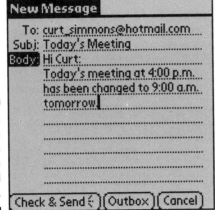

Figure 6-10:
Wireless
PDAs
provide
basic e-mail
functionality.

With the e-mail application, you can receive messages, send messages, reply to messages, store messages, and do just about anything else you can do with a typical e-mail program. However, you cannot send and receive e-mail attachments, such as documents or pictures, via your PDA's wireless e-mail features. Also, some PDA e-mail applications place restrictions on message lengths. Any messages you send or receive that exceed the allowed length get truncated. Remember to ask the salesperson about this issue before you make a purchase!

At the time of this writing, the exception to this rule is the Compaq iPAQ Pocket PC, which can send and receive attachments. You can find out more about the IPAQ in the next section.

Why can't you send and receive attachments on most PDAs? First, attachments take up disk space, and most PDAs do not have enough extra storage space to hold attachment files. Next, the PDA needs applications that can open attachments. For example, if you download a picture file, the PDA needs a program that can read the picture file. The desktop computer has these programs installed when you purchase it, but the PDA does not have enough storage room for regular desktop applications. The IPAQ is the exception to this rule, and as I explain in the following section, the IPAQ acts more like a desktop computer than a handheld device, anyway.

Quick Catalog of Web-Enabled PDAs

In this section, I point out the primary wireless PDA options and give you quick and easy information about them so you can choose one that is right for you. First, however, I must offer the obligatory warning: This section offers a brief overview of popular wireless PDAs, not a comprehensive directory. Use this section as a guide to help you know what is available. However, you may find the perfect PDA from another manufacturer that I do not cover in this section. Also, products and service plans change quickly, so visit the manufacturers' Web sites noted throughout this section to get the most up-to-date information and possible sales or discounts.

With that obligatory warning out of the way, check out the following sections to read about several popular wireless PDAs.

Palm: Wireless Internet and e-mail

The Palm, or Palm Pilot, is the most popular PDA on the market. Palm was one of the first true PDAs on the market, and you can choose from several Palm models. The Palm VIIx, m500, and m505 are currently the only Palm models that provide wireless Internet access straight out of the box, although I expect more models to provide wireless Internet access by the time you read this book. The wireless Internet Palm models cost approximately $399 to $500, depending on the model and excluding Internet setup and usage fees. You may be able to upgrade other Palm models with a wireless modem and Internet connection kit, usually for around $200. See the Palm Web site for details.

The Palm , is a compact PDA that uses a stylus for communication with the system. It also provides an on-screen keyboard for easy input, but it does not have an external keyboard. The Palm is very easy to use, and Internet activation is a real snap — just raise the antenna and follow the instructions that appear. The unit connects with a tower, gathers information from you, sets up your e-mail address and connection, takes your credit card number, and you're all set. I was able to activate my account in less than five minutes with no problems at all.

Palm PDA features

The wireless Internet Palm models provides the functionality of most other Palm handhelds, plus they provide you with 8 MB of RAM or more. The unit weighs only 6.7 ounces with the batteries installed. It's easy to carry and easy to use. Here's a quick rundown of the Palm's primary features:

- Preinstalled with the Palm operating system and the capability to synchronize with your desktop computer.

- Preinstalled primary applications, such as Date Book, Address Book, and To Do List. You can install other applications from the Palm Web site.

✔ An easy search feature with which you can find any data on the PDA by simply typing a keyword and performing the search for the information.

✔ An infrared port so you can beam files and applications to other infrared-enabled Palms. An infrared port uses an infrared beam, much like grocery store scanners, to send information wirelessly to another Palm device. Of course, the devices must be close to each other, but the infrared transfer gives you a quick and easy way to move data between two devices.

✔ Graffiti software, which is a handwriting recognition program, so you can write on screen with the stylus. This takes a little practice, but it is very effective after you master some of the strange lettering.

✔ Automatic Internet connectivity — simply raise the antenna.

Palm wireless Internet features

The Palm uses the Palm.net service as your Internet service provider (ISP). In other words, you use the Palm.net service to establish Internet connectivity and send and receive e-mail. When you sign up with the Palm.net service, you receive a Palm e-mail address, such as `yourname@palm.net`. Can you use a different ISP, you might wonder? No, you must use Palm.net. This approach is the norm for PDAs. The ISP must support the PDA communication, so you usually can choose from only one ISP, or at most two.

Palm.net service gives you three Internet connectivity options. You pay a one-time setup fee of $9.99. You then choose from one of the plans I describe in Table 6-1.

Table 6-1: Palm.net Wireless Internet Plans

Wireless Plan	What You Get	Monthly Fee
Basic	50KB of information per month (about 50 Palm screens)	$9.99, plus $.20 for each KB in excess of the monthly 50KB limit
Extended	150KB of information per month (about 450 Palm screens)	$24.99, plus $.20 for each KB in excess of the monthly 150KB limit
Unlimited	Unlimited Internet and e-mail usage	$44.99

The Palm.net service is available in more than 260 metropolitan areas throughout the United States. It has no roaming fees. In other words, you can use the Palm.net service in any area where it is available without additional charges. For more information about the Palm VIIx, visit `www.palm.com`.

RIM BlackBerry: Access to corporate e-mail

Research In Motion (RIM) has gained a lot of attention with its BlackBerry product during the past year. As shown in Figure 6-11, this PDA ships as two different models: the 957 standard handheld size and the 950 pager size. They both do the same thing — the size you prefer determines which one you pick. The 957 has a bigger display and more memory. Unless you specifically need a pager-sized model, the 957 is your best pick. The 950 costs around $400, and the 957 will cost you around $500.

As you can see in Figure 6-11, the RIM BlackBerry uses a QWERTY keyboard instead of a stylus. It has a sleek design and is very easy to use. The BlackBerry offers built-in wireless connectivity that is always available when the unit is on. You don't even have to raise an antenna. The wireless connectivity provides e-mail, messaging, and some Internet content. That may not sound like much, but the BlackBerry also can integrate seamlessly with corporate e-mail systems. This factor alone makes BlackBerry very popular as a corporate PDA, and more than 7,000 companies have adopted it since its introduction into the market.

Figure 6-11:
The RIM BlackBerry 950 and 957.

BlackBerry PDA features

The BlackBerry PDA contains the typical features that you expect to find in a PDA. Here's an overview of its more interesting features:

- A full set of organizational software, such as calendar, address book, task list, alarm, and related applications.

- A 386 processor for plenty of speed.

- An "always on, always connected" wireless approach, with neither an antenna to raise nor a modem to activate. When the unit is turned on, it is connected to the wireless network.

- Advanced security features, including the industry standard Triple Data Encryption Standard (TDES). This feature enables the BlackBerry to meet corporate network security requirements for remote e-mail.

- Full desktop computer synchronization using Puma Technology's Intellisync software. When you place the BlackBerry in its cradle, Intellisync automatically synchronizes your PC with any changes you made to your BlackBerry's calendar, task list, and address book.

BlackBerry Internet and e-mail features

The BlackBerry was designed with corporate e-mail and seamless connectivity in mind. The BlackBerry comes in two basic flavors: the Enterprise edition and the Internet edition.

The Enterprise edition enables the BlackBerry to function natively with networks that use Microsoft Exchange or Lotus Domino. BlackBerry Enterprise Server is additional software that networks can deploy so that messages received for a BlackBerry user are redirected wirelessly to the BlackBerry handheld. So, with this model, you do not actually check your e-mail; it arrives automatically to your BlackBerry. When you send a message, it goes to the Exchange Server or Lotus Domino server on your corporate network, which forwards it on to the appropriate location on your network or via the Internet.

The Internet edition of BlackBerry functions like the Palm. You purchase an ISP account and use an Internet e-mail address that you can access from the BlackBerry. You can synchronize e-mail, calendar data, and other types of information with your desktop PC.

For Internet content, you use a few different services that are available with the BlackBerry. Although these services give you access to the Web content you want, the content offered caters to business and travel. All of these are optional services, and you may be charged extra for using them.

- **Ask@OracleMobile:** With this free service, which was created for BlackBerry, you can ask for stock quotes, traffic reports, flight information, dictionary translation, and other types of services. To get the desired information, you send a short e-mail message to ask@oraclemobile.com, which replies with the answer to your question. You can learn more about this service at `www.oraclemobile.com/mymobile/register1.jsp`

✔ **Go.Web:** With a subscription to this service, you can gather and customize Web content, such as news, travel, sports, and stocks. Depending on the options you select, this information can be readily displayed to you as it is needed. If you choose to subscribe to Go.Web, the first month is free, but after that, you'll be charged $9.95 per month for the first 25KB of data and $.30 for each additional kilobyte (there's a monthly cap of $19.95). You can learn more about this service at `www.goamerica.net/htm/blackberry/index.html`.

✔ **PocketGenie:** This subscription-based Web service connects with BlackBerry so you can view Internet content via a micro-browser. You can get all kinds of Web content using this service, including restaurant and movie guides. This service costs $9.95 per month for 50 uses, then $.25 for each additional use, or you can just pay $14.95 for unlimited use. You also have to pay a $9.95 setup fee. You can read more about this service at `www.wolfetech.com`.

You don't use Web clippings, as you do with the Palm , but you can get essentially the same information using these services. However, getting that information may cost you a little more because you must subscribe to each service.

The BlackBerry Internet edition uses Aether Systems, found at `www.aethersystems.com`, for its wireless service plan. You pay a flat rate of $39.99 per month for wireless access, but that fee is for e-mail access only — paging and roaming are not included. As with all wireless plans, you need to check out the coverage maps and make sure service is available in your area.

Watch for even more BlackBerry product/service combinations as other vendors adopt BlackBerry and combine it with their products and services. For example, RIM and AOL currently offer a co-branded product, and you'll soon see RIM working with Compaq and other vendors. RIM will also support Java in the near future., For business users and corporate networks, the BlackBerry is an exciting one to watch. Read more about the BlackBerry at `www.blackberry.net`.

Compaq iPAQ: Versatile and powerful

Before you start sending me angry e-mail messages, I do realize that the Compaq iPAQ is not really considered a PDA, but rather a handheld PC or a pocket PC. The Compaq iPAQ is more than a PDA; it is a complete computer system that can do just about everything a desktop system can do. I include it here because it fits into this chapter's coverage of handheld devices and wireless Internet connectivity.

The Compaq iPAQ ships in several different models — even a desktop version that essentially provides Internet connectivity. Running Windows CE, it has the power to run mini versions of major applications, such as Microsoft Word, Excel, Internet Explorer, and even Outlook. It sports a color screen, a 206 MHz processor, and 32MB of RAM, depending on the model you purchase. This model costs around $500.

iPAQ features

The Compaq iPAQ is a true PC that fits in your hand. It has Pocket Word, Excel, Outlook, Internet Explorer, and even Windows Media Player. The unit features handwriting recognition, soft keyboard, and even voice recording. The iPAQ is a powerful personal computer that truly brings the Windows CE operating system to life because it has enough processing power and RAM to run the system. Most things you can do on a regular desktop PC, you also can do on the iPAQ.

iPAQ Internet and e-mail features

The iPAQ, at the time of this writing, does not ship with built-in wireless Internet and e-mail capabilities. You can turn the iPAQ into a wireless hand-held by using a wireless modem, which will cost you around $300. Then, you can purchase a designated ISP service with a flat-rate monthly access fee. So, you pay more up-front money because you need the wireless modem. However, after you have the modem, you have many different options for using wireless Internet and e-mail. You can even use the iPAQ to synchronize and work with Microsoft Exchange environments, in much the same way as the RIM BlackBerry. So, the iPAQ can be a personal machine or a business machine, depending on your needs.

 As with all products, you should spend some time talking to a customer service representative if you are interested in an iPAQ because so many options are available to you. You can find out more about the iPAQ by visiting www. compaq.com.

HP Jornada 540 Series: Complete computing in your hand

The HP Jornada is a pocket or handheld PC. As with the iPAQ, you can choose from several different models, all of which are very cool and may meet your needs. The HP Jornada, shown in Figure 6-12, runs the Windows CE operating system and uses a 133 MHz processor with up to 32MB of RAM. (I still have a desktop PC lurking around my house that isn't that fast.) It contains typical Windows applications, will synch up with your desktop PC, and even supports the Universal Serial Bus (USB), which is an easy-to-use port found on most desktop computers. The 548 color model costs $500 and has a 133 MHz processor and 32MB of RAM, while the 720 color model costs $900 and has a 206 MHz processor and 32MB of RAM. Neither includes a wireless modem or Internet access out of the box.

Jornada features

Using the Windows CE operating system, the Jornada provides the Pocket applications from Microsoft, such as Word, Outlook, Excel, and Windows Media Player. The unit contains a built-in sound recorder, an infrared port, a touch-sensitive screen, and an on-screen keyboard. Essentially, the Jornada can do almost everything a desktop PC can do. These features vary, depending on the model. For example, the 720 contains a physical keyboard instead of an on-screen version.

Jornada Internet and e-mail features

The Jornada does not natively provide wireless Internet access, but you can get it by purchasing the Minstrel 540 Wireless modem, which costs about $350. You can then use the modem to connect to ISPs or even a corporate network.

Spend some time talking to a customer service representative if you are interested in the Jornada — it has various different options available that you'll want to spend time researching. You can find out more about the Jornada by visiting www.hp.com.

Figure 6-12:
The HP
Jornada 540
Series.

Chapter 7

Wireless Devices of the Future

. . . .

In This Chapter

▶ Thinking about where we've been and where we're going

▶ Moving into the future with wireless devices

▶ Taking the Internet everywhere

▶ Exploring possible new devices

. . . .

Ah, the future . . . a perfect world of peace, love, and harmony — we hope. What the future holds remains uncertain, but I think we can safely assume that the Internet and computing technology are here to stay and will only become more complex, yet more fantastic, in the years ahead. Competition will spur developers and manufacturers to give us more, and the Internet, its usage, and the devices we use to access it will become more sophisticated, easier to use, and more convenient.

To understand how quickly technology can evolve, consider the computer sitting on your desk — a seemingly simple piece of machinery, right? However, only a few years ago, you would have needed an entire room or maybe even the entire floor of a building to house a computer that could pack as much processing power as you now have sitting on your desk. Or, consider the handheld computer. It fits in the palm of your hand, but it is more powerful than the desktop computers most of us used only a few years ago.

In this chapter, I explore what you may see in the future of the wireless Internet. I've taken the liberty to let my imagination run a bit wild, but I base my predictions on current industry trends. So remember that you read it here first.

Where Have We Been?

Before I peer into the future, I want to take a brief look at where we've been. To get a good handle on the future of the wireless Internet, you need to understand where we stand today, in terms of two key components: the Internet itself and the tools you use to access the Internet.

Remembering the Internet

If you've joined the Internet revolution recently, which most of you probably have, you may not have any frame of reference for understanding where the Internet comes from or where it is headed.

The origins of the Internet came during the 1960s, in work by a US government research group. The military wanted a computer network that could communicate in times of war. This network would have to function regardless of damage done to one city or another. In other words, the military wanted a network that did not rely on one central location or centralized computers controlling it. The end result of the work by this research group was a network in which different computers could send and receive data using various network pathways. If one pathway was unavailable, the network would simply use a different pathway to get the data to its intended destination.

The Internet officially began in 1969 and was called ARPAnet. ARPAnet was funded by the U.S. Advanced Research Projects Agency. The first tests of the Internet occurred with only a few universities connected to each other. The National Science Foundation later began working with the Internet, and it did not become a public entity until 1992. In 1995, commercial Internet service providers (ISPs) took control of the major Internet links, and the public Internet was born. In other words, the Internet is an adolescent — a wild and scary thought, in my opinion.

During the 1980s, when the Internet was still private, the research efforts continued, and different network protocols were introduced. A *network protocol* tells computers how to communicate with each other. Just as you and I rely on the rules of the English language to communicate, computers rely on standard sets of rules, or protocols, for communication so they know how to move data from one computer to the next. The Internet is built on TCP/IP (the Transmission Control Protocol and Internet Protocol), a powerful protocol suite that contains hundreds of protocols that computers can use. All these different protocols in the TCP/IP protocol suite enable you to do all sorts of different things on the Internet, such as read Web pages, listen to music, watch movies, send e-mail, and chat.

Whew! If that isn't enough fry your brain, the Internet primarily uses the TCP/IP protocols known as HyperText Transfer Protocol, or HTTP. You may recognize the abbreviation HTTP from surfing the Web. A typical Web address looks like this: `http://curtsimmons.hypermart.net`. The HTTP at the beginning of the address tells the computer what kind of protocol is in use for the address. HTTP is the standard protocol for moving Web pages from one computer to another.

As you may have already guessed, the standard for Web pages on the Internet is the HyperText Markup Language, otherwise known as HTML. HTML is a text-based computer language that your browser reads in order to display a Web page to you. HTML pages move from one computer to another via HTTP.

If you're new to these abbreviations, and you suddenly feel as if you are set-tling to the bottom of the ocean, don't worry — a simple example will make it all clear. Perhaps you want to visit `http://curtsimmons.hypermart.net`. (Hey, it's my book — I can use my Web site if I want!) You sit at your computer and open a Web browser, such as Internet Explorer or Netscape Navigator. In the address line, you type **http://curtsimmons.hypermart.net** and then you press Enter on your keyboard.

In most browsers, you don't have to type the `http://` part of the address. Your browser already knows that you are visiting an Internet site using HTTP, so that part is understood. For example, you can just type **curtsimmons. hypermart.net**, or **msn.com**, or **espn.com**, or whatever address you want to visit, without the **http://**, which is great because typing the **http://** is always a drag, anyway.

After you type the address and press Enter, your Web browser uses HTTP and a few other protocols, all of which are too gory to mention here, to find the Web site you want. The Web site processes your request and then sends the requested HTML document over the Internet to your computer. Your computer reads the HTML it receives, and then your browser creates the nice graphics and pictures you see in your browser window from the HTML it reads. Figure 7-1 shows an example of the HTML coding that your Web browser reads. Figure 7-2 shows how your browser interprets that HTML code.

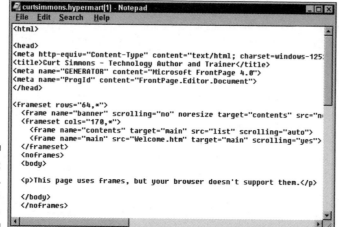

Figure 7-1:
The HTML code of a Web site.

```
curtsimmons.hypermart[1] - Notepad
File  Edit  Search  Help
<html>

<head>
<meta http-equiv="Content-Type" content="text/html; charset=windows-125
<title>Curt Simmons - Technology Author and Trainer</title>
<meta name="GENERATOR" content="Microsoft FrontPage 4.0">
<meta name="ProgId" content="FrontPage.Editor.Document">
</head>

<frameset rows="64,*">
  <frame name="banner" scrolling="no" noresize target="contents" src="n
  <frameset cols="170,*">
    <frame name="contents" target="main" src="list" scrolling="auto">
    <frame name="main" src="Welcome.htm" target="main" scrolling="yes">
  </frameset>
  <noframes>
  <body>

  <p>This page uses frames, but your browser doesn't support them.</p>

  </body>
  </noframes>
```

You can see the HTML code of any Web page you want. If you're using Internet Explorer, just click View⇨Source, and if you're using Netscape, just click View⇨Page Source.

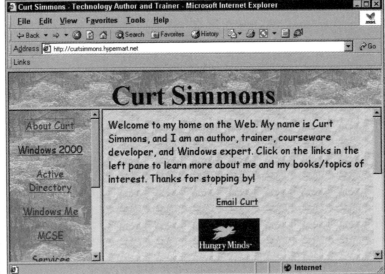

Figure 7-2:
The interpreted HTML code displayed in your Web browser.

I should back up for a moment, however, and point out that the early days of Internet browsing were not as much fun. In fact, they were downright boring by today's standards. Originally, HTML provided a means for transferring documents over the TCP/IP network. The documents had no pictures, and they were not adorned with the cool graphics that you see today. However, HTML could *hyperlink* to other documents. A hyperlink, often called a *link,* is a way to jump from one page to another. When you click on a link with your computer's mouse, you are taken to a different page or even a different Web site altogether. In Figure 7-2, the underlined phrases listed in the left pane are links. If you click on one of those links, you are taken to a different page. So, these early HTML documents were plain and boring, but they could link items together so you could jump between documents all over the Internet — which was very cool and exciting at the time.

Today's Internet technology provides new HTML and HTTP standards, but the basic technology is still in place: You view Web pages through a browser and use hyperlinks to move from page to page or from Web site to Web site. The difference today is that the Internet has become a multimedia animal. You can see pictures and graphics, watch movies, listen to music, and interact with Web sites through dynamic HTML. For example, you can search for information on a Web site or purchase an item by giving the Web site your address, credit card number, and so on.

So, the Internet has evolved from a private entity to a public entity, and from static, flat HTML pages to dynamic, exciting HTML content. That content continues to develop so that you can interact with the Internet more freely and access the Internet from all kinds of devices. And that is where Wireless

Access Protocol (WAP) comes into play. These new protocols enable Internet access for people on the go — an important capability in these mobile days.

Remembering the computer . . . from surfing to crawling

When the Internet became public in 1995, nerds like me immediately wanted to join up and play. We could read information, e-mail each other, and all was great. The Internet began growing at an alarming rate — one that continues today. I remember first connecting with the Internet using a Macintosh with a 14.4 Kbps modem. I was in heaven! Today, I would rather watch paint dry than use a 14.4 Kbps modem.

But at that time, 14.4 Kbps was sufficient. After all, Web pages were primarily text, with few or no graphics. Web browsers were simple and did very little except interpret HTML. As the Internet continued to grow, however, Web sites became more complex, and pictures and other graphics became more common. Modem speeds continued to improve, and we all kept waiting for modem upgrades so we could surf faster and faster.

We soon hit a wall with 56 Kbps modems, maxing out the current analog phone lines, which were never designed to carry Internet traffic. (In fact, those 56 Kbps modems really give you only about 47 Kbps on a perfect day.) Web sites continued to grow, multimedia continued to boom, and the 56 Kbps modem started to get left behind.

And that's basically where we are today. Most of you probably still use a 56 Kbps modem, and that's okay. But I predict that the modem will die a slow death in the next few years as DSL, cable, and the new Internet satellite products become less expensive and easier to use. High bandwidth solutions, such as DSL, cable, and satellite Internet access can provide transfer rates in excess of 500 Kbps, breaking free of the modem and dial-up connections.

From the desktop, we search for high bandwidth and easy, interactive Web sites. In the past two years, however, a great shift has occurred, with the Internet evolving from a PC-only network to the wireless Internet, which is the subject of this book. The wireless Internet gives us the freedom to use the Internet while we're on the move. At this time, the wireless Internet is limited and primarily text-based. But you know as well as I do that consumers are going to demand more and more from the wireless Internet. We'll want the wireless Internet to look and act just like the regular wired Internet, and we'll want it to be fast. And guess what? We'll get it, eventually!

What Do Wireless Internet Users Want?

You may feel like you are at the mercy of the computing and Internet technology giants, but those big companies actually listen carefully to consumers. After all, if a company can meet our needs, we buy its products, and the company makes money. So, how can I predict what might be on the horizon for the Internet users — in particular, wireless Internet users? Simply look at what consumers want and then look at technologies that are being developed to help consumers get what they want.

So, what do consumers want from the Internet, computers, and wireless devices? In the following sections, I make some predictions about what consumers want, based on my own experience and needs as a consumer, as well as my observations of industry developments.

Freedom from desktop PCs

I spend most of my day pecking at a computer keyboard, and I bet that many of you do the same. I don't want to spend every waking moment sitting at a computer, but I want to use the Internet for my daily life. In other words, the Internet needs to integrate with my life — not vice-versa. After all, technology is supposed to make our lives easier and more enjoyable, and sitting in front of a computer screen all the time is not very fun.

So, I want more devices. Specifically, I want devices that I can use and carry with me so I can get my e-mail, check my stocks, and buy stuff on the Internet no matter where I am. The current wireless Internet and wireless devices represent only the beginning of movement toward satisfying this demand. I offer some speculations about the types of devices you might see in the near future in the section "What Can We Expect from Wireless Internet Devices of Tomorrow?," later in this chapter.

Quick, easy searches for Internet information

Consumers don't want to spend all day trying to locate information they want; they want it quickly and easily. After all, who wants to spend hours fumbling with search engines? Several existing technologies can help you customize the Internet and access information more quickly, especially personal information, such as stocks, accounts, and shopping carts. However, that isn't enough, and consumers want a friendlier, more helpful Internet that enables them to find information quickly.

Want to get rich quick?

Hey, all you entrepreneurs out there. I have a suggestion for a guaranteed get-rich-quick scheme: Build a better search engine. Internet search engines have come a long way in the last few years, but they still leave a lot to be desired. How many times have you tried to find something on the Internet, only to search until your eyes began to burn? Or, you search for something, such as "where can I buy tomatoes?" and your search results include such topics as "The Tomato Nuclear Project" or "Using vegetables in human genetic research."

You know the information is out there, but you just can't find it. Internet directories and search engines have long been a problem due to the vast amount of information and correct cataloging and keyword searching. The person who finally figures out how to create an Internet search engine database that quickly and accurately helps you find the information you want will be a very wealthy person, indeed. But just remember, if you're that person, I expect a 10 percent cut of your profits because I gave you the idea.

Real content, pictures, and files

At this time, the wireless Internet doesn't provide much in the way of digital content and downloads. With the exception of handheld computers, today's wireless devices simply cannot store much information at one time. I want a Web-enabled wireless device that can do just about anything on the Internet. Give me the Internet — and give me *all* of the Internet!

Small devices that can do everything

The world's first computer took up an entire floor of an office building. Subsequent computers brought the space requirements down to one room. Later enhancements brought computers to the desktop, then the laptop, and then to handheld devices. See the pattern?

With advances in chip technology, devices, including cellular phones and pagers, are getting smaller and smaller. You can safely tuck your tiny Web-enabled phone in your pocket and go on your way. However, that still isn't small enough. I want an even smaller device that can do everything. In fact, I want to be able to choose from different combination devices that meet my needs. Make it small, powerful, and simple to use!

One simple interface — not a bunch of applications

You can find all kinds of Internet content, and for some of that content, you must have a certain application to read the file. For example, listening to some audio files requires RealPlayer, while others need Windows Media Player. Downloading different applications so you can view content can be real drag, especially if you have a slow connection. I want to experience everything the Internet offers via one simple device. I don't want to download and use five different applications. I want one simple interface that does everything.

Control over the content that enters our homes

The Internet offers all kinds of information — some of it good and some of it not so good. I want to use the Internet without the potential for seeing violent, pornographic content. I especially want my children to be able to use the Internet without seeing stuff they should not see. In other words, I want to control the information coming from the Internet — I don't want it to control me or have me worried all the time about what my children might see. Some programs can help block this kind of content, but I want more control than those programs offer — and I want it to be foolproof. I also want to control advertisements. I shouldn't have to read advertisements on the Internet if I don't want to.

An Internet that knows who we are

Here's a question for you: How many times have you typed the same information about yourself while using the Internet? In other words, how many times have you typed a user name, password, your address, credit card information, and so on? Personally, I have entered this information over and over and over . . . .

I want the Internet to know who I am, and I want it to remember all my information. Then, I want the Internet to keep my information absolutely safe from other people. In other words, the Internet should know me, help me, and protect me. I want to go from site to site without reentering my e-mail address and password, and I want to shop at different sites without entering my name, address, credit card number, and so on. I am important, my information is important, and I want it safe and always available to me.

Where Is the Internet Headed?

I admit that predicting what the Internet will be like in a few years is virtually impossible. Why? The Internet, like all technologies, is constantly growing and changing. You never know who is working on a new device or technology that will radically change the way things are done on the Internet, so you cannot accurately predict where the Internet is headed.

However, I can make some general predictions about how the Internet is going to change, based on the wants and needs of consumers and the technology that is currently being developed. Of course, I cannot guarantee that the Internet will meet all of these wants and needs in the near future, but I think you're likely to see some of the following changes very soon.

Automatic recognition

One of the biggest headaches about doing anything online is entering personal information. Many Web sites ask you to enter information about yourself. Then, if you want to buy something from the site, you have to enter additional information. And of course, you probably have to repeat the entire process at the next Web site you visit.

This incompatibility between Web sites is tiresome and a waste of time. Technology developers recognize this problem, and you'll soon see online services that all Web sites recognize. For example, you can sign up with one of these services, give the service all kinds of information about you, such as your name, e-mail address, mailing address, credit card number(s), and just about anything else. Then, the service stores this information in a file that your browser can transmit to any Web site. The site can read the information and automatically recognize you, and you can use the site without any further distractions. If you want to buy a product, just click it and choose to buy it — you won't have to enter information over and over because it is all contained in your personal file.

So what happens if you move, your e-mail address changes, or your credit card number changes? No problem. You just visit the service site and update your information. Then, any Web sites you visit will get your updated information. This way, the Internet always knows who you are, and you can easily visit and use sites.

But what if you don't want to give away all your personal information? That's no problem, either, because your service site can simply ask you which information you want to provide to a Web site when you first visit it — particularly if it is a new Web site that you have not visited before. The result: Web sites can quickly identify you, you can give them the information they need, and you don't get carpal tunnel syndrome by repeatedly typing in the same boring information.

Universal data manipulation

Consider this scenario: You want to visit a single Web site and pay your car note, your house note, and your telephone bill using two different credit cards. Where can you go to do this? Answer: You can't — at least, not yet.

One of the problems with the Internet is that you cannot manipulate data easily. In fact, the Internet as we know it is rather static, effectively treating your PC as a dumb terminal that simply displays information from the Web sites you visit. You may say, "Wait a minute — I can do lots of things on the Internet." True enough, but all you are really doing is gathering information that already exists. You cannot create new information (unless you own a Web site), and you cannot synthesize information by combining bits and pieces of it — for example, accessing a single page on which you can pay all your bills using different accounts and information.

You can gather information from a search engine (information that already exists), view movies or listen to music (files that exist on a server), fill out customer service forms (a static database transaction), and perform a myriad of other tasks, but when you really boil it all down, your browser acts like a dumb terminal that reports static, existing Internet content back to you. You cannot change that content to suit your needs. But hopefully, that will soon change.

Various developers, including Microsoft, are currently working on technologies that will help transform the Internet into a place where users can manipulate and change information, as needed. Using technologies, such as Extensible Markup Language (XML), developers are writing programs and coding that can work with any application and on any platform. These technologies will enable different Web sites to be completely compatible with one another. As a user, you can then combine parts of different Web sites in a way that meets your needs. Want to combine several different sites so you can pay your bills on one easy screen? The emerging Internet technologies hold great promise that you will be able to do just that — and lots more.

Customizable user experience

I want my own user page on the Internet — a place where I can see my e-mail, get a weather report, view stocks and bonds, and keep tabs on products that I want to buy. I want these items updated regularly, and I want the ability to change them at any time I want. Guess what? Those features are coming soon!

Some Internet service providers (ISPs) offer personal, customizable home-pages where you can gather a set of data that is prepackaged for you, such as the weather in your area, news in your area, and so on. However, the experience is rather limited. The goal is to have a single Web page where you, as the user, can decide what you want to see and what should readily appear there for you — completely up-to-date and accurate. This customizable user experience is getting lots of attention, and I think you will see more and more services like these catering to the needs and whims of the user. After all, the users keep these companies in business, and most ISPs and services are trying to provide personal, rich user environments where you get what you want and how you want it. Competition between companies is fierce, and that's good news for you and me — the consumers.

More interactivity

The big promises from the technology world today are personalization and interactivity. In other words, I don't want boring, static Internet sites served to my browser; I want interactive content in which I can get exactly what I want and need from the Web site. For example, I want to be able to read a news story and then ask a question about that story. The server should be able to read my question and intelligently answer it. In other words, I want Internet servers that truly interact with me — not just hand me static pages. You'll see technology continue to provide ways to make the Internet more tailored to you and more interactive. In this way, the Internet can truly become a place that serves your needs and makes your life easier and more fun.

Where Are Wireless Devices Headed?

Before I speculate on some of the wireless devices you are likely to see in the near future, this section considers some of the concepts and consumer needs that will help drive the invention of new devices. As any inventor or developer knows, if you build something that people either want or need, you have a winner. Technology is certainly no exception to that rule, and in the ever-competitive computing market, companies must develop products that users need or at least believe they cannot live without. Take cellular phones, for example. Only a few years ago, almost no one owned a cellular phone. Today, millions of people own cellular phones, and we marvel that we were able to exist without them. In reality, we got along just fine without them, but the perception in the marketplace is that cellular phones make your life easier and safer if you are traveling. That may or may not be true, but consumers have decided it is true, and that's all that matters. If consumers had not climbed on the cell-phone bandwagon, the concept would have quickly died away. The fact is, businesses spend millions of dollars every year trying to identify and then develop products that consumers will buy.

In the wireless device and computing device market, what do consumers want? I can identify a few known items that the industry is working very hard to produce. Some require technology that is not quite up to par yet, but we'll get there soon. The following sections explore some of those device concepts you are likely to see manufacturers leaning toward in the future.

Space savers

Over and over again, consumers tell computer and device manufacturers that smaller is usually better. Remember those bulky cellular phones that looked a child's plastic toy? Some of us owned them, but they have been replaced by ultra-small, sleek phones that can easily fit in our pockets. Or, what about the personal computer? The personal computer tower sitting under your desk probably contains twice as many cards and drives as PCs did a few years ago — and it is typically smaller. Devices will continue to be small, easy to carry, and easy to store. Computers will continue to offer more functionality and take up less and less room.

Multiple-function products

In the wireless Internet device market, consumers want more freedom over products. They want products that can do multiple things and products that combine features. For example, why not offer a PDA that is also a cellular phone? These multifunction devices will enable consumers to choose a device that is just right for them, and — you guessed it — reduce multiple devices to a single, small device that meets all of their needs. This is one need that is currently being met, and you can see an example of a phone/PDA combination device in the section, "Combination devices," later in this chapter.

Appliance-based computing

How would you like to own a computer that has only a screen, a keyboard, and a mouse? You never have to install any applications, and the system never crashes. You don't use any disks or CD-ROMs, and nothing ever malfunctions, unless you stick it under a water faucet. Does this sound too good to be true? It's not!

As shown in Figure 7-3, a concept known as *appliance-based computing* gives you a simple window to the Internet. You pay a monthly fee to subscribe to a service that provides you with an operating system and the applications you want. You can subscribe to different applications as you need them and change the way your user interface works. Using this method, all the computer's work actually gets done on a server on the Internet. You use the operating system and applications as if they reside on your computer, but they actually reside on the server. Your system never crashes because it runs on the server. You don't have to upgrade applications because a server administrator automatically does the upgrades.

You simply subscribe to what you want, use what you want, and make adjustments as your computing needs change. You pay according to your subscription, and you don't have the hassle of solving problems and the expense of buying costly applications. At first glance, you may think, "I don't want to lose control of my computer." That's true; someone else actually manages the computer, and you simply access a window to that computer. However, that's the great thing about service-based computing: You get what you want, and someone else does the dirty work of making a computer function the way it should. Think of it this way: You could buy a generator, connect it to your house, and generate your own electricity. However, paying a monthly service fee to the electric company and having someone take care of the electricity generation for you is much easier and more practical. The same is true with appliance-based computing. You can get all the power of computing without all the technical headaches.

Of course, this level of functionality is not available yet, and you would need a constant and very fast connection to the Internet for it to work well. However, this kind of computing is coming, and you can already buy Internet appliances that simply connect you to the Internet and enable you to use it, such as Compaq's iPAQ Home Internet Appliance.

Human interface

I have a love/hate relationship with my computer keyboard. I love it because it enables me to write books for a living, but I hate it because it wears out my fingers. Wouldn't it be great if we could just talk to our computers and have them do exactly what we say? In other words, a machine should communicate with us on our terms; we should not be forced to communicate with the machine through input devices. If that sounds too Star Trekish to you, you might be surprised that human communication with the computer is just around the corner.

In fact, you can talk to your computer now, on a limited basis. Language interface software enables you to issue spoken commands to your computer and even write documents. I haven't found it to be as fast as I can type, so I haven't made the transition yet, but language interface, sometimes called natural interface, is receiving lots of attention.

Although computers are complex, they do not come close to matching the complexity of our brains and our language skills. So, computers have taken some time to catch with us so that we can communicate with the computer through natural, human communication, such as speech or vision. Exactly what the human interface will entail remains to be seen, but it's a coming thing and you may see your keyboard and mouse become less and less important!

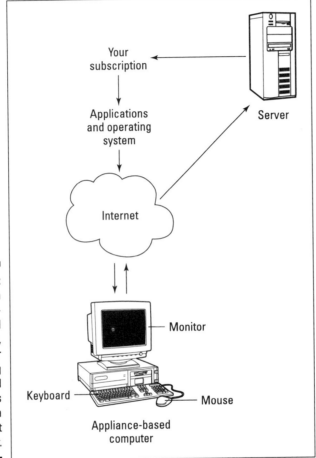

Figure 7-3:
With
appliance-
based
computing,
your
operating
system and
applications
reside on an
Internet
server.

What Can We Expect from Wireless Internet Devices of Tomorrow?

So, you're looking at your Web-enabled phone and pager or PDA and wondering what the future of wireless Internet devices might hold. Well, several cool and exciting developments may be coming your way in the near future, and they all focus on the needs of consumers and our "information on the go" lifestyles. Take a look at the following sections for speculations on what you may see in the very near future.

Combination devices

Several leading manufacturers already have devices in the works that combine existing devices that we already know and love. A natural merger involves the cellular phone and the PDA. You need the power of the PDA, and you must carry a cellular phone in order to make calls, but carrying two devices is no fun. So, the natural next step is a combination cellular phone and PDA with a stylus or even a keyboard, as shown in Figure 7-4.

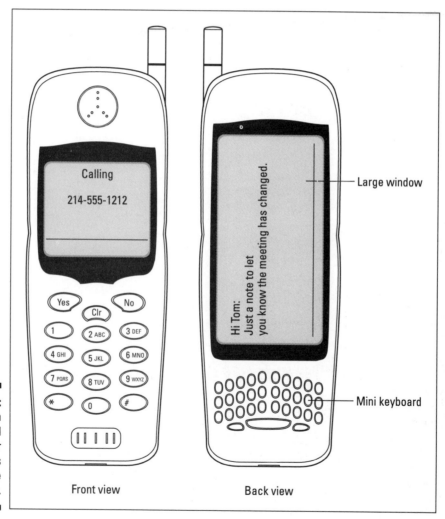

Figure 7-4: Combination PDAs and cellular phones are sure to be a hit.

Front view   Back view

The phone might reside on one side of the device and the PDA on the other, or the device might work like those toys that transform from trucks into robots: Slide a few levers, and your cellular phone converts into a PDA. Of course, all kinds of styles and models may be available, but the important object is to marry the power of the PDA with the features of the cellular phone. This way, you can talk, surf the Internet, or get your e-mail, all on one smooth device. Figure 7-5 shows another example of the PDA/cell phone/pager of the future.

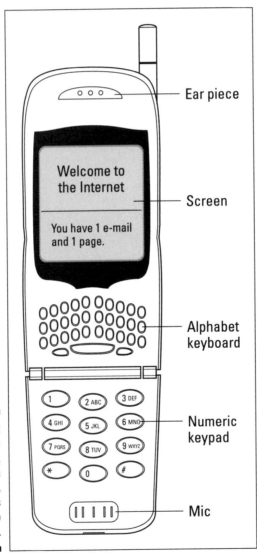

Figure 7-5: Get phone service, wireless Internet, and pages in one interface.

You may think these cool items are a long way off, but you can already get a combination phone/ PDA. The Kyocera Smartphone, shown in Figure 7-6, is both a cellular phone and a PDA. The Smartphone runs the Palm operating system and does everything that Palm devices and phones can do. I predict that this product will become the device of choice in the very near future.

Information on the move

Wireless Internet access will get easier, and the coverage areas will reach even remote locations. As more and more people use wireless, the coverage expands. This expansion will help lead to wireless Internet devices that are implanted in all kinds of products. After all, why limit wireless devices to phones and PDAs? The next natural step is to begin embedding wireless Internet devices into other kinds of products. What kinds of products, you might ask? Anything that moves and that people typically carry with them.

The first example that readily comes to mind is the automobile. People spend lots of time in their cars, so why not put a wireless Internet device in your car's dashboard or console, as shown in Figure 7-7?

Figure 7-6:
The
Kyocera
Smartphone
is a PDA
and a
phone.

© *Photo used by permission, courtesy of
Kyocera Wireless Corp.*

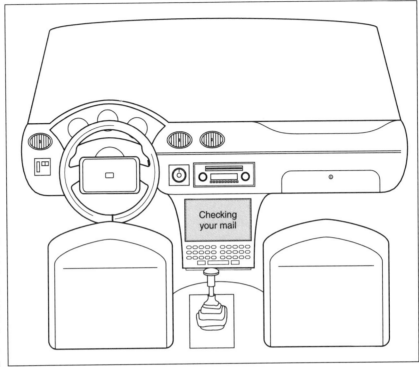

Figure 7-7:
Get any
information
you want
from inside
your
automobile.

Now, before you get angry with me and cry out that this is not safe, remember that I'm just the messenger, and in fact, computer screens are already available in many higher end automobiles. I recently took a cruise with my aunt in her new Mercedes, which has a large screen positioned in the console where she can get driving directions and all kinds of other information using wireless technology. The next step is to provide Internet content and access to your e-mail from inside the car. In fact, I expect automobiles to come equipped with read/write CD-ROM drives so you can save e-mail files and related Internet downloads and documents. Want the latest version of a new operating system? Hey, just download it in your car on your way to work!

Moving from the automobile, various other potential products quickly come to mind, as shown in Figure 7-8. Anything that people usually carry with them could include an embedded wireless device. What about clothes? I can see a jacket with a small screen built into the sleeve with which you can access the Internet using a stylus. Or, how about a wrist device that looks like a watch? Get your e-mail and manage it with a stylus. How about a briefcase, purse, wallet, or even a wireless PDA the size of a credit card? You name it, and a wireless Internet device can be implanted in it.

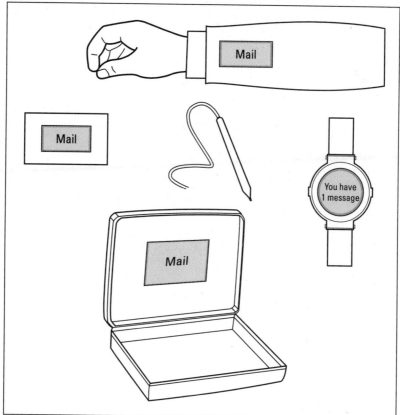

Figure 7-8:
Any article
of clothing
or
accessory
may be a
target for
the wireless
Internet.

In fact, some of these items are already becoming available. Royal Philips Electronics and Levi Strauss & Co. have worked together to create the first wearable products to enter the market. The product range is branded Industrial Clothing Design (ICD+), and consists of jackets that contain a "body area network." The jackets integrate wiring so that the Philips Xenium GSM mobile phone and Rush MP3 players are unified with the clothing.

Natural communication

Still a little ways into the future are devices that give you Internet access via natural communication. Perhaps you want to go for an evening walk, but you still need to get some work done. No problem. Simply wear a wireless Internet headset, as shown in Figure 7-9. Using natural language, you can talk to servers on the Internet, retrieve your mail and information, and then have it read back to you over the earphones. You can even use the voice controls to locate and purchase items.

Or maybe you're sitting in the airport waiting for your flight. You put on your sunglasses and press a button, and a small antenna appears and connects you to the Internet. The inside of your lenses becomes dark enough to display content from the Internet and check your e-mail, as shown as Figure 7-10. You can then control what you see through your eye movements.

Sound crazy? Maybe, but crazier ideas than these have come to pass, and if consumers want these products, they will appear in the marketplace. This is the true power of the wireless Internet — the Internet that will completely integrate with your life and always be available to you various ways. The future is total wireless Internet access — and the future will arrive very soon!

Figure 7-9:
Voice-
controlled
access to
information
on the
wireless
Internet.

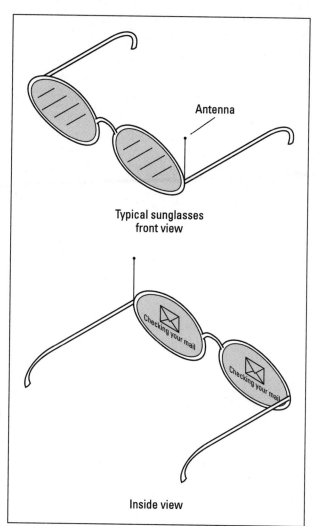

Antenna

Typical sunglasses
front view

Checking your mail

Checking your mail

Figure 7-10:
Eye-
command
wireless
Internet
access.

Inside view

Part III
Communicating on the Wireless Internet

The 5th Wave   By Rich Tennant

"It's an e-mail from my mother. She wants me to know how happy she is for us."

In this part . . .

You're connected, you have your device, and you're ready to go. So what can you actually do on the wireless Internet? In this part, you explore the different ways in which you can stay in touch via the wireless Internet. Specifically, you find out how to use wireless e-mail, instant messaging, and wireless calendars.

Chapter 8

Using Wireless E-Mail

In This Chapter

▶ Getting your wireless e-mail

▶ Sending wireless e-mail

▶ Managing contacts

▶ Accessing corporate e-mail via the wireless Internet

▶ Getting your e-mail from any mail account

My wife says I'm addicted to my e-mail. That is not true, of course, but I do admit that e-mail consumes a significant amount of my daily time. I depend on it for my business and to keep in touch with family and friends. That's why I check my e-mail every ten minutes. Okay, maybe my wife has a point.

In all honesty, I'm amazed that I was ever able to survive without e-mail. You probably share that same sentiment. Of course, e-mail has been available for only a decade or so and widely used during only the past few years. Now, millions of messages are sent and received daily, and many businesses depend on e-mail within their private networks and on the Internet.

Thanks to the wireless Internet, you can get your e-mail anywhere and at any time. In this chapter, I explore wireless e-mail, show you how it works, and give you some smart tips and tricks for getting your mail on the wireless Internet.

E-Mail 101: Reviewing the Basics

Whether you're sending e-mail via the wireless Internet or the regular wired Internet, e-mail works in almost the same way. Before I jump into the nitty-gritty of wireless e-mail, I want to spend a few moments exploring the basics of e-mail and e-mail accounts.

Understanding how e-mail works

I use e-mail so often that I rarely think about how it works. Don't worry, I'm not going throw a bunch of (yawn) technology terms at you, but I think that understanding what you're doing makes life a little easier. It's like driving a car: You don't need to know everything about the car in order to use it, but if you understand a few basics, you're less likely to run out of gas.

So, how does a computer send an e-mail message to another computer? It's not magic, but it can be rather complex. Most Internet e-mail is sent using a *protocol,* or a rule of behavior, called *Simple Mail Transfer Protocol* (SMTP). SMTP enables one computer to send an e-mail message to another computer without regard for the type of computer or the type of e-mail program being used. For example, I can send an e-mail message using Microsoft Outlook on my Windows Me computer, and you can receive that message via Netscape mail on your Macintosh. We use completely different computers and e-mail programs, but our machines can still talk to each other without any problems.

When you type and send an e-mail message, your computer puts that message in a very basic text format — a format that any computer can read. Your computer then takes the message and breaks it apart into little computer pieces called *bytes.* Then, the computer sends those bytes to the mail server at your Internet Service Provider (ISP), which sends them over the Internet. The intended recipient's ISP receives the mail message and then sends the mail message to the user you are trying to contact. The user's computer reassembles the bytes and displays the message — and all of this happens rather quickly.

Consider an example. Assume that I want to send you an e-mail message. My e-mail address is curt@myisp.com, and your e-mail address is you@yourisp.com. Here's what happens when I send a message to you:

1. **Using the e-mail program on my trusty computer, I type the message and then click the Send button.**

2. **My computer takes the message, strips it down to a basic level, divides the message into little chunks of data, and then sends it over the phone line to my ISP, DSL link, satellite link, or whatever kind of transmission medium I am using.**

3. **The mail server at my ISP checks the message address and then uses other Internet servers to find your ISP.**

4. **After the mail server finds your ISP, it sends the message to your ISP over the Internet.**

5. **Your ISP gets the message and looks at the address. The mail server at your ISP says, "Hey, I know you."**

6. **Your ISP's mail server sends the message to your computer. Or, if you're not connected, the mail server holds the message until you connect and download it.**

7. **Your computer gets the message and reassembles it so you can read it.**

Figure 8-1 depicts this process. Of course, the process includes numerous technical details that I am happy to avoid bothering you with here, but you now know the basics of what happens.

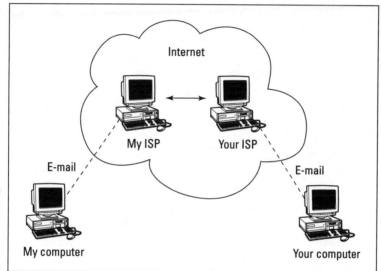

Figure 8-1:
Sending
e-mail via
the Internet.

Growing attached to e-mail attachments

I enjoy receiving e-mail messages, but I like e-mail attachments even more. After all, who doesn't want to see an instant photo of little Johnny's birthday party or Aunt Ruth's new cat? How about a document or spreadsheet for work, or a PowerPoint presentation? How about a music file or even a movie clip? You name it, you can send it with an e-mail message, and these files are known as *attachments*.

Attachments can be literally any kind of file. If you have a computer program that can make it and save it, you can send it via e-mail. However, you need to remember a few important caveats regarding e-mail attachments:

✔ **E-mail attachments can be *bandwidth intensive*.** In other words, these files may be several megabytes in size and may take a long time to send and receive, unless you have a DSL, cable, or satellite connection to the Internet. PowerPoint presentations and video files can be really big, and some ISPs do not allow a single user's mailbox to hold files that large. So, before you get too happy about e-mailing attachments, keep the size issue in mind.

✔ **E-mail attachments are *application specific.*** The recipient must have an application that can read the attachment. Picture files usually aren't a problem because most people use standard picture types, such as JPEG and GIF files. Any Internet-ready computer can read these types of files because — you guessed it — they're used on the Internet. However, what if I send a file that I created in PhotoShop and saved as a PhotoShop file? The recipient must have PhotoShop in order to open the file and see it. The same is true for word processing documents and other types of files. Try to send files in common file formats that your recipients probably can read.

Reviewing the basics of e-mail accounts

All e-mail accounts work in basically the same way, and they all work through an ISP. When you decided to jump onto the information superhighway, you found an ISP in your area that could connect you. The Internet is free, but you must pay an ISP a monthly fee in order to connect with the Internet. That monthly fee probably costs you somewhere between $19.99 a month and $60.00 a month, depending on the type of service you have (dial-up, DSL, cable, satellite, and so on).

Along with access to the Internet, you probably received one e-mail address, or maybe more. That e-mail address has the following format: `your_user_name@ your_ISP's_name.domain`. For example, my ISP is MSN. I use the MSN satellite Internet service, which costs me about $60.00 per month. (Yes, that's expensive, but it's fast and I live out in the boondocks, so it was my only high-speed option.) The ISP is MSN, and the domain for MSN is .com. (Yours may be .net, .mil, .gov, or .edu.) My user name is curtsimmons, so my complete e-mail address is `curtsimmons@msn.com`. (Don't send me spam, or junk e-mail, please.)

When I want to get my e-mail, how do the mail servers at MSN know that I am who I say I am and that they should give me my mail? My computer logs on to the MSN mail server using my username (curtsimmons) and a password (which I'm not telling you). The MSN server checks my username and password against its database and says, "Yep, this is Curt and he can have his mail."

Your e-mail account consists of your e-mail address, your username, and your password. With these three components, you can connect with your ISP and then send and receive e-mail.

Wireless E-Mail 101: Understanding the Differences

In a nutshell, wireless e-mail works just like regular, wired e-mail (see the previous section), with some basic differences. You use your wireless device, such as your Web-enabled phone or PDA, and get your e-mail over the air instead of through a wire. With wireless e-mail, you still have an ISP, a username, and a password, just like you do with a wired mail account.

For example, users on the Internet send mail to your wireless ISP account. At the moment, I'm using a Palm.net account. So, if a friend sends e-mail to curtsimmons@palm.net, the e-mail is sent on the Internet to a mail server at Palm.net. When I use my Palm VIIx to check for e-mail, the mail is transferred wirelessly from the Palm.net server to my PDA, as shown in Figure 8-2. From the PDA, I can receive my e-mail, send e-mail, and manage my e-mail messages and contacts, just as I would with a computer.

In reality, your phone or PDA may first connect with some kind of wireless tower, which then sends the e-mail to your ISP. But for simplicity's sake, just know that your wireless ISP is a part of the wired Internet — and that is why you can get e-mail from anyone, not just other wireless customers.

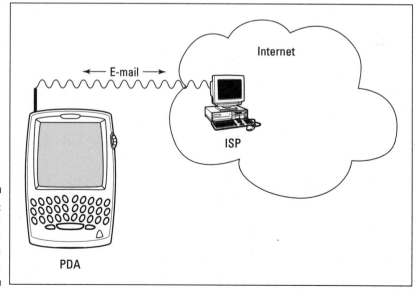

Figure 8-2:
Sending e-mail via the wireless Internet.

E-mail on the wireless Internet is designed for short messages. You can write a novel in an e-mail message and send it from your computer, but your Web-enabled phone or PDA is limited in memory and cannot handle extraordinarily long messages. Of course, inputting messages into a Web-enabled phone or PDA isn't exactly fun anyway, so typical e-mail messages are short and to the point, such as the example shown in Figure 8-3.

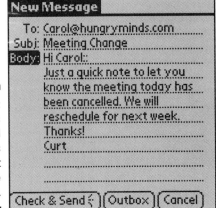

Figure 8-3:
Wireless
e-mail
messages
are short
and to the
point.

Another important difference between wired e-mail and wireless e-mail involves attachments. With wireless e-mail, you can't get them and you can't send them. Wireless devices do not have the storage capabilities, memory, or applications to open and read or create and send e-mail attachments. So, with e-mail attachments, you are limited to the wired world — at least for the time being.

Otherwise, wireless e-mail works just like wired e-mail, and you can manage e-mail in just about the same way.

Getting Connected to Your Wireless E-Mail

Getting connected to your wireless e-mail is usually a snap because your e-mail is included in a typical account that you purchase. Of course, this depends on your provider and the type of device you use, so follow your provider's instructions about getting set up with your e-mail account and getting connected. Typically, however, you get set up and connected in one of the following ways:

✔ **Sign up for a service, such as a phone service with a provider like Sprint or AT&T.** You decide on a service plan and the kind of Internet service you want and then you get an e-mail account on that service. For example, if you decide to sign up with AT&T, you get a PocketNet e-mail account. If you sign up with Southwestern Bell Wireless, you get a Southwestern Bell wireless account, and so on. After you activate your account, your e-mail is activated, and you can use it by turning on the phone and following the instructions to connect to your mail account.

✔ **Get the device and then use the device to sign up for an account.** With some PDAs, such as the Palm VIIx, you use the device itself to set up your Internet access and e-mail account. Simply raise the antenna, connect to the network, pick a username and password, enter your credit card info, and you're all set. From then on, you just raise the antenna to connect and you can use e-mail.

✔ **Get the device, sign up on the wired Web, and then activate the device.** With some PDAs, you must visit a Web site on the wired Web, select a service plan, and sign up. Then, the service contacts your PDA directly and sets it up to start working with the wireless service. Then, you can simply turn on the PDA and you're already connected. At the time of this writing, the BlackBerry Internet edition works this way.

Connecting to the wireless Internet is actually much easier than connecting to the wired Internet. No phone line and modem nightmares, error messages, and other frustrating hassles. With most wireless devices, you simply turn on the device or raise the antenna, and you're automatically connected — no fuss and no hassles!

Using Your Wireless E-Mail

Sending and receiving wireless e-mail involves just a few easy steps — and that's good news. After all, when you're on the move, you don't want to worry about a bunch of different functions and instructions.

The actual steps you follow to send and receive mail will differ, depending on the device you use. If you use a Web-enabled phone, you need to use some select buttons and use your keypad to type a message. On a PDA, you use a stylus or the miniature keyboard. Either way, the process is basically the same, and the following sections show you how to use e-mail on your wireless device.

Creating and sending an e-mail message

To create an e-mail message, use your wireless device to access a new message window. Usually, you open this window by clicking a button or a link called Mail or New Mail. Check your device's manual or instructions for specific steps. After you open the window for creating your new message, complete the following steps:

1. **In the To line, type the e-mail address of the recipient. If you want to send the message to more than one person, just enter additional addresses.**

   You probably need to separate multiple addresses with either a comma or a semicolon; check your documentation for details.

2. **Type a short subject for the message.**

3. **Enter the text of the message in the provided space, as shown in Figure 8-4.**

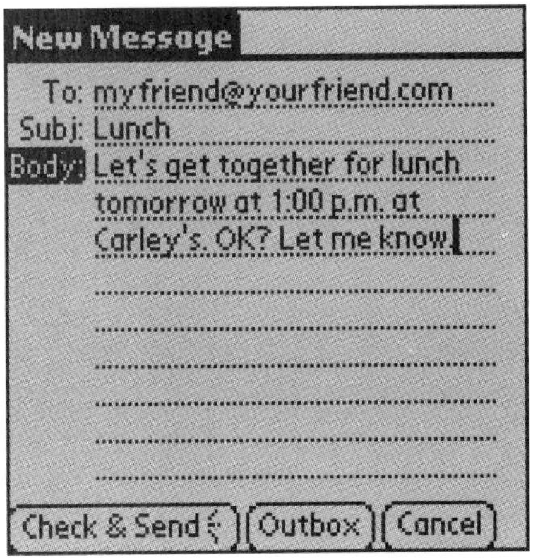

Figure 8-4:
Enter an address and a subject and then type your message.

```
┌─────────────────────────────────┐
│ New Message                      │
│   To: myfriend@yourfriend.com    │
│ Subj: Lunch                      │
│ Body: Let's get together for lunch│
│       tomorrow at 1:00 p.m. at   │
│       Carley's. OK? Let me know. │
│                                  │
│                                  │
│                                  │
│                                  │
│                                  │
│                                  │
│ (Check & Send )( Outbox )( Cancel )│
└─────────────────────────────────┘
```

4. **After you finish your message, click the Send button (or Send Message, Check & Send, or something similar).**

   Your wireless device sends the e-mail message to the specified recipient(s). However, some mail clients keep a "sent" message in an outbox or folder until you choose to "send mail." Check your mail client's documentation for more details.

Receiving e-mail

Receiving e-mail on a wireless device is usually a piece of cake because you really do not need to do anything. Depending on the type of wireless device and service you use, you simply turn on the device or raise the antenna, access the e-mail portion of your interface, and either read the mail that appears or click a Check or Check For Mail button. Your device retrieves your wireless e-mail, which shows up in your inbox.

TIP

Wireless Internet mail-etiquette

Okay, all you wireless e-mail users, listen up! You should observe some basic wireless e-mail "mail-etiquette" in order to make your life easier and avoid aggravating the people who receive your messages. Just remember these quick guidelines for wireless e-mail:

- ✔ Type a descriptive subject. The mail recipient should be able to look at your subject line and know what the mail is about. Don't use generic subjects, such as "Hello" or "Guess Who." For people who receive a lot of mail, these flimsy subject headings are annoying.

- ✔ Don't type long, descriptive subjects. Sure, you want your recipient to know what the message is about, but don't put the entire message in the subject line. For example, here's an example of an overly long subject line: "Wanted to mention that we're having a barbeque at Karen's house at noon on Tuesday." If you must put details in the subject line, condensed them as much as possible. For example, a recipient can easily decipher a subject line such as "Noon Tues — Barbecue at Karen's." Keep the subject lines short. When you're using wireless devices, you don't have a lot of subject line room to work with anyway, so less is always more.

- ✔ Keep your messages short and to the point. Avoid long descriptions and unnecessary words. For example, the following message

has lots of words, but it really doesn't say much: "Hi, John, I was looking back over the work we did this week, and I was curious about the possibility of adding another account to the organization structure. When you get into work tomorrow, please come see me so we can visit about this possibility." You could just as easily say, "Hi John: We may be able to add another account to the org. structure — let's talk tomorrow."

- ✔ DON'T TYPE IN ALL CAPITAL LETTERS. CAPITAL LETTERS ARE AGGRAVATING AND HARD TO READ. AND AFTER ALL, WHAT ARE YOU SHOUTING ABOUT ANYWAY? NO ONE CAN HEAR YOU — THIS IS E-MAIL FOR GOODNESS SAKE!

- ✔ don't type in all lowercase letters and ignore every punctuation and sentence rule you have ever learned in your entire life this makes you look like you don't know what you are doing and you don't want everyone to think that e-mail has made you lose your mind

- ✔ Use common abbreviations where appropriate, but make sure everyone can understand your abbreviations. For example, if you type, "Meet me today @ 3 pm at office," everyone will know what you mean. If you type, "M tdy @ 3pm @ off," you may be twiddling your thumbs, waiting for someone to show up.

Depending on your device, you can choose to delete messages after your read them, or you may be able to store messages in mini-folders. You can also reply to and forward messages as you would with a typical e-mail account.

Wireless e-mail is meant for messaging and not for life management. Here's what I mean: On my PC, I use Microsoft Outlook 2000 to manage my e-mail. With this application, I can store all my received e-mail in folders, keep every deleted message and sent message that ever entered or existed in my computer, and maintain a list of every contact I ever made. That's a lot of information — roughly 100MB of hard disk space. Your wireless device cannot hold all that information.

If you get lots of e-mail, you still need a computer to keep up with it. Use your wireless device for quick messages and to keep in contact with people when you're away, but remember that your wireless device does not have the power to keep up with the volume of mail you may receive on your computer.

Managing Contacts

A *contact* is person on whom you keep information, such as phone numbers, e-mail addresses, physical addresses, and other relevant information. Virtually every wireless device has the capability to manage contacts — and that's good news. After all, remembering Uncle Joe's e-mail address or even one of your colleague's can be quite a challenge. So, to help you avoid the `whoareyou@ idon'tknow.com` syndrome, Web-enabled phones and PDAs provide address books and contacts lists.

As I explain in the following sections, these contact management tools come in two flavors: PDA local management and Web site management.

Storing contact data on your PDA

All PDAs have address books, and that was one of the reasons that PDAs first came into vogue. After all, you need data management and storage that is quick, easy, and electronic — and not pencil driven. PDAs give business-people an easy way to keep with a bunch of contacts.

Most PDAs contain a category just for addresses or contacts. Using the PDA software, you can add, remove, and edit contact information at any time. For example, in Figure 8-5, I am adding a contact to my PDA.

In addition to simple address lists, PDAs enable you to create folder structures so you can organize your contacts, create additional information about them, and easily manage them as they change. Most PDAs also contain a search feature so you can quickly find the contact you need.

Figure 8-5:
All PDAs
offer
tools for
managing
addresses
and contact
information.

Storing contact data with a Web-enabled phone

Web-enabled phones can store some contact information, but they offer only limited storage space, so you cannot store lots of contacts. Okay, that's all fine, but what if you must have 100 important e-mail addresses and phone numbers with you while you travel? Fortunately, you do not need to revert to the paper address book, because your Web-enabled phone gives you another alternative. Why not store your information on the Internet and then just get it when you need it?

Various companies provide Web storage solutions so you can store contacts and address book data on a Web server and then get that data wherever you may be. As you might guess, several of these sites are wireless savvy and will work with your Web-enabled phone or PDA. For example, Figure 8-6 shows the Web site at `http://www.webaddressbook.com`, a company that provides these storage solutions. For more options, check out `http://corp.visto.com`, `http://www.eorganizer.com`, and `http://www.interplanner.com`. Also, on any search engine, search for "free address book."

Some carriers even provide this service to their customers. For example, if you sign up for AT&T's digital PocketNet service Premium plan, you get your own personal Web site that can store as many as 5,000 entries. Then, using your Web-enabled phone, you simply access your personal Web site and get the information you need. Pretty cool, I must say!

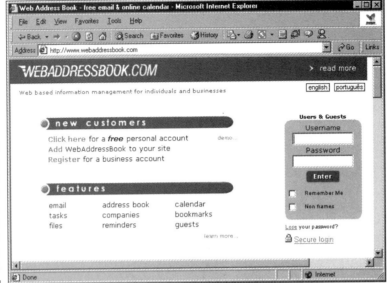

Figure 8-6:
Use Web
sites, such
as this one,
to store
information
on the
Internet.

Getting Other Internet Mail on Your Wireless Device

I know what you're thinking. No, I'm not a mind reader, but let's face the facts. All this wireless e-mail stuff is great, but it usually means that you need another e-mail account. For example, if you want to use a Palm PDA, you need a Palm.net e-mail address. Or, if you want to use AT&T, you must have a PocketNet address — right?

Not exactly. Your options vary according to the device you use. For example, the RIM BlackBerry can connect with corporate e-mail systems that use Microsoft Exchange Server or Lotus Domino, both of which are types of messaging servers. BlackBerry users who use Lotus Notes or Microsoft Outlook for their business e-mail may need only one e-mail address. If their e-mail administrators give them the necessary rights, they can access their standard business e-mail via their BlackBerry. So, for the corporate user, a wireless device may include some very cool integration options.

However, what about the rest of us? What about the typical user or even businessperson who does not use a RIM BlackBerry? For example, I work for myself and use several different e-mail addresses, in addition to using my Palm.net account when I'm away from home. How can I get my other e-mail on the wireless device? After all, the point is to stay connected to all my mail while I'm away. My Palm.net account is not my primary account where all my e-mail goes. What to do?

You have two very important options. First, if you use a Web e-mail service, such as Yahoo!, Hotmail, Go, or Netscape, you can probably access that Internet mail from your wireless device. Check your wireless device to be sure, but most of them support WAP applications that enable you to get your mail. For example, when I'm away from home, I can use the Palm to access e-mail on my Yahoo! address. From that access point, I can manage the e-mail just as though I were sitting at my computer.

Fair enough, but what if you're not using Web mail? What if you use an ISP account, and your mail is downloaded to your computer into a mail client, such as Outlook, Eudora, or Netscape? You're out of town and your mail is stuck at home. Or is it?

In most typical mail client applications, you can create rules that will send your e-mail to your wireless-enabled mail account or a Web mail server when you are away from home. These rules are very easy to create and they simply tell your mail client to send a copy of all messages to another e-mail address. For example, I can create a rule so that when I am not at home, all messages that arrive at my computer get forwarded to my Palm.net e-mail address, or even to a Web e-mail server such as Yahoo! or Hotmail. Then, I can check my messages wherever I happen to be.

You can also play the e-mail forwarding game in a smarter way by forwarding messages from certain people to your wireless account, instead of forwarding all messages. This tactic ensures that you only receive important e-mail on your wireless account, which may have limited e-mail storage space.

Of course, you must take a few important steps to make this work:

- **Turn on your computer.** In order to receive your e-mail when you are not home, your computer must be turned on. Some ISPs enable you to create rules on their servers that will forward your mail, but you will have to check with your ISP about this option. If your ISP offers this option, you do not need to leave your computer turned on because the mail gets forwarded from your ISP.

- **Configure your computer to check for mail.** Most mail applications enable you to set an auto-check option. For example, I can configure Microsoft Outlook so it automatically checks for mail messages every 10 minutes or so.

- **Connect to your ISP from your computer.** If you have an "always-on" connection, such as cable, DSL, or satellite, you have nothing to worry about. However, if you connect to your ISP using a modem, you need to configure your dial-up connection and mail client so they work together to create a dial-up session, download your mail, and then automatically disconnect. Most computers and mail applications support this configuration, but you'll need to check your documentation to make sure.

After you decide that you want to forward your mail to an account that you can access from the wireless Internet, you need to set up a rule to make it happen. Exactly what you need to do will depend on the mail client you use, but I can offer a couple of examples — one from Outlook Express 5 and one from Eudora mail. Check the Help file on your mail client if you're using something different.

To create a forwarding rule in Outlook Express 5, follow these steps:

1. **In Outlook Express 5, choose Tools⇨Message Rules⇨Mail.**

2. **In the New Mail Rule dialog box that's displayed, under Select The Conditions For Your Rule, select For All Mail Messages. Then, under Select The Actions For Your Rule, select Forward To People, as shown in Figure 8-7.**

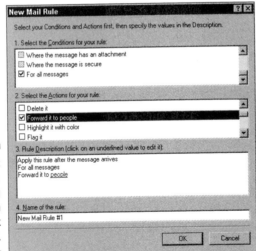

Figure 8-7: Setting a forwarding rule in Outlook Express 5.

3. **In the Rule Description portion of the dialog box, click the People link.**

    A dialog box appears where you can enter an e-mail address or a bunch of e-mail addresses, if you so choose, as shown in Figure 8-8.

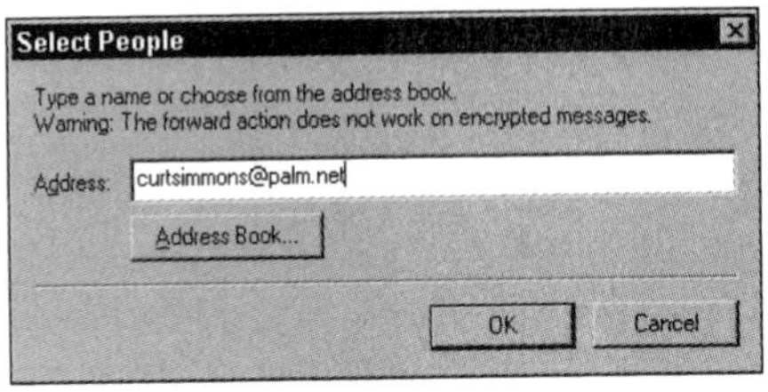

Figure 8-8: Enter the desired e-mail address.

4. **Enter the e-mail address(es) to which you want messages forwarded and then click OK.**

5. **Click OK to save the rule.**

To configure a mail forwarding rule in Eudora, follow these steps:

1. **In Eudora, click Tools⇨Filters.**

2. **In Match section of the Filters window, select Incoming.**

3. **For the Header settings, select To: and Is from the drop-down lists (if they aren't already selected), and then enter your e-mail address, as shown in Figure 8-9.**

4. **In the Action section of the Filters window, select Forward To from the drop-down list and then enter the e-mail address to which you want the e-mail forwarded.**

    This configuration will ensure that all your incoming mail gets forwarded to the address that you have specified.

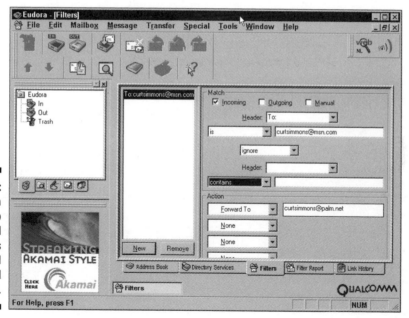

Figure 8-9:
Creating a filter to forward all messages to a desired e-mail account.

Chapter 9

Having Fun with Instant Messaging

In This Chapter

▶ What is instant messaging?

▶ What is it good for?

▶ How does it work?

▶ How can you get the most out of it?

The wireless Internet provides all kinds of fun and exciting things that you can do online. For example, most wireless devices support a very cool feature known as instant messaging. Instant messaging enables you to send short text messages to other people using your phone, pager, or PDA.

Instant messages differ from e-mail because the messages immediately appear on the recipient's screen. The recipient can read the message and immediately reply to you. It's great for short, quick, almost conversational exchanges. It's also very easy and fun!

So, how can you use instant messaging, and what steps can you take to make the most of this wireless Internet feature? In this chapter, I explore these questions and provide you with some tips for instant messaging usage.

Getting to Know Instant Messaging

Instant messaging is a simple, real-time communication feature that enables you to send a short text message to anyone who uses a messaging service with a phone or pager number, or anyone who has an e-mail address. In effect, the instant messaging feature enables your phone or PDA to act like a pager.

Instant messaging enables you to send brief messages to other people in a chat-like fashion. In case you're not familiar with this *chat* concept, I will give you the skinny. On the Internet, users can communicate instantly with one another using a certain protocol, usually Internet Relay Chat (IRC). This protocol enables the Internet to act as an instant message center. Users can enter a chat room and exchange messages with other users within the chat room. Those messages appear instantly, based on the user's name or *handle*. It's easy and fun, but can be highly addictive. However, in order for chatting to work, both parties must be logged on to the same chat room, so using chat requires a fair amount of coordination.

Recognizing the popularity of this chat feature among Internet users, many ISPs — including MSN, AOL, Yahoo!, Netscape, and many others — now provide instant messaging software with which you can instantly communicate, or chat, with other users of that ISP software.

This concept naturally gives way to instant messaging, which gives you a chat-like setting via your Internet phone, pager, or PDA.

Why Use Instant Messaging?

When assessing the value of new technology, I typically think in very practical terms. Sure, instant messaging is a cool idea, but what is it really good for? The answer to that question lies in your use of the wireless Internet and the way you communicate with other people.

Frankly, instant messaging may not be that useful to you, especially if you use your phone primarily for voice communication. However, for some individuals and businesspeople, instant messaging provides a quick, easy, and inexpensive way to communicate.

Most Internet phone plans charge extra for instant messaging. (With pagers, the service is wrapped together with your plan, and for a PDA, you typically download a utility that enables you to send messages at no additional charge.) To keep Internet phone rates at a competitive level, you normally pay extra for the service, per your phone plan. However, the service is usually inexpensive. For example, most phone services can give you instant messaging capabilities for as little as $5 to $10 per month. For this fee, you can send and receive instant messages, often with no limit on the number of messages — especially if you can find a good promotional deal.

So, why would you want to use instant messaging? Check out the following sections for details.

Saving money

Instant messaging can save you money, especially if you communicate frequently with people outside your local calling area. Keep in mind that phone plans have local calling areas, roaming areas, and long-distance areas. Depending on your area, those long-distance charges can soar and quickly turn into a lot of money. If you need to contact a friend who lives outside your service area, why not just send the friend a quick message instead of paying for the long-distance call?

Communicating on the run

In some cases, placing a phone call can take up lots of time, especially if the person you are calling expects quick information from you. Consider this scenario: You call a friend to make lunch plans. The friend wants to go, but needs to check her schedule, so she has to call you back. Your friend calls back and gives you a time range, but you can't decide on a restaurant. You decide to look on the Internet and call her back . . . and so on, and so on.

If you get stuck playing phone tag or making lots of calls back and forth, you quickly burn your monthly minutes for no good reason. Rather than waste your time making calls over and over again, you can use instant messaging to trade these communication quips back and forth with friends.

Making work easy

In large buildings or factories, instant messaging offers a great way to communicate with other employees. In businesses with workers on the move, you can send quick messages to people as needed instead of spending all your time on the phone.

How do instant messages differ from e-mail?

Instant messages differ from e-mail in several ways. Instant messages act more like a page — they are immediately sent to the recipient and are immediately displayed on the recipient's screen. In contrast, a recipient must manually check for e-mail and then download it. Also, instant messages are for quick communication on relatively unimportant topics. You cannot save instant messages and you cannot forward instant messages to other people as you can an e-mail message. Remember: Use instant messages for brief communications, and use e-mail to send longer, more organized messages.

Talking to people who can't talk

Have you ever been stranded in a meeting in which you could not place or receive a phone call? In such cases, you can quickly type a short message and send it via your phone or pager. For any cases in which you can't talk but need to communicate, instant messaging can help you out of a jam.

Having fun

Hey, instant messaging simply can be lots of fun. It's just like chatting on the Internet. And having fun is often the only reason you need!

Understanding How Instant Messaging Works

Although the process varies somewhat, depending on the product you use, instant messaging typically involves just a few simple steps. In order to send an instant message to another person, you need

- ✔ The phone number, pager number, or e-mail address for the person to whom you want to send the message
- ✔ The message that you want to send

To send an instant message, complete the following steps:

1. **Follow your wireless device's instructions to open a new message window.**

2. **Enter the phone or pager number, or the Internet e-mail address for the person you want to contact.**

3. **Using the keypad on your phone or pager, or your PDA's keyboard or stylus, type the message.**

4. **Click the wireless device's Send option.**

Depending on the type of wireless device you use, you are limited to a certain number of characters when entering or even receiving text messages — typically, around 100 characters, although some devices allow even fewer characters per message. Consequently, you must be succinct and possibly even creative when entering your message. You want to send as much information as possible with the fewest possible words. However, with a 100-character limit, you actually have quite a bit of freedom. For example:

What about SMS?

SMS, or Short Message Service, is a term you may see thrown around in the wireless Internet world. SMS is used with GSM phones and has become very popular in Europe, the middle East, Asia, and Africa, and is beginning to make its way into North America, too. SMS provides text messages up to 160 characters. The good thing about SMS is that it provides a delivery receipt. Instead of just sending your messages into outer space and hoping that they arrive at the desired destination, SMS ensures that they are delivered and sends you a receipt notification. In order to use SMS, your phone needs the correct hardware and a subscription service. Although SMS is not very popular in the US at this time, keep your eye on it during the coming year. If you are a Nextel customer, or you are considering Nextel, remember that Nextel supports SMS.

```
Tom: We have changed the meeting to 4:30 this afternoon. Meet
     in the Dallas room with the slides of last month's
     report.
```

This message contains 99 characters, so I'm just under the limit. As this example shows, you can say quite a bit, but you do have to get to the point. The good news is that you can use keyboard characters or abbreviations to shorten your messages, as necessary. As long as the other party can understand you, use as much shorthand as you want — for example:

```
Meet @ Joe's @ 4 pm
```

or . . .

```
RE: Area dist meeting @ 11
```

Sending Messages via the Wired Internet

A cool feature of instant messaging on the wired Internet is that you can access various Web sites and directly send an instant message to someone who uses an Internet phone, pager, or PDA. In other words, you can use the wired Internet to send instant messages to people on the wireless Internet. For example, if your friend uses a Sprint Internet phone, you can access www.sprintpcs.com and send an instant message to that person's phone number or e-mail address. AT&T, Verizon, and other services also offer these wired services.

You can send instant messages only to people who subscribe to the same service as you.

Quick Tips for Instant Messaging

Instant messaging is fun, easy to use, and can be helpful in various scenarios. However, as with all services on the wireless Internet, use this feature wisely. Here are some tips for getting the most out of instant messaging:

- In order to use instant messaging, you need the phone number, pager number, or e-mail address of the person with whom you want to communicate. Make sure you have this information available in your device's address book.

- Keep text messages short and to the point.

- Use abbreviations when needed, but make sure they are understandable. Don't create messages that look like gibberish to the recipients.

- Use messaging freely, but beware of "messaging spam." Don't send messages to people all the time, because you are likely to be ignored — and considered an annoyance.

Chapter 10

Using a Wireless Calendar

In This Chapter

▶ Understanding electronic calendars

▶ Working with wireless calendars

▶ Using Web-based calendars

▶ Getting some quick tips for calendar users

*Q*uick: Where are you supposed to be two weeks from today at 10:30 in the morning? If you were to ask me that question, you'd get a blank stare as my reply. Keeping up with your daily routine can be quite difficult with so much to do and so little time to get it all done. Between work, taking care of the kids, and my church, my calendar is always overloaded with events I must attend and jobs I must complete.

Fortunately, technology steps up to the plate to help you manage your business and your life more effectively. Electronic calendars have become very popular and very useful during the past several years by providing a way to keep you organized. For work and your daily life, the calendar software on your PC or your wireless device offers an effective means for keeping track of where you need to be and when you need to be there.

Of course, wireless devices and calendar software represent a winning combination for on-the-move people. In fact, calendar capabilities and the ability to synchronize with your PC's calendar are essential features of any wireless device. In this chapter, I explore electronic calendars and explain how you can use them on the wireless Internet.

Getting to Know Electronic Calendars

Various PC-based programs include electronic calendar features. For example, most major e-mail programs, such as Outlook and Eudora, contain built-in calendars. Linking calendar and e-mail functions offers a very effective combination in corporate settings. You can schedule appointments and tell the calendar to send you e-mail reminders, and in a network setting, you can even add items to another person's calendar.

For example, if I want to schedule a meeting with four colleagues, I can use my e-mail program to send a special meeting notice to those four people. The message specifies the time and date of the meeting, and the other four people must respond to my e-mail and agree to attend. After they agree to attend, the calendar software automatically places the time, date, and reminder on my calendar, which is very cool and very helpful.

Electronic calendars, such as the Microsoft Outlook example shown in Figure 10-1, are very easy to use. You can schedule appointments as needed, remove them, or do just about anything else related to calendars.

As shown in Figure 10-1, the calendar lists important tasks that I have scheduled for the day, even personal items. Outlook reminds me about each task as its time approaches by giving me e-mail reminders and computer sound warnings. I can view my calendar in daily, weekly, or monthly formats. With only a little effort, I can configure everything I need to help keep me on track.

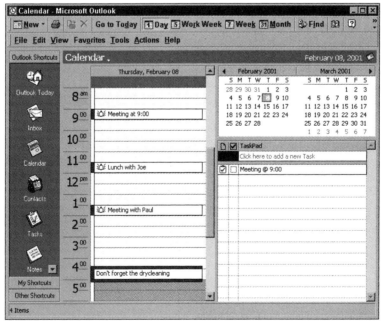

Figure 10-1:
Microsoft
Outlook
provides a
built-in
electronic
calendar.

Making Dates with Your PDA

When PDAs first arrived on the scene, calendar software ranked among their more important components. With PDA-based calendar software, if you're away from your computer, you can make changes to your calendar and keep track of where you're supposed to be. Then, you can synchronize your PC's calendar with any changes that you make on the PDA.

Figures 10-2 and 10-3 show daily and monthly views of a PDA calendar (on a Palm device, in this example). As you can see, the PDA's calendar works in basically the same way as the PC version. I can enter appointments on an hourly basis, and I can see different views of my calendar, such as weekly and monthly.

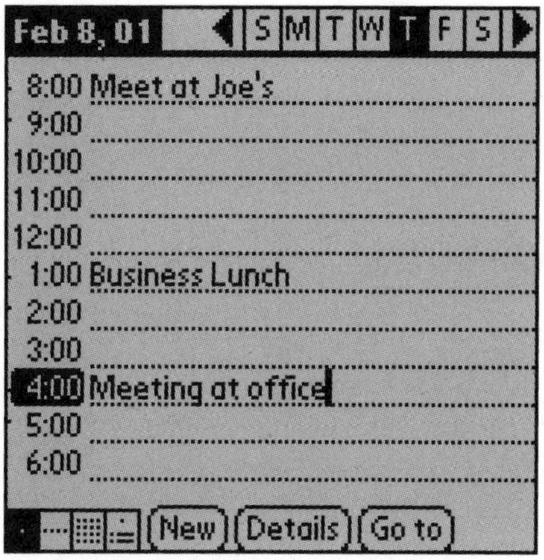

Figure 10-2:
Daily view
on a Palm
PDA.

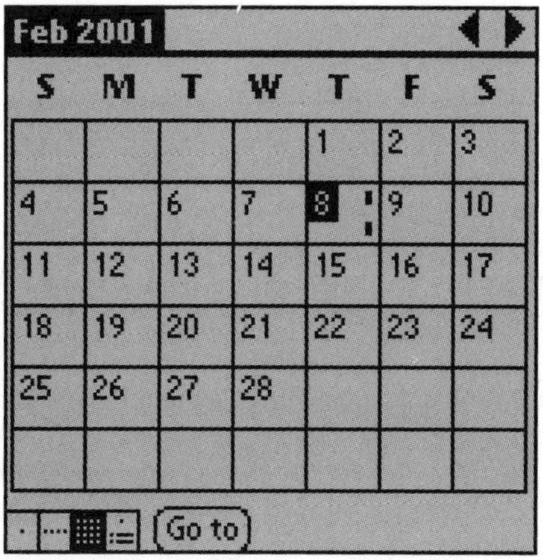

Feb 8, 01	S M T W T F S
8:00 Meet at Joe's	
9:00	
10:00	
11:00	
12:00	
1:00 Business Lunch	
2:00	
3:00	
4:00 Meeting at office	
5:00	
6:00	

(New) (Details) (Go to)

Figure 10-3:
Monthly
view on a
Palm PDA.

Feb 2001						◀ ▶
S	M	T	W	T	F	S
				1	2	3
4	5	6	7	8	9	10
11	12	13	14	15	16	17
18	19	20	21	22	23	24
25	26	27	28			

(Go to)

Each PDA ships with software that enables it to connect with your PC. This process, called *synchronization,* enables the PC and the PDA to exchange information. Specifically, you can synchronize your PDA's e-mail and calendar information with the corresponding information in a PC-based program, such as Outlook. With this great feature, you ensure that you always have complete, up-to-date calendar information on every device you use. What if you enter a bunch of information into your computer that you want on the PDA? No problem, you can also synchronize calendar data from your PC with the corresponding information on your PDA.

PDAs offer a very effective electronic calendar solution, and virtually all PDAs work in the same way. You can easily synchronize your PDA's calendar with your PC's calendar.

Although PDAs have built-in calendar features, most cannot synchronize wirelessly with the PC. The exception to this rule is the BlackBerry, which now provides "over the air" calendar synching with your PC. If you're not using a BlackBerry, however, any changes made to your calendar must be manually synchronized using PDA software and synchronization cradles and cables.

Calling up a Calendar on Your Web-Enabled Phone

If you use a Web-enabled phone and you want to manage your calendar information from that wireless device, I have some good news and some bad news. The good news is that most Web-enabled, or Internet phones can maintain personal information, such as calendars and to-do lists (which may be called by various other names, depending on your service provider). The bad news is that you may pay extra for this service, depending on your plan.

With most service plans, you store your calendar data on a central Web server. Or, depending on the model, your phone may store that data. You can make updates or changes to your calendar as needed and use your Internet phone to keep you on track throughout the day.

But what about synchronization? Can you synchronize the calendar on your Web-enabled phone with data from PC-based applications, such as Outlook. Yes, but not natively.

Typically, Internet phones do not ship to you with the capability to connect with your PC, nor do they include software that enables your PC and the phone to communicate with each other. In order to get this synchronization, you must rely on third-party software called FoneSync Pro, produced by Openwave Systems. This software, along with a tether cable, enables you to connect the phone and your PC, and then synchronize calendar information, e-mail, and to-do lists with other personal information management software. FoneSync works with all kinds of PC applications, and you can read more about it in Chapter 11. You also can get more information by visiting www.fonesync. com. The software and equipment will cost you about $80 dollars, so you have to part with a little hard-earned cash in order to synchronize your phone's calendar with the calendar on your PC. Of course, if you don't really care about synching up with a PC, you do not have to incur this additional expense.

As with PDA calendars, you cannot use your phone to synch up with your PC calendar over the wireless Internet. Synchronization is limited to a physical connection with your phone and your PC.

Considering Web Calendar Options

As you think about your calendar needs and mobility, consider some other options that are available on the Internet. If you travel a lot, or if calendar synchronization with your PC isn't all that important to you, you may want to consider some other free or at least inexpensive options that enable you to store calendars, to-do lists, address books, and other types of data on the Internet so you can access it anywhere from your wireless device.

Interested? It's actually very easy. Free Internet mail providers, such as Hotmail.com, Yahoo.com, Netscape.com, and the host of others that are available all provide free Web calendars. After you create an account, you can manage your calendar, contacts, and other types of personal information directly on the Web — no matter if you are using your PC or wireless device.

Various other sites also provide personal information management services, for free or for a fee, to the wireless Internet community. Check out www.visto. com or www.room33.com, just to name two. Also, check with your wireless provider for additional sites or information about online calendar management. These are great solutions for the mobile calendar user!

Curt's Calendar Quick Tips

Believe me, I've used plenty of electronic calendars, and although they are very helpful, they also can be a real drag if you do not manage them well. So, here are my quick tips for getting the most out of electronic calendars:

- **List all the appointments you need, but avoid *overlisting*.** If you try to list every single task you need to accomplish, you are likely to end up with a calendar so full of information that it becomes more confusing than helpful.

- **Keep entries short and to the point.** List only the pertinent information.

- ✔ **Use time entries when possible.** You can watch the clock throughout the day and make certain you are accomplishing your tasks in a timely fashion.

- ✔ **Remove items after you complete them.** Give yourself a sense of accomplishment and cut down on confusion.

- ✔ **And here's the big one: Use only one calendar.** Do not use a phone calendar and a Web calendar and a PC calendar and a paper calendar. Keep all your information in one location Otherwise, you'll start beating your head against the wall trying to figure out where you are supposed to be and what you are supposed to be doing!

Part IV
Working and Playing on the Wireless Internet

The 5th Wave   By Rich Tennant

"Oh wait – this says, 'Lunch Ed from Marketing', not 'Lynch', 'Lunch'."

In this part . . .

*W*eb surfing enables you to jump from Web site to Web site so you can quickly find the information you need or want. However, surfing with a wireless device is significantly different from surfing with a Web browser on your desktop computer. In this part, you explore surfing the wireless Web, including keeping up with your money online, shopping on the wireless Internet, and using various other wireless surfing features.

Chapter 11

Surfing the Wireless Internet

In This Chapter

▶ Understanding how wired surfing works

▶ Surfing with a PDA

▶ Surfing with a Web-enabled phone

I don't know who coined the phrase *surfing the Web,* but it certainly has stuck over the past few years. *Web surfing,* also called *browsing,* refers to the process of accessing Web sites and moving from one Web site to another, or even among individual Web pages within a site. For example, while checking out your favorite sports Web site, you realize that you need to buy dear old dad a birthday present. With a few mouse clicks and keystrokes, you can easily jump from the sports site to an online store and purchase the gift. Then, you can jump back to your sports site and continue reading about the big game.

But what about surfing the wireless Web? Does it differ from surfing the wired Web? Yes, surfing the wireless Web differs quite a bit from surfing the Web in the wired world. The functionality of wireless devices makes for a whole new experience in surfing around your favorite Web sites. So, this chapter explains how you can surf the Internet with your wireless Internet device.

Surfing in the Wired World

You surf the wired Web using a program called a *Web browser.* A Web browser, like Netscape or Internet Explorer, enables you to view Web documents and pages. Your browser uses HTTP (HyperText Transfer Protocol) to retrieve HTML (HyperText Markup Language) documents.

HTTP defines the rules that enable computers to move Web documents from one place to another on the Internet. HTML is a simple, text-based computer language used in all Web pages. Your browser reads the HTML code, interprets it, and then displays the resulting Web page in your browser's window. It's quick, simple, and effective.

But how does surfing work? How can you move quickly and easily from one Web page to another? In order to understand surfing in the wireless world, you need to understand how surfing works in the wired world. The following sections explore the design of the Internet that enables you to surf the Web quickly and easily when you're using your desktop computer.

Understanding Web addressing

To understand how surfing works, you need to understand two basic Internet components: Web page addressing and hyperlinks. *Web page addressing* refers to the names of Web pages. Your Web browser uses a Web page's name to get that page from the Internet. For example, you could direct your browser to visit www.dummies.com.

After you access this initial page, called an *index page* or simply a *home page,* you can then access additional pages within the site. Each page you access has its own name. For example, perhaps the Web site at www.dummies.com contains two other Web pages called page1 and page2. To keep things organized so your browser can access the pages, each page has its own address. In this case, the addresses would be www.dummies.com/page1.htm and www.dummies.com/page2.htm. You can type these addresses directly into your browser's address box and visit those pages.

To understand the structure of the pages within a Web site, think of the Web site as a book. While books contain individual pages of information organized by page numbers, a Web site also contains pages of information, but organized by addresses.

Of course, a book's structure includes other elements in addition to simple page numbers. Specifically, an author may divide a book into several parts, and each of those parts may contain two or more chapters, each of which consists of multiple pages. Similarly, a Web site typically has a hierarchical structure that consists of directories, subdirectories, and individual pages. For example, the Web site at www.dummies.com might contain several sales-related pages, which the site stores in one folder. To access the first of those sales pages, you might tell your browser to display the page at www.dummies.com/sales/page1.htm.

Now, you may be thinking, "Wait a minute, when I access Web sites, I don't have to type all these different addresses into my browser's address line That would take too much time!" And you're right. Typing those lengthy addresses would take too much time and it would get really aggravating. So, if each page has its own address, why don't you have to type each address? Because you are surfing, and you surf from one page to another by clicking on hyperlinks, as I explain in the following section.

Hyperlinking around the world

Hyperlinks enable you to move from one Web page to another, or from one Web site to another. If you've spent any time on the Internet, you're familiar with hyperlinks — also known simply as *links*. Web pages usually display hyperlinks in a bold color, such as red or blue, and the links are normally underlined, as shown in Figure 11-1. When you point at a hyperlink, the mouse pointer changes to a little finger icon, indicating that you can click on the link and go to a different page. In Figure 11-1, all the underlined words in the left column are hyperlinks, as well as other underlined words within the main part of the page. By clicking on one of these words, you can jump directly to the desired page.

So why use hyperlinks? The answer lies in accessibility. As I explain in the preceding section of this chapter, each page on the Internet has its own address. Without hyperlinks, you would have to enter the address of each page to move around. Returning to the Dummies.com example, the left-hand pane of the Web page shown in Figure 11-1 contains a list of links, including one for the Dummies Answer Network. If you click on this link with your mouse, you immediately go to the Dummies Answer Network page, which is actually found at `http://answers.dummies.com`. Without the link, you would have to type in the address to access that particular Web page. Similarly, clicking on the Technology link in the left-hand pane of the Dummies.com home page takes you directly to the Dummies Technology Catalog at `http://catalog.dummies.com/section.asp?section=17`. As you can see, without hyperlinks, moving from page to page is very tedious, headache-ish, and fraught with errors.

So, you surf the wired Web via hyperlinks. Just point and click, and your browser takes you directly to the page you want, with no typing and no fumbling with a bunch of addresses.

Okay, how does this magic work? Hyperlinks function through very simple HTML commands underlying each Web page that you see. When Web designers create a Web page, they specify the actual Web address associated with each hyperlink on the page. You can't see the actual address because it is embedded in the HTML code. However, your Web browser can read the address and take you directly to the page using the address. In other words, the browser does all the dirty work, entering the address for you and then moving you to the desired page. Figure 11-2 shows how this process works and even lists a sample of the HTML hyperlink code that your Web browser sees.

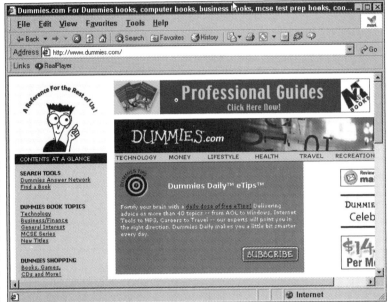

Figure 11-1:
Hyperlinks
point the
way to all
kinds of
information
at Dummies.
com.

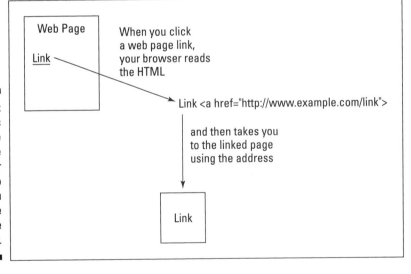

Figure 11-2:
Hyperlinks
in the
HTML code
enable your
browser to
take you
from one
Web page
to another.

Your Web browser reads links whenever you want to move from one page to another, or even from one Web site to another. For example, when you use a search engine, such as Google.com, you see the search results displayed as a series of hyperlinks. If you click on one of the links in the list of search results, your browser takes you directly to the corresponding Web site. The entire Internet and the concepts of surfing and browsing all rely on this simple hyperlink technology.

As you surf the Internet, remember that virtually any word or object can function as a hyperlink, including pictures, buttons, icons, and anything else you may see on a typical Web page.

Surfing in the Wireless World

Okay, hyperlinks serve as the basis for surfing in the wired world. Do they also work on the wireless Web? Well, yes and no. As I mention earlier in this chapter, surfing on the wireless Internet differs from surfing on the wired Internet. Don't worry; hyperlinks are still alive and well on the wireless Internet. However, they do not work in the same way and they do not work between different Web sites.

Now that may seem confusing, but I can clear up this hyperlink business. In the wireless world, hyperlinks do not work the same way because wireless devices do not have Web browsers that can manage them. For this reason, you cannot jump from one wireless Web site to another via hyperlinks. However, you can maneuver among pages within the same Web site on your wireless device.

For example, Figure 11-3 shows the mySimon.com wireless Web clipping, as it appears on a Palm VIIx. The categories listed are hyperlinks. I can click on a link on this page — for example, Books, Movies & Music — and check out listings in that category.

However, from within a wireless Web site, I cannot jump to a different Web site. The mini-browser in a wireless device has no place to enter a URL and physically move to a different Web site. So, your surfing via hyperlinks is limited to pages within a Web site. For example, you cannot jump from mySimon. com to MSN.com or another Web site via links. I don't mean that you cannot visit other sites; you just can't surf over to them.

So, why can't you surf the wireless Web via hyperlinks? Wireless Web sites use small Web applications that enable you to get information from the Web and move around within it. Each application works on its own because not every site on the Internet supports wireless access. Consequently, each site must produce its own wireless Web application and then deliver that software to you through your ISP.

Figure 11-3:
Use internal hyperlinks to maneuver within a wireless Web site.

REMEMBER

The mini Web sites that you see on your wireless device are really applications. Each one works on its own to communicate with the actual Web site on the Internet. To get a clearer picture of what I mean, assume that you want to visit mySimon.com using your wired, desktop computer. You type **www.mysimon.com** into your browser's address line, and your browser pulls the mySimon.com home page to your computer from the Internet and displays it to you. However, if you want to access mySimon.com on your wireless device, the simple home page is stored locally on the device — you don't surf to it. From this mini-application, you can use links and search for information by communicating with the mySimon.com Web servers on the Internet.

If that is the case, how can you get from site to site on the wireless Internet? The process differs a little, depending on whether you use a PDA or a Web-enabled phone. In the following sections, I explain how you surf the wireless Web using each type of device.

Surfing on a PDA

You can surf the wireless Internet using a PDA, depending on the make and model. However, PDAs do not use a typical Web browser. Instead, you download mini-applications from the provider's Web site to the PDA (or install them from your Palm CD) and then use each mini-application to access a specific Web site. In other words, you cannot surf from one Internet site to another on your PDA. You specifically install the application or application set that enables you to visit each Web site you want to use.

For example, Web surfing on the Palm VIIx uses a technique called Web clipping, which uses mini-applications called Palm Query Apps (PQAs). When I first got connected to the Internet with my Palm VIIx, I had a mail application and a few Web applications preinstalled. I can access the Palm.net Web site to download more PQAs. Alternatively, I can download those applications to my desktop PC and then synchronize with the Palm VIIx.

PDAs provide a synchronization cradle and software so the PDA can communicate with the PC. Consequently, I can easily download the Palm PQAs I want and then transfer them to the Palm at my leisure. I can access any Web site that supports the Palm platform as long as I have installed the appropriate PQAs for those sites.

Check out this book's Wireless Internet Access Directory for a listing of Web sites that are compatible with your wireless device.

After I download the applications I want, I can access those sites as desired. The following steps show you how this process works on a Palm VIIx:

1. **In the Palm handheld, access the main menu that lists your current Web applications, along with the other standard Palm applications, as shown in Figure 11-4.**

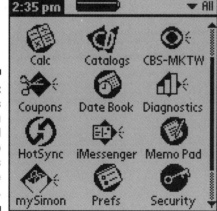

Figure 11-4:
The Palm's main menu lists all the Web applications you have installed.

2. **To visit a Web site, simply tap that site's icon with the stylus.**

   The Web application connects you with the wireless Internet and opens the main page, such as the mySimon site shown in Figure 11-5.

3. **Use the Web site as desired.**

   For example, in Figure 11-6, I am searching for this book on the mySimon Web site.

4. **When you finish with the Web site, simply access the Palm's main menu. Then, you can select another site to visit from the menu listing.**

Figure 11-5:
Viewing
the Web
application's
main page.

Figure 11-6:
Searching a
Web site
via a Web
application
on a PDA.

As you can see, surfing wireless Web sites works almost the same way as surfing on a desktop PC. Surfing in the wireless world differs from wired surfing in two fundamental ways. First, you must access a main menu to select the Web site you want to visit. Second, to have that Web site appear in the PDA's main menu, you must download the application that enables you to access the site.

Don't worry about wasting lots of time downloading these Web applications. Most of these PDA applications weigh in at less than 15KB in size — about the size of an average e-mail message with no attachments. So, downloading a typical Web application takes less than a minute.

Deleting wireless Web applications

So, what happens if you decide that you no longer need a Web application that you downloaded to your PDA? Can you get rid of it? Sure. The following steps show you how to delete an application from a Palm device (and other PDAs use a similar process):

1. **Tap the Application soft button to open the main application screen. Then, tap the menu soft button at the bottom of the screen.**

   An App menu appears with a Delete option, as shown in Figure 11-7.

Figure 11-7:
Use the App menu to delete an item.

2. **Tap Delete.**

   A Delete window appears, as shown in Figure 11-8. The Free Memory bar shows how much memory you have available, and you also see how much memory each application uses.

3. **To delete an application, select it with the stylus and then tap the Delete button. Then, tap Yes in response to the warning message that appears.**

Figure 11-8:
Select an item and click Delete.

Surfing on a Web-enabled phone

Surfing on a Web-enabled phone is not much different from surfing on a PDA. You still have access to certain Web sites that support Internet communication via a wireless phone, and you operate the wireless sites by using a microbrowser (which is a mini-Web browser) — namely, the Openwave Mobile Browser.

The Openwave Mobile Browser is the de facto standard for Internet-enabled phones. In fact, most wireless phones that provide Internet service use the Openwave Mobile Browser so that you can visit Internet sites. These Internet sites typically appear on your phone in the form of a menu, as shown in Figure 11-9. This example shows the Openwave Mobile Browser displayed on NeoPoint's 2000 model.

Almost any Web-enabled phone you choose to purchase probably uses the Openwave Mobile Browser. So, I want to spend a moment here pointing out some of its features. The Openwave Mobile Browser is a Wireless Access Protocol (WAP) compliant browser, which means it adheres to all of WAP's standards. That's good news for you because the Openwave Mobile Browser is designed to take full advantage of the wireless Internet. Check out some of its features:

- ✔ **Local home page:** Openwave Mobile Browser contains a home page from which you can access your favorite Web sites. It also contains a favorites list so you can easily list sites you want to revisit, in much the same way as you use Favorites and Bookmarks in Internet Explorer and Netscape Navigator.

- ✔ **Local cache store:** The microbrowser uses the phone's local memory to store temporary Web information, such as Web page data that you are currently viewing.

- ✔ **Good security:** The Openwave Mobile Browser makes full use of WAP and WAP security protocols.

- ✔ **Display:** The microbrowser is designed to make the most of small hand-held displays by using smart scrolling features to conserve space.

To find out more about the Openwave Mobile Browser specifications and all the phone models that use it, visit `www.openwave.com`.

When you decide on a service plan (see Chapter 2), take a look at the Web functionality for that service provider. Your surfing abilities may work a little differently, depending on which provider you choose and which make and model of phone you purchase. In short, do your homework and know what you want before you purchase a plan.

Figure 11-9:
Accessing
the wireless
Internet via
a NeoPoint
2000.

When you purchase your Web-enabled phone, it will ship to you configured with e-mail access and access to some popular Web sites. You can then use the wireless phone's keypad to maneuver through the home page and access wireless Web sites of your choice.

But what if you want different Web sites that are not listed? Can you access other Web sites using your Web-enabled phone? Sure. With the wireless Internet, you have a rich landscape of WAP-enabled Web sites ready for use. You can find out more about those sites by visiting this book's Wireless Internet Access Directory and then you can take a look at your provider's online listing of supported Web sites. Service providers continually update these lists as more and more Web sites join the wireless Internet.

If you want to choose different Web sites for your list, you need to check out your phone's instructions because each provider and phone model works somewhat differently. However, for the purpose of helping you understand how this process works, I can show you how to access other sites with AT&T

Wireless. The following steps show how you get a different group of Web sites, called a *homedeck*. Each homedeck provides different groups of Web sites that can appear on your home page. The following example demonstrates how you choose a new homedeck with AT&T Wireless:

1. **On your AT&T Internet-ready phone, select Data Mode.**

2. **Use the Up/Down arrow keys to access item 8, AT&T. Press the Yes button.**

3. **Use the Up/Down arrow keys to select item 2, Settings. Press the Yes button.**

4. **Use the Up/Down arrow keys to select item 4, Change Homepage. Press the Yes button.**

5. **Use the Up/Down arrow keys to select item 2, AT&T Surf Lounge. Press the Yes button.**

6. **Press the Yes button to select Make AT&T Surf Lounge your home page.**

7. **Press the Menu key and select the Reset Cache option. Press the OK softkey.**

Synchronizing your phone and your PC

While I am talking about the Openwave Mobile Browser, I also want to mention phone and PC synchronization. Can you synchronize the e-mail, address book, contact list, and other information in your Web-enabled phone with the corresponding information in your PC? What about synchronization with a PDA? I can answer those questions with a qualified yes, depending on your phone model.

In addition to the Openwave Mobile Browser, Openwave (formerly two companies, Phone.com and Software.com) offers another product called FoneSync Pro, which enables you to synchronize information on your phone with information on your PC or PDA. FoneSync Pro provides software for your computer and a tether connection that enables you to physically connect your phone with your PC's serial port.

After you connect the phone and the PC, you can perform synchronization. For example, you can import e-mail into a PC-based mail client, such as Outlook or Eudora. Or, you can synchronize the phone and the PC to maintain a back-up copy of all the information from your phone. That way, you don't have to worry about losing your phone. When you get your new phone, simply synchronize it with the data from your PC.

FoneSync is compatible with more than 350 models of phones. You can find out more about FoneSync Pro by visiting www.fonesync.com. You also can check out a cool demo at that site. FoneSync Pro costs about $80 for the software and cable, and you can order the product directly from the FoneSync Web site.

Some providers also give you a personalized Web site where you can configure the options you want on your Web-enabled phone directly from your PC. After you configure this new home page for your phone, you can access this home page and use the sites you selected on your home page from your phone. For example, the Southwestern Bell wireless service, now called Cingular Wireless, provides its users with an Internet window at www.mywirelesswindow.com. You can download a utility for your PC so you can manage your wireless window for the wireless Internet phone.

Surfing on a wireless Web phone involves choosing the sites that you want to visit, configuring your home page so you can access those sites in a menu, and then using your phone's menu and arrow keys to maneuver among Web sites — not as smooth as surfing with a Web browser, but not too shabby when you're on the move and need information quickly!

Chapter 12

Keeping Up with Your Money

· ·

In This Chapter

▶ Managing your money with the wireless Internet

▶ Keeping track of your accounts online

▶ Accessing wireless investment and stock sites

· ·

*M*anaging your expenses, income, and investments doesn't have to be a pencil-and-paper process anymore. These days, you can tackle money management with the help of many different tools, including various software packages and Internet sites. Your wireless device gives you access to all kinds of money management tools and resources that can help you keep track of what you have and where it all goes.

Now, if the idea of managing your money over the Internet gives you a sinking feeling in the pit of your stomach, let me reassure you. Money management and financial transactions over the Internet are safe and secure, and they can certainly make your life a lot easier. Like the wired Internet, the wireless Internet provides numerous money management features and financial information sites that can help you earn more — and keep it!

In this chapter, I explore the basics of online money management on the wireless Internet. I show you what the wireless world offers and how you can use the Internet to make money management easier and more productive.

E-Money and You!

Why allow the Internet to invade your finances? The real question is, why not? After all, the Internet is becoming more and more integrated into our lives all the time. Why not use the Internet — and even the wireless Internet — to manage your money?

I understand that you may be worried about the security of managing your finances on the Internet. Is some geeky techno-criminal lurking out there in cyberspace, just waiting to steal your money? Although that type of crime is technically possible, your money is much safer as *e-money,* or electronic money, than it is when you handle it using a checking account or other paper means.

Web sites that enable you to make financial transactions or view financial records use an encryption method that scrambles the data while it travels to and from your wireless device or PC. This encryption method — typically, Secure HTTP (SHTTP) — makes it impossible for another person to view your online information. This same encryption method is used for online shopping, enabling you to buy something online without worrying much about someone stealing your credit card number. Am I saying that encryption makes it absolutely impossible for someone to steal money or other information? No, but these secure, online transactions are much safer than physically visiting the bank. So, use the Internet with confidence. Your money and personal financial information are much safer in the electronic world than they are in the world of paper-and-pencil transactions.

Okay, your money is safe, and you are unlikely to experience any kind of theft when using the wireless Internet. That's all well and good, but why should you handle your finances online? That's a good question, and here are my top five reasons for using the Internet for money management:

- ✔ **Management anywhere:** Your money should follow you; it should be an integral part of your hectic life and should not sit idly in some bank's vault. You should be able to access your money and get information about it anywhere. The wireless Internet can provide this capability because the wireless Internet always follows you. However, your bank must support wireless access to its Web site. Most major banks now provide online money management, but your bank's Web site must support WAP in order for your wireless device to access it. So, you'll need to do a little homework to see if your bank supports wireless access. Many major banks, such as Bank of America, USAB, Harris Bank, Texas Credit Union, and others support money management via your wireless device.

- ✔ **Information on the fly:** Waiting for bank statements and other financial information is a drag. You should be able to get information about your money at any time, and the wireless Internet can make that happen, but the same issues apply — your bank must support WAP in order for you to gain access.

- ✔ **Transactions anywhere:** The wireless Internet enables you to initiate all kinds of wireless money transactions, anywhere and at any time of day. Pay bills, apply for loans — you name it. Visa, MasterCard, Discover, and most major credit card companies support wireless access so you can check out your account anytime and even make wireless transfers. Also, use Mastercard.com and Visa.com to locate a nearby ATM so you can get cash when you need it.

- ✔ **Instant investments:** You can use your wireless device to make instant investments, buy and sell stocks, and perform other financial transactions immediately, no matter where you are. Online investing has become very popular, and most major investment sites are now WAP compatible. Check out CharlesSchwab.com, CNBC.com, Etrade.com, Tdwaterhouse.com, and Prudential.com, just to name a few. Also check out the financial listings in this book's Wireless Internet Access Directory.

- ✔ **Real-time information:** The stock market changes constantly, and you cannot stay glued to a TV or a wired computer, or wait for the morning paper. Use your wireless device to watch the stock market and get information immediately as it happens. Visit BeyondtheBull.com, CBSmarketwatch.com, Bloomberg.com, and many other stock market and investment sites to keep up with the market. Armed with real-time information, you can make financial decisions that are right for you.

The wireless Internet is your ticket to fast, immediate financial information and transactions. Use it to keep your money and interests following you around — you don't have to follow them!

Managing Your Money with the Wireless Internet

These days, personal money management means much more than simply depositing money in the bank and then withdrawing it via a checking account or in cash. Of course, we also use credit cards (unfortunately, too many of them) and ATMs, and now wireless devices have joined the party. No matter how many gadgets you add to the mix, however, the same basic principles still apply: Deposit more than you withdraw, and make sure the money you spend goes to the places it should.

Banking at the lake

The wireless Internet does not free you from your money management responsibilities. You still have to earn the money and control your spending. However, the wireless Internet can make money management easier in various ways because you can manage your money on your wireless device instead of traveling to banks and ATMs to take care of it.

So, how does it work? To manage your bank account via your wireless device, your bank must have an Internet site that supports wireless devices (via the Wireless Access Protocol — WAP). To find out whether your bank's Web site supports wireless devices, simply enter the bank's URL in your wireless device. If the site does not support wireless devices, you'll get an error message.

If your bank does not support wireless Internet access, ask your banker about wireless support for the bank's Web site. Customers drive business, so let your bank know that you want wireless access.

Using your bank's wireless Web site, you can check the status of your account, transfer money from one account to another, and perform any other type of business you would perform if you actually walked into the bank. The benefits are quite clear: You save lots of time and aggravation. You do not have to rush to the bank before it closes. Just use your wireless device to manage your account at any time of the day or night, whether you are at home, at the office, in a cab, or even at the lake!

Finding an ATM

Another great benefit of the wireless Internet is finding an ATM. Consider this scenario: You're out on the town in an unfamiliar city and you realize that you are running low on cash. What can you do? With your wireless device, you can access various ATM finder tools that can help you locate an ATM in any desired city. As you might imagine, this feature can be very helpful, especially for travelers. Visit Mastercard.com or Visa.com to find an ATM near you. If you're using a Palm device, you can download an ATM Finder from the Palm.net site. Also, if your bank is on the wireless Internet, you may be able to find an ATM from your bank's site.

Check out the financial section in this book's Wireless Internet Access Directory for a listing of helpful financial sites that may be compatible with your wireless device.

Managing cards and accounts

Various wireless Internet sites can help you manage your bank account as well as credit card accounts from one Internet site. You can log on and then use the wireless site to access your accounts. For example, at AccountMinder (www.accountminder.com), you can easily set up an AccountMinder account and then pull your other banking and credit card accounts into a single management location — very helpful!

Exploring other money management tools

With your wireless device, you may be able to pay your utility bills, credit card bills, and any other charges you incur. To find out whether you can use this feature, visit the Web site for each company to see if wireless access is available.

The wireless Internet also offers various other financial tools. For example, check out www.countrywide.com to keep track of today's interest rates or even apply for a loan. Progressive.com gives you the ability to shop for insurance rates, pay your Progressive bill, and get additional information on your account, all from your wireless device. Rovenet.com gives wireless users several different information pages about online investing and money management. If you're a Palm user, you can even download a Currency Calculator PQA so you can convert currency and find out information about fluctuating currency values.

These are just a few examples, and the list of sites and management tools grows longer everyday. Be sure to check out the financial section of the Wireless Internet Access Directory in this book for more site options, and check your wireless provider's Web site for new sites and information. As more and more Internet sites join the wireless world, your handheld device will be able to manage your money and your life with ease!

Investing Online via the Wireless Internet

You can use the wireless Internet to buy and sell stock, manage investments, and even manage retirement accounts. These services work in the same manner as they do on the wired Web, except you perform them using your wireless device. The good news for you online money investors is that many popular online investment companies are available on the wireless Internet.

On the wireless Internet, you find popular sites, such as www.cbsmarketwatch.com, www.ameritrade.com, and www.beyondthebull.com. You can use these sites to set up an account and then manage trading from your wireless device. These sites are also great for watching the market, typically giving you various types of charts and reports.

Numerous sites enable you to closely monitor your investments in a real-time manner. This way, you always know exactly what is going on with the market. For example, you can watch the stock market and manage your investments at sites such as www.cbsmarketwatch.com and www.beyondthebull.com.

Remember to check out this book's Wireless Internet Access Directory for a listing of financial sites that may be available on your wireless device.

And if you want to find out more about online investing, check out *Investing Online For Dummies,* 3rd Edition, by Kathleen Sindell (published by Hungry Minds, Inc.).

Chapter 13

Shopping on the Wireless Internet

. . . .

In This Chapter

▶ Checking out the benefits of Internet shopping

▶ Shopping safely

▶ Dealing with shipping and returns

▶ Using stores and finding products

▶ Buying stuff online

. . . .

*O*kay, I'll admit it. I love buying stuff on the Internet. I can sit comfortably in my own home, browse all kinds of products, buy the one I want, and then have it arrive at my home in a few days. No traffic, long lines, or screaming kids — I think shopping on the Internet is the best thing since apple pie. Of course, not everyone agrees. After all, you can't hold the product in your hand before you buy it, and some people get the willies thinking about giving their money to a faceless machine.

Still, Internet shopping grows more popular every year, as more and more people discover the ease of use, the safety, and the fantastic number of products that they can buy online. As you might guess, the wireless Internet includes online shopping, and you can use your Web-enabled phone or PDA to shop and buy products no matter where you are. You can order some books while you wait in rush-hour traffic. Or, send birthday flowers to dear old mom before you board the plane. Wireless Internet shopping is safe and it can save you time, aggravation, and money.

In this chapter, I explore wireless Internet shopping, showing you all the ins and outs of shopping the wireless world when you're on the go.

Shopping at the World's Biggest Mall

I like to think of the Internet as the world's biggest mall. It contains all kinds of stores selling all kinds of products from all over world, and each store has the biggest selection of merchandise available.

If you recently joined the wireless Internet, or even the regular wired Internet, maybe you're curious about online shopping, even though you have never actually purchased an item. Maybe you feel a little trepidation about buying a product from a machine. In the following sections, I describe ten great benefits of Internet shopping.

You can find anything and everything

If you walk into a bookstore looking for a book on the mating habits of goldfish, you probably will be disappointed. Typically, you will not find a book on such a specialized topic. However, in an e-commerce (electronic commerce) environment, you are not limited by a store's physical inventory. At a typical online bookstore, such as www.amazon.com or www.barnesandnoble.com, the only limits you face are the Web site's database and publishing houses' inventory. If the product exists anywhere in the world, you can probably find it for sale on the Internet.

This feature is what I love most about Internet shopping. At my fingertips, I can find all kinds of products that I could not otherwise find without lots of frustration and wandering around the city. Need a certain outfit or a really cool retro CD? No problem, you can find it. Need an out-of-print book? You can probably find it. What about groceries, flowers, and sporting goods? Again, no problem — the Internet has them all.

You can shop anytime, anywhere

I am a morning person. I like to get up with the chickens and I do my best work before noon. One morning at about 5:30, I decided that I needed a null modem cable to connect two non-networked computers. I located the product I wanted on the Internet and quickly purchased it — while the rest of the world slept.

My wife, on the other hand is a night owl. Her day really gets going about the time I'm falling asleep. During the writing of this book, we're expecting a new baby, so she surfs the Internet during the middle of the night, shopping for baby comforters, clothes, and all those other goodies.

The key point here: The Internet never closes. You can visit online stores 24 hours a day, seven days a week, 365 days a year, without fail. You can shop at any hour, and the Internet servers and technology do not care.

The Internet is not grouchy

I avoid last-minute Christmas shopping like the plague. I know that many people enjoy the hustle and bustle, but I don't like the waiting in line and the irritable salespeople who are overloaded on Christmas cheer. Now, please don't send me a nasty e-mail message — I know that salespeople have a tough job. However, I like to get answers to my questions without loads of attitude.

The Internet never has an attitude. You can shop for all kinds of products online, perform numerous searches, and ask the same questions over and over again, and the Web site will never say, "Just find it yourself."

The Internet remembers you

For some holiday reading last year, I bought a bestseller at an online bookstore. About nine months later, the online bookstore sent me an e-mail message telling me about a new book by the same author, and even gave me an e-coupon for $3 off. Now that's customer service!

I think my money is important, and if I spend my money at a particular store, I believe the store should remember what I have bought and help me find the kinds of things I like. How many regular stores remember everything you've bought or ever considered buying? I thought so.

Many online stores use technology that remembers you. The Web server's database keeps up with your username and password and remembers the items you purchased as well as every item you have ever viewed. Then, judging from your shopping patterns, the Web site recommends products to you and lets you know when new products are available.

It never rains, snows, or hails on the Internet

Here's an all-too-familiar scenario: As you head into the mall, the weather is fine. However, by the time you check out and head to the exit with all your purchases, it's pouring rain, snowing, or a sudden freak hail storm is pounding the parking lot. What can you do? You stand under the canopy of the storefront with all the other customers, staring longingly at your car and wishing you were already home.

Guess what? It never rains, snows, or hails on the Internet — and that's enough said!

Products are always where they are "supposed" to be

Consider this familiar refrain:

> Customer: Excuse me. Do you sell house slippers?
>
> Merchant: Yes, we do.
>
> Customer: Where can I find them?
>
> Merchant: On aisle 17.
>
> Customer: Where on aisle 17?
>
> Merchant: Midway down, third shelf. You can't miss them.

The customer travels to aisle 17, and house slippers are nowhere to be found.

> Customer: I didn't find house slippers on aisle 17.
>
> Merchant: Hmmm. Maybe we don't carry them after all. But you might want to check aisle 18, just to be sure.

In all likelihood, you have suffered through similar scenarios. You never have shopping experiences like this on the Internet. The Web site always knows what products are available and what products are not available. You don't have to wander around looking for things that should be on aisle 17. You simply search for an item, and if the Web site has the item, you go directly to it.

Prices are usually lower

I'm not going to tell you that the Internet always has the best prices. Regular stores and Internet stores all compete with one another, so you have to look carefully before buying a product. However, as a general rule, I find that I can buy the same product cheaper online than at most stores. True, I have to pay shipping, but reputable online stores keep their shipping costs to a minimum, and you may not have to pay state sales tax on items. (Check on this issue, though, because some states do charge sales tax for your online purchases.) Of course, a smart consumer shops around to be sure, but my experience is that online prices are usually a little lower.

You can comparison shop in one place

Maybe you want to buy a pair of ski boots. Three different stores in your city sell the ski boots, and you want to know which store has the best price. You can either call each store to find the lowest prince, or drive to each store and examine the price for yourself. This whole process can be very time consuming and aggravating.

Or, you can do your comparison shopping via the Internet. You can quickly find the same product on several different Web sites and easily compare prices. Some Web sites even compare the prices for you — for example, www.mysimon.com.

You can shop at stores in distant locations

I live in a small town about an hour from Dallas. I don't have a lot of stores to choose from unless I want to trek to Dallas, spend all day driving all over the city, burning up a lot of gasoline and giving myself severe heartburn. Or, I can use the Internet and shop at stores that are not in my area. I don't have to drive anywhere, the shopping experience is not stressful, and I can surf from store to store with great ease.

You can shop in your underwear

Maybe you think I am stretching a point here, but there's a lot to be said for comfort shopping. You can shop privately from your own home or any other location with a wireless Internet device, and you don't have to look presentable. In fact, by the time you get all gussied up and drive to the store, you could have already shopped online and been done!

Practicing Safe Shopping

Many people who refuse to shop online have said to me, "There's no way I would ever use my credit cards on the Internet. Someone might steal my numbers." That's true, but those same people will calmly hand their credit cards to store clerks and gas station attendants without a thought about how honest those salespeople may be.

Shopping online with a credit card is much safer than shopping in a regular store. When you shop online, you do not deal with humans and potential human error and theft. Web servers on the Internet will not steal your credit card number and charge you for a bunch of items that you did not purchase.

More mind-boggling security stuff

The type of encryption used to transfer personal information to and from a Web a site depends on your device. Several different types exist, and different companies develop encryption methods. However, many wireless Web sites also use their own encryption on top of the device's standard encryption. So, at any given time, your credit card information may be encrypted twice or even more during transit using different encryption methods. A thief would have to sort out all that mess to figure out your credit card numbers. So, shop with confidence — your credit card is much safer on the wireless Internet than it is in your purse or wallet.

In fact, to steal your credit card online, a thief would have to intercept your computer's TCP/IP communication with the Web site and decipher it in order to discover your account numbers. That may not sound too difficult, but credit card numbers and personal information are almost always encrypted by your Web browser and the Internet Web server. *Encryption* involves the scrambling of data so that it cannot be read without a key. The Web server and your Web browser work out an encryption method so the data can be safely sent to the Web site and decrypted, as shown in Figure 13-1.

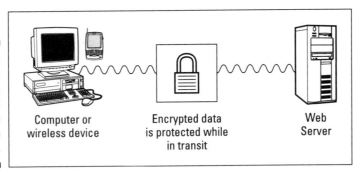

Figure 13-1:
Credit card
information
is encrypted
and sent to
the Web
server.

Computer or wireless device

Encrypted data is protected while in transit

Web Server

So, to steal your credit card information online, a thief would have to intercept your encrypted data and break the encryption code — a process that can be accomplished, but not easily. You may have seen advertisements that involve getting protection from people online stealing credit cards, but I'm here to tell you that your credit card is much safer buying items online than in a regular store.

By following a few simple tips, you can greatly reduce the likelihood of having any problems with credit card theft online:

✔ Remember that the wireless Internet sites that currently support credit card transactions are major sites that provide highly secure transactions. From a wireless device, you are basically safe.

✔ From a wired computer, stick to well-known Web sites. I'm all for new Internet sites, but to be entirely safe, stick to major sites that are recognized by the general public. Also, watch for site notices, such as `Secure Server` or `Secure Shopping Cart`.

✔ The Web site should give you information about its privacy policy and security methods. In fact, some sites guarantee that you will never be responsible for anything charged to your account that you did not want to buy. If you can't find any of this privacy and security information at the Web site, move on.

✔ Watch out for "too good to be true" deals and other promotions that just do not sound plausible. If you are suspicious, follow your instincts and move on.

✔ Obtain a credit card that is designed for Internet usage. For example, I have a credit card from a major bank that was made for online use. The card uses chip technology and guarantees that I will never be held responsible for any transactions that I do not authorize. In fact, the credit card even gives me a 5-percent discount on all items at certain online partner stores — which more than makes up for the usual shipping charges.

Many Web sites and credit cards guarantee safe Internet shopping, freeing you from all responsibility. This is a sure sign that Internet shopping is generally safe and problem free.

Understanding Internet Shipping and Returns

I think Internet shopping is a great thing. It's easy, fun, and involves very few security risks. However, Internet shopping falls short of shopping at a typical store in terms of shipping fees and time as well as the handling of returns.

I do not mean to say that you will pay outrageous shipping rates nor that you are stuck with what you purchase. On the contrary, reputable Internet stores are very happy to work with you and usually give you various options. So, the trick is knowing what to look and for and how to make the best use of Internet store policies. The following sections explore these issues to help ensure that you enjoy positive online shopping experiences.

Managing Internet shipping

Most online stores charge you a shipping fee for sending the products that you purchase. That's reasonable, but fees vary from store and store, and you can even choose the type of shipping that you want. Of course, the faster you want the item, the more you pay. Some stores charge a higher price for the product but do not charge a shipping fee, so your total price may be less. But, getting the product may take longer than it would from another vendor . . . and so on and so on. As you can see, shipping charges can get confusing, and you want to make certain you get the best deal possible.

Here are some practical tips you should keep in mind as you consider Internet shipping charges:

- ✔ **Compare the price of the product, plus the standard shipping charge, against the same product and shipping charge at another site. Then, examine the shipping time.** For example, assume that Site A sells this book for $19.99 with a $2.49 shipping charge. Delivery takes four to seven days. Site B sells this book for $18.88, with a $4.20 shipping charge, and the book is guaranteed to arrive within four days. So, Site A's total price is $22.48 while Site B's total price is $23.08 — a difference of 60 cents. However, you may wait longer to get the book from Site A. So, which is a better deal? That is up to you in the end, depending on your patience and how important 60 cents is to your pocket book. The point is to look at the price, shipping cost, and delivery time, and determine which combination best suits your needs.

- ✔ **Look for shipping options.** Many online sites give you such options as U.S priority mail, UPS ground, FedEx overnight, and so on. Faster shipping costs more, but may be worth the price if you're in a hurry.

- ✔ **Before you place an online order, make sure the shipping fee is clearly stated.** Do not buy products from sites that do not tell you upfront the shipping fee.

- ✔ **Make sure you give the online store enough information to correctly ship your order.** Include your full name and complete shipping address. Also, remember that UPS, FedEx, and others do not ship to post office boxes.

While I am on the topic of shipping fees and price comparisons, I want to mention a Web site, available on most wireless Internet devices, that helps you examine the purchase price and shipping cost of a product from several sites. The mySimon To Go wireless portal, shown in Figure 13-2, and found on the wired Internet at `www.mysimon.com`, explores the Internet for you and compares the prices and shipping fees of items across a wide number of Internet sites. You can browse different categories of products, search for the product of your choice, and then buy the product that meets your price and shipping needs.

Although some Internet sites sell products at a low price and then gouge you with the shipping fee, most are honest and do not make their money from shipping charges. As with all things in life, though, be a smart consumer and check the facts before you make a purchase.

Returning items purchased online

All reputable online stores have return policies, just like a store you might visit at the mall. Those return policies vary from store to store, but they have common and reasonable provisions so you can return an item that was delivered in error or one that you do not want. Here are some common return policy clauses that you are likely to see for Internet store purchases:

✔ Most online stores give you a time period in which you may return items, typically 30 days. After that time, either you can't return the item or you do so under significant restrictions. A 30-day limit is fair, though, and helps the store avoid getting ripped off by dishonest customers.

✔ You should be able to return items that were erroneously shipped to you for a full refund plus the cost of return shipping.

✔ You should be able to return any unopened item for a full refund, but you are responsible for the return shipping. For example, you decide to purchase a music CD, but change your mind after it has been shipped. If you don't open it, you can return it for a full refund minus your cost to ship the item — which is fair because you changed your mind. If the Internet store also has a physical store in your area, such as Barnes & Noble, Wal-Mart, Target, and so on, you can probably return the item directly to the physical store as well.

Every online store should have a page that describes its return policy. Check out this page to make sure you understand how things will work if you need to return an item. Also, if you can't get the return information you need quickly and easily, move on to another site.

If the time comes for you to return an item, you typically visit a specified page on the Web site, fill in the information, and the store will generate a return number and mailer label for you to use. When you receive an item you have purchased, your invoice and other paperwork included in the package usually tell you how to handle returns.

Shopping the Wireless Internet

Are you ready to shop? The following sections help you get started. In the following sections, I explore Internet shopping and how it works. I also give you shopping tips and information about using the wireless Internet. Keep in mind that the procedure may differ slightly, depending on which wireless device you use, so check your device documentation for any specific details you may need to remember.

Finding shopping sites

To start shopping on the wireless Internet, you must first find Internet stores that your particular device supports. Each wireless Internet device, such as a Web-enabled phone or PDA, may support different Web sites. Typically, however, most wireless devices support the more popular sites on the Internet.

New wireless Web sites are being added all the time, so check your service for more information. If you are an AT&T Wireless customer, check the AT&T Web site for updates. If you are a Palm customer, check the Palm Web site for new Web clippings that will be available.

Also, be sure to check out this book's Wireless Internet Access Directory. You'll find a Shopping section that lists typical wireless Web sites you may be able to visit on your device.

Remember, when using the wireless Internet, you do not surf the Web for sites. Instead, you determine the Web sites or block of Web sites that you want to use and have them downloaded to your phone or PDA. The specific instructions for your device will vary, but you typically can add more sites by following these steps:

1. **On your phone or PDA, open the application that enables you to connect to the wireless Internet.**

2. **Using your function keys, keyboard, or stylus, navigate to your service provider's site.**

3. **Select the option that provides access to additional Web sites.**

4. **Select the Web site or block of Web sites that you want to use.**

   The new Web sites that you select appear in your Internet menu or Favorites folder, depending on the type of device you use.

Searching for products on wireless Internet shopping sites

After you select the shopping site or store you want to use (see the preceding section), you can search the Web site for the product you want. If you have used the Web site before, you may be prompted to log on. This is okay, so go ahead and provide the user name and password if the site requires them.

Now, you're ready to look for the product you want. First, check the site's interface; some have a drop-down menu that enables you to select the kind of product you want to find.

When searching for items at online stores, follow these simple guidelines:

✔ If you are looking for a particular product, enter the exact name of the product, or in the case of a book, you can search by using the author's name. For example, if you want to look for the movie "Castaway," select the site's video store and then type the exact name of the movie.

✔ Be concise. For example, if you wanted to find this book, you would enter **Wireless Internet Access For Dummies**, not **I want to find Wireless Internet Access For Dummies**. Keep your search very specific and simple.

✔ If you're not sure of the product's name, be as specific as you can when entering information. For example, if you want to buy a new watch, but you're not sure what you want, just make sure you are in the correct category or store and then type **watch** or **wrist watch**. Keep it short and specific.

If your search fails and you can't seem to find the item you want, try using different keywords. If that doesn't work, try choosing a different online store that is more likely to have the product that you want.

As you access different online stores, remember to play around with each site so you can discover all that it has to offer. Some sites can give you the top ten items in various categories, help you find a physical store in any city, and enable you to send free electronic cards to friends and family (provided you have their e-mail addresses).

Spend time looking around each store. You can find all kinds of interesting and fun things to do.

Purchasing an item

After you search for an item, the store displays the results of your search. Depending on your search criteria, the database may have guessed and given you several items to choose from. If you find what you want, select it using your phone keypad arrows or via your PDA's stylus or keyboard. More information about the item appears, including the price and possible reviews from other customers. After you decide that you want to buy the item, follow these quick and easy steps:

1. **Locate a button on the Web site that says** `Purchase`, `Add to Basket`, **or some other similar term. Click that button to begin the checkout process.**

2. **If you see a button that says something, such as** `Proceed to Check Out`, **select that option.**

3. **If you have an existing account with the online store, verify that your account information is accurate, if you are prompted to do so. If you do not have an online account with the store, follow the site's instructions for entering your personal information, such as your name, e-mail address, shipping address, phone number, and credit card information.**

   This process may take a few minutes, and you may need to complete several screens. Remember that the information you enter is encrypted before it is sent to the Web site.

4. **After you enter the required information, check the instructions and the final price tally, which includes the shipping fee. Then, follow the Web site's instructions to complete the purchase.**

   After you purchase the item, you typically see a thank-you page, and the site sends you an e-mail message confirming your order.

Checking the status of your order

After you purchase an item from a Web site, you can check the status of your order at any time. You can check the status of the order on the wired Internet by checking your e-mail and following a Web link that the store provides in the e-mail message that confirms your order. This link takes you to your account on the store's Web site.

You can also check the status of your order by using your wireless device. Most online stores give you an option, such as My Account or Order Status. By selecting that option, you can see all the items you have ordered and find out whether the items have been shipped to you. If the items have not been shipped, the account information will usually tell you why.

Most online stores enable you to cancel an order with no penalty until the order is shipped. So, if you purchase an item using your wireless device because you're bored out of your mind while waiting on a meeting, you can always access your account and cancel that order later if you change your mind — unless the item has already shipped. Follow the site's instructions for canceling orders.

Having even more shopping-related fun on the wireless Internet

In addition to searching for and buying items on the Internet, you can do a few other interesting things that fall into the shopping realm. Check with your provider to find out which sites are available for your device, but these ideas will get your mind moving:

- **Auctions:** At online auction sites, such as eBay, you can find items, bid on them, and even manage your own account if you are a seller or a buyer. You can bid on hot items while connected to the wired Internet and then use the wireless Internet to keep track of your bids while you are on the move so you don't get outbid.

- **Gifts:** Forgot mom's birthday, or maybe you need to send a thank-you gift? No problem. The wireless Internet includes numerous Web sites from which you can order flowers and send cards and gifts, such as www.ftd.com. Check your service provider for wireless Web sites.

- **Catalogs:** Do you love to get catalogs in the mail? No time to look for new catalogs? Then visit a catalog site such as CatalogDirect.com. You can easily sign up to get catalogs of your choice from this site while you are on the move.

- **Coupons:** Like to save money? Then visit a coupon site such as ClipACoupon.com, shown in Figure 13-3. At this site, you can browse different categories and locate all kinds of coupons that will save you money. It's fun and rewarding!

ClipACoupon

ClipACoupon.com(sm)
Local Area – Specify Location
▼ –All Categories–
OR Search: ....

Your Registration Info
Email: ....
Password: ....
☑ Remember Registration Info
Tell me about Registration info
(Find Coupons)

Courtesy of Tom Ridinger, CTO, ClipACoupon.com, Inc.

Figure 13-3: Coupon sites like ClipACoupon.com can help you save money.

As you can see, you can do all kinds of fun and interesting things while shopping on the wireless Internet. So, get moving, find some sites, and start shopping!

Chapter 14

Wireless and Your World

In This Chapter

▶ Keeping up with the news

▶ Traveling

▶ Watching the weather

▶ Making plans

▶ Getting information

▶ Having fun

S ure, the wireless Internet is great for your business and other aspects of your life: You can send and receive e-mail, manage your money, shop, and stay connected when you're on the move. However, you also can do lots of other things on the wireless Internet — and new sites and new options are being added daily!

In this chapter, I explore various additional, interesting, and fun things you can do on the wireless Internet. Discover how the wireless Internet can be a constant source of information, help, and entertainment.

Getting the News

One of the great things about the wireless Internet is that it enables you to keep up with the latest news — even when you are away from your computer or the television. While you sit in a cab or on the bus, you can use the wireless Internet to access all kinds of news and information sites.

The wireless Internet includes many major news sites, such as ABCnews.com and CNN.com. You can access these sites and see the major headlines, or you can visit various subsections and find science, entertainment, technology, and all kinds of other news. It's like reading a newspaper that fits in the palm of your hand.

Also, many other news sites focus on certain specifics, such as your geographic area. You can find out about local news and issues specific to your region.

Additionally, you can find various other sites that fall into the news and information category. For example, the Body1.com site, shown in Figure 14-1, enables you to research all kinds of medical and psychiatric conditions as well as learn about first aid and doctor profiles.

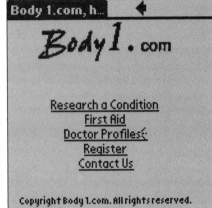

Figure 14-1: Body1.com provides all kinds of medical news and information.

As you can see, you can find news on just about any topic you want. From national, to regional, to local, to topic specific, the wireless Internet makes the information you need available at your fingertips.

Following Sports

All right, sports fans, here's the big question: What can the wireless Internet do for you? The answer: a lot! You can keep up with sports teams, games, scores, and other sports-related information on the wireless Internet. No more biting your nails, waiting to find out what's going on with the big game. Just use your wireless device and access any number of sports sites to find out what's happening.

For you football fans out there, keep track of all the games and all the news at Joe Bryant's Cheatsheets.net, which is becoming FootballGuys.com as of this writing. At the Cheatsheets.net wireless site, shown in Figure 14-2, you can get all kinds of game projections, player rankings, and other information. You can even search for rankings and projections quickly and easily, as shown in Figure 14-3.

Figure 14-2:
Follow
football at
Cheatsheets
.net.

Figure 14-3:
Check out
rankings,
projections,
and all kinds
of stuff.

Football is not the only sport to arrive on the wireless Internet. You can access all kinds of sites to keep up with sports news and related information. For example, the 2wayNews.com wireless Internet site gives you a unified place to keep up with all kinds of sports results, as shown in Figure 14-4.

So, rest assured sports fans — if you want quick news on your favorite sports team or games in progress, the wireless Internet is for you.

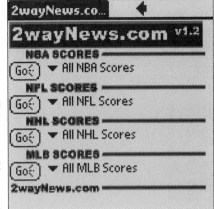

Figure 14-4:
Get scores quickly and easily at 2wayNews. com.

Watching the Weather

I live in Texas, and the saying here is, "If you don't like the weather, just wait 10 minutes because it will change" — and that's not much of an exaggeration. I like to use my wireless PDA to keep track of the weather, especially when I am traveling around the state. Quick access to weather news helps you avoid all kinds of problems and may get you out of many jams. So, for the traveler, or just someone who likes to stay in tune with the weather regularly, the wireless Internet is certainly your ticket.

For example, the infoBrand My Weather Center, shown in Figure 14-5, gives you a quick way to find out about weather conditions in any desired city or ZIP code. Simply enter the city or ZIP code, and the Weather Center retrieves the information for you.

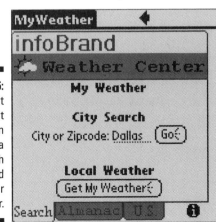

Figure 14-5:
Find out about weather in your area with infoBrand My Weather Center.

The infoBrand My Weather Center also gives you a national summary of
weather conditions in major cities, as shown in Figure 14-6, as well as an
almanac that chronicles weather history.

Figure 14-6:
Check out
the National
Summary
on the
infoBrand
My Weather
Center.

© 1998–2001 Silicon Dreams Interactive and Wendy Jones

In addition to sites like this one, you can find numerous weather sites and
weather information specific to your region. You also can get information
about specific weather events, such as hurricanes or tornados, or you can
check on the snow at your favorite ski slope. From your wireless device, you
always have access to the latest weather information.

Getting Travel Help

Wireless devices are made to go with you, and the wireless Internet offers
plenty of sites that can help you when you're traveling. In the past, you had
to rely on information from gas station attendants and other local people —
some helpful and others maybe not so helpful. Now, however the wireless
Internet puts you in charge because you can find all kinds of travel-related
information right on the Internet.

You can use your wireless device to check on the status of your plane flight
or call a cab — all from the palm of your hand. For example, visit
Travelocity.com's wireless Internet site to check out flight departure information, flight schedules, existing itineraries, and all kinds of other information
about your flight, as shown in Figure 14-7.

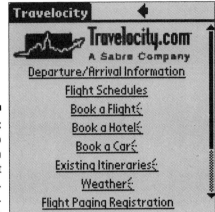

Figure 14-7:
Get help with travel at Travelocity. com.

These services are very helpful to the busy traveler. You can also access numerous hotel sites and even locate hotel finders so you can get the best deal on a place to stay.

What if you get lost? Can you get a map of city or driving directions? Sure, no problem. One wireless Internet site that provides travel assistance is MapQuest — found on the wired Web at www.mapquest.com. MapQuest provides maps of virtually any area and even step-by-step driving directions. Figure 14-8 shows the MapQuest interface from a Palm VIIx.

Figure 14-8:
Use MapQuest to find maps and get driving directions.

The wireless Internet even contains boating and fishing sites, and plenty of related information for anyone who needs directions on the water. Use your wireless device to call a limo, find a gas station, locate a bus, or find just about any other kind of service you might need when you're on the road. The wireless Internet puts you in control of your travel plans and ensures that help is just seconds away.

Planning an Evening Out

How do you find out what's cool and new to do? Or, how can you keep up with coming attractions in the city where you live? What if you're visiting a city and you need to a find a really great restaurant? No problem. Use your wireless device to track down what's cool, new, unusual, or tasty in virtually any city.

The wireless Internet includes all kinds of restaurant guides, attraction guides, concert information, and much, much more. You can even read theme park reviews and find the closest Starbucks. Everything you need to plan an evening out is at your fingertips — even where to find a new suit or dress.

This book's Wireless Internet Access Directory lists sites in various helpful categories. Be sure to read through this directory to find all that is available to you.

Getting Information

Imagine that you're sitting in a hotel room working on a presentation. You need to find information about a particular topic, but you have no books available. Solution? Use the wireless Internet. The wireless Internet offers a plethora of information about all kinds of topics.

You can find great online resources via the wireless Internet. You can access encyclopedia sites, newspapers, magazines — you can even search through the Bible!

What if you're struggling for a certain word or need to know how to pronounce *zwieback* (a type of German bread, if you're dying to know). No problem, just visit Merriam-Webster Dictionary on the wireless Internet, as shown in Figure 14-9. Find the definitions to words, use the thesaurus, and check out the pronunciation guide.

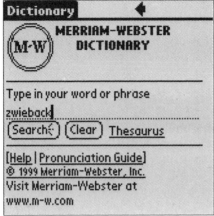

Figure 14-9: Find definitions, use a thesaurus, or access a pronunciation guide.

What if you need a little help? Need a good quotation to get your day off to the right start? You can find quotation sites and other unique sites. For example, you can access the MyMotivator.com Web site on the wireless Internet, as shown in Figure 14-10. Get all kinds of success quotes and even create your own GoalTree. Very cool!

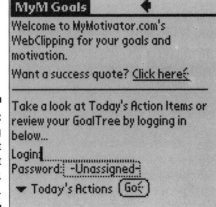

Figure 14-10: Get moving and get motivated at MyMotivator. com.

Having Fun

What? Have fun with a wireless device? Absolutely. The wireless Internet includes lots of great sites for passing the time and having lots of fun. Read stories, find jokes, see what's happening in Hollywood, check out movie and music reviews — you can even play games and trivia. The wireless Internet can meet your needs and your wants. It's all there for the taking, so get connected and start living the wireless life!

Part V
The Part of Tens

In this part . . .

The Part of Tens is that fun-filled place you find in every *For Dummies* book — a place where you can gain lots of quick and insightful information. In this part, you can check out ten common questions and answers about wireless Internet access, almost ten things you can't do on the wireless Internet, ten cool Web phone accessories, and ten great wireless Internet-related Web sites.

Chapter 15

Ten Common Questions and Answers About the Wireless Internet

In This Chapter

▶ Accessing corporate e-mail

▶ Choosing a service plan

▶ Understanding connectivity

▶ Exploring devices and services

▶ Getting more information

*W*ireless Internet access isn't all that difficult to understand, but filtering out some of the misconceptions and advertising hype can get rather aggravating. So, in this chapter, I answer ten common questions I often get asked about wireless Internet access. As you'll see from my answers to these questions, always make sure you do your homework before you sign up with a particular plan or decide to use a particular device.

Can I Access Corporate E-Mail via the Wireless Internet?

Maybe. The RIM BlackBerry PDA can access your mailbox in corporate environments that use Microsoft Exchange or Lotus Domino mail systems. You can use the same e-mail address on the BlackBerry as you use for your corporate e-mail. Or, if that is not practical, you can create an e-mail rule to forward all your corporate e-mail to another e-mail address. For example, if you use a Web-enabled phone, you could create an e-mail rule that forwards your mail to a Web account so you can still read your corporate e-mail using the wireless device.

Depending on the device you use and the type of mail server your corporate network uses, you may choose other solutions as well. Ask your network administrator for more information.

See Chapter 8 for more information about using e-mail rules and corporate e-mail access solutions.

Can I Send and Receive E-Mail Attachments?

With a PC-based mail program, you can attach all kinds of files to your e-mail messages — important documents, programs, games, or even a picture of little Janie's birthday party. In contrast, wireless Internet access uses devices that support only text messages. So the long-winded answer is no, you cannot send and receive e-mail attachments with your wireless device.

To open an attachment that you receive on your PC, you need the right software on your computer. For example, if I send you a Microsoft Word document, you must have Microsoft Word installed on your computer in order to read that file. The same point holds true for pictures and other types of files that you receive as e-mail attachments: Your computer must have the right software in order to read them.

Web-enabled devices do not run these programs and cannot display e-mail attachments for you, such as pictures or word processing documents. Besides, wireless Internet access typically churns along at about 9 Kbps, so even if you could download attachments, doing so would take forever. Save the attachments for the computer and use the wireless Internet for simple text messages.

How Am I Billed for My Wireless Internet Access?

The billing method depends on the type of device and the service you ordered. Basically, you are billed in one of two ways. If you purchased a Web-enabled phone, your wireless Internet usage is included as part of your wireless phone bill. Depending on the type of service you purchased, you may be billed on a per-usage basis, or you may have a blanket plan that gives you a certain amount of time. If you're using a Web-enabled pager, the Web usage is included as part of your monthly bill.

The second option involves charging your credit card automatically. For example, I'm currently using a Palm VIIx wireless PDA. When I purchased the device, I followed the instructions and connected wirelessly to Palm.net, where I set up my account and provided my credit card number. Each month, my credit card statement includes the monthly access fee for the plan I purchased.

What Kind of Internet Access Plans Are Available?

You can choose from two basic types of Web access plans. One type gives you a specified number of minutes of Internet access for a certain fee. The second type of plan charges you for Internet usage by the minute, similar to how you would be charged for a phone call. Web-enabled phones and pagers often use the per-minute charge plan, but some carriers offer a blanket plan that gives you more time freedom.

If you use a PDA, you usually have different plans available. Some give you a certain amount of data download while other plans are unlimited. If you surfed the Internet when it first became popular a few years ago, these "time plans" may sound vaguely familiar. With regular wired Internet access, most plans sold today are unlimited, and I expect this same unlimited service to eventually prevail in the wireless world as well.

Why Doesn't My Wireless Internet Device Work in All Locations?

Wireless Internet access is available in most parts of the United States. However, if you live or travel in a very remote part of the country, you may lose connectivity. The "No service available" message simply tells you that you are out of reach of a wireless tower.

Before you purchase a Web-enabled device and a service plan, check the coverage maps for that service, which are typically available on the carrier's Web site. Or, quiz the sales associate about the coverage map before signing on the dotted line and giving away your hard-earned money.

Can I Access Any Web Site on the Internet?

No, wireless Internet devices technically do not enable you to browse the Internet. In other words, you cannot move from site to site via external hyperlinks as you can when using a computer. Not all Web sites provide compatibility with wireless devices, so you can access only certain sites with your wireless device, but you cannot surf by typing in URLs as you would with a typical browser. Still, you can access many sites from your wireless device. Check your device's documentation for more details and be sure to check out this book's Wireless Internet Access Directory.

Do Wireless Devices Provide Any Security?

Your wireless device may not be as secure as a computer, but most wireless devices do use encryption technology to encrypt credit card numbers and related data to prevent access during transmission on the Internet. Generally, you do not need to worry about unauthorized access to sensitive information. Using your credit card on the Internet is much safer than using it at a typical department store. Also, many credit cards today offer free Internet theft protection. With this feature, if your credit card number is ever stolen on the Internet, you are not at all responsible for the charges. Check your credit card's Web site to find out whether your card offers this free service.

Which Wireless Internet Service Is Best?

I wouldn't say that any one service is best. All the services provide quality Internet access. Choosing the right one for you is just a matter of deciding what you want and how much you want to pay. For example, I have an AT&T Wireless Internet plan for my Web-enabled phone, and I also use Palm.net for my Palm VIIx — two different plans with different rates and services, but both very good. Like most things in life, the trick is to spend time shopping around. Find out what's available and then compare the various choices with your needs and your budget. Then, you choose a service plan that is right for you.

What Is the Coolest New Wireless Device Coming onto the Market?

Well, we all have our own opinions about what's really cool, but I'll tell you what I think. I prefer using a PDA instead of a Web-enabled phone, but I also need a cell phone. So, I'm stuck carrying two different devices, which is a real drag. However, some great combination products are already on the market, providing both phone and PDA functionality. Look for Web phone/PDA combinations that include larger pop-out screens and even convertible keyboards — in other words, look for devices that can be everything you need and fit nicely into your purse or pocket.

Where Can I Get Current Information about Wireless Devices?

In free enterprise, nothing stays the same for very long, so you should check the various Web sites of wireless Internet providers for the most up-to-date information. Also, see Chapter 18, which lists ten helpful Web sites for wireless Internet information; you can browse these sites to find out what's new and cool!

Chapter 16

Almost Ten Things You Can't Do with Wireless Internet Devices

In This Chapter

▶ What happened to all the graphics?

▶ No surfing

▶ Forget about e-mail attachments

▶ Access everywhere — not!

*O*kay, I've sung the praises of the wireless Internet and those nifty wireless Internet devices throughout this book, but I want you to know that I do not have my head stuck in the wireless clouds. Wireless Internet devices have quite a few limitations, and their convenience does come with a cost. However, I do think the benefits far outweigh the cost because wireless devices do offer all the major functionality of e-mail and Internet usage. Still, I don't want you to think I have a wireless brain, and I don't want you to be fooled about wireless device limitations. So, I give you almost ten things you can't do with wireless Internet devices.

Welcome to a Barren Graphics Landscape

Do you love the cool graphics, pictures, and colors of the Internet? Well, you can forget them in the wireless world. Why, you might wonder? Those pretty pictures, animated graphics, and colors are all great for your home computer, but most wireless devices simply cannot support all the Web files and content necessary to download and display them to you. In fact, most wireless devices have monochrome screens with only limited ability to display pictures.

Another aspect of this limitation involves the speed at which these devices download information. Most wireless devices can only download information at about 9 Kbps, as opposed to the 56 Kbps of a typical computer modem. So, even if your wireless device could download graphics, you would be drawing your Social Security check before the download ever completed. So, for the most part, your Internet usage is limited to monochrome, text-only pages. Don't worry though; at the rate of wireless device development, I expect this will change in the near future.

No Web Surfing

As I explain a few times throughout this book, you cannot surf the Web with wireless devices. True, you can access the Internet and view predefined Web pages that your wireless devices support, but you cannot actually surf the Internet and view any Web page that you want. This is kind of a drag and one of those problems that will eventually go away as more and more Web sites support wireless devices. For now, though, you can access only a limited number of Web sites.

No Favorites or Bookmarks

Internet Explorer and Netscape Navigator give you the option to save URLs in the browser as you find ones that you like. These browsers call this option Favorites or Bookmarks, respectively. After you save the address for a Web site in this way, you simply access the Favorites or Bookmarks menu and click on the name of the Web site that you want to revisit. This is a great tool so that you do not have to remember the URLs for Web sites that you find.

Wireless devices do not offer this option because you can't technically surf the Internet with your wireless device. Any Web sites that are available for you to visit are already specified in the device. Some devices, such as Web-enabled phones, provide you with a predefined favorites list that you can customize, but you cannot surf the Internet and bookmark sites that you find along the way. Check out Chapter 11 to find out more about using these lists of favorite sites with Web-enabled phones.

May I Have a Cookie?

No, I'm afraid you cannot have a cookie. Web browsers, such as Netscape Navigator and Internet Explorer, use small files called *cookies.* For example, when you visit Amazon.com, you can enter information about yourself so that Amazon.com can track you, your purchases, and the items you like to view. The Web site stores this information in a cookie file within your Web browser. Each time you visit the Web site, your browser sends the cookie to the Web site. (And you thought the Web site was able to identify you because it was just that smart.) Most wireless Internet devices cannot store cookies because they do not actually use Web browsers. So, information that appears automatically in your PC's browser may not do so using a wireless device.

No File Downloads Allowed

Many Web sites enable you to download different kinds of files. For example, you may download a Word document or another type of document file to your PC. Your wireless Internet device can read Web site data and display it to you, but you cannot download any files of any kind, including pictures or programs. Wireless devices cannot read these files, nor do they have the disk space to store them. So, the information you access must live on the Internet — no files allowed.

No E-Mail Attachments

Just as you cannot download files, you cannot send or receive e-mail attachments with your wireless device. This limitation includes documents, pictures, programs, or anything else you might attach to an e-mail message on a typical computer. However, this rule has one exception: Some PDAs can download an ASCII text file (a simple, basic text file format) and append the file to the end of the message. Then, you can read the text file as if it were part of the message. Of course, most files sent via e-mail are more elaborate than simple ASCII text, and you can't read anything beyond this basic text format.

If someone sends attachments to you, your device displays a message telling you that it cannot read the attachment. You can work around this problem by sending a copy of each wireless e-mail message you receive to a different e-mail address that you can access from a computer. Some services support this feature, and you can find out more about it in Chapter 8.

No E-Mail Formatting

Some e-mail applications enable you to format your e-mail messages with particular fonts, colors, background images, and signatures. However, wireless Internet devices do not support these formatting capabilities.

Little to No Support for Internet Multimedia

I love the multimedia nature of today's Internet. I like to watch movie trailers, listen to music samples, and even listen to the radio on the Internet. The multimedia features of the Internet are readily available on a PC, but you are out of luck with wireless devices. In order to play movies, listen to music, and display other types of multimedia, your computer uses applications that can download the data and interpret the data for you. A Web-enabled phone or PDA does not yet have this capacity. The applications do not exist for these small devices, and the devices cannot handle the amount of data needed to play multimedia. So, for multimedia use, you're still stuck to your PC. Don't worry, though — I expect the wireless devices of tomorrow will support multimedia applications.

Black Holes Abound

The marketing catch for the wireless Internet says that you can access the Internet and your e-mail everywhere. That is not quite true. You can access the Internet and your e-mail if you are in an area supported by your wireless device. Fortunately, you can access the wireless Internet in most major cities, but if you are traveling, you should expect blackouts in which you simply cannot use your wireless device. In fact, you may even experience blackouts in other areas, like the subway or a freeway tunnel, even if connectivity is available in the area. The simple reality is that you cannot access the wireless Internet from every location, but the wireless network is growing every day and this is one of those problems that will be resolved in the near future.

Chapter 17

Ten Great Web-Enabled Phone Accessories

In This Chapter

▶ Understanding why phone accessories are so cool

▶ Finding out where to get phone accessories

▶ Checking out ten great phone accessories

*W*eb-enabled phones are cool devices, and as you might guess, you can purchase some very cool accessories to make your life even easier — or at least, more interesting. So, I present in this chapter a list of ten great accessories for your Web-enabled phone.

You can find these accessories in most places where Web-enabled phones are sold. I've seen these items sold at various stands in the mall, so they're fairly easy to locate. However, if you prefer to avoid the mall, you can also find these products at online merchants, such as www.buy.com, www.amazon.com, and www.radioshack.com.

Getting a Cool Removable Faceplate

Nokia started a trend with its 5100 series phones. You can purchase the phone and then pick all kinds of cool, wild, and inexpensive (less than $20) faceplate covers so your phone stands out in the crowd. Do you like neon orange? No problem. What about tiger skin? No problem. You can get whatever kind of faceplate you want. However, faceplates are designed for specific phone models, so make sure you buy one that is designed for your phone.

Talking Freely with a Headset

Let's face the facts: We all like to talk on our wireless phones while driving , and we all know that we shouldn't because the distraction is dangerous. I shudder to think of how many accidents have occurred because of cellular phone use. However, you can purchase a hands-free headset so you can talk on your phone and keep both hands on the wheel. The headset attaches to your ear and places a microphone in front of your mouth. This way, you can talk, drive, and look like a telephone operator, all at the same time. Headsets are available for most models of Web-enabled phones by both phone manufacturers and various third-party manufacturers, but make sure you buy one that is compatible with your phone make and model. Prices for this accessory range from $20 to $30.

Going Hands-Free in Your Car

You can purchase a hands-free headset that enables you to talk without holding your phone, but why not go completely hands-free? Various phone manufacturers also offer hands-free kits that enable you to completely manage your phone calls without handling the wireless phone. The hands-free unit plugs into a cigarette lighter port or other electrical port. It includes a lapel microphone and volume control, and charges your phone while you use it. For about $50, you can find these hands-free wireless solutions for several phone brands, including Motorola, Nokia, and Samsung.

Keeping Charged and Ready

When you're traveling, you use your wireless phone a lot, and the batteries don't last forever. So, you need a travel charger. Depending on your phone model, you may have a small travel charger that shipped with your phone. If not, however, you can buy a small travel charger for less than $20. The charger fits neatly in your suitcase and can charge your phone in your hotel room. The standard phone battery charger that comes with your phone may work just as well, but in either case, make sure you have a charger with you when you travel.

Getting a Charge from Your Car

If you often travel in your car for long distances, buy a handy charge cable that plugs into the car's cigarette lighter or other available power port. You can then keep your phone charged while you drive. If you travel a lot and depend on your wireless phone, the travel charger is a great and inexpensive (less than $20) investment.

Living Longer with a Lithium Battery

Your phone comes to you with a standard, rechargeable battery. However, for many models, you can upgrade to a lithium ion battery that will last longer (and usually weighs less). Of course, you need to check your phone model to see if a lithium battery is available for your phone, but if you use your phone a lot during the day, the lithium battery may relieve some of your low-charge worries.

Displaying Your Phone on a Belt Clip

Wireless phones are great, but keeping track of them often becomes a hassle. However, you can wear your phone while you are on the move with a belt clip or a holster. These products clip onto your belt, your purse, your pocket, or just about anything else. At its simplest level, the clip is just a plastic holder for your phone that keeps it securely in place on your person. However, you can buy various clip models — some even vibrate when you get a call so as not to disturb important meetings. As with most other wireless phone products, you need to carefully check out the clip before you buy it to make certain it will hold your model of phone. Prices for these clips range from $10 to around $30.

Keeping Your Phone Secure with a Case

Quick, how many things do you have in your purse or briefcase? If you are like me, *quick* does not accurately describe the speed at which you can answer that question. If your purse or briefcase is in perpetual avalanche mode, consider buying a protective case so your phone doesn't get crushed or the shuffling of debris doesn't make long-distance calls for you. Most phone cases are available in hard plastic or rubber that is durable enough to protect the phone stored inside. If you carry a bunch of junk around with you and your phone is always getting crammed, stuffed, dropped, and abused, the hard case is well worth your investment of roughly $10 to $30.

Using a Replacement Antenna

So you're about to get into your cab, you drop your phone on the sidewalk, and then someone steps on your phone and breaks off the antenna. You were supposed to call the office in ten minutes for a telemeeting. What to do? Well, without a replacement antenna, you can't do much, so I recommend keeping a replacement antenna with you at all times, because you never know what life may do to your phone.

Most phone antennas are very durable, but people have a way of breaking things. With a replacement antenna, your phone will always be available to you. On the lighter side, some replacement antennas are even decorative and some even light up. Check your phone manufacturer for replacement antennas that will work with your phone model. You can probably buy one for less than $20.

Working at Your Desk

You have an office, you use your wireless phone a lot during the day, and batteries never seem to keep up with you. Does this describe your life? If so, consider a desktop charger kit. A desktop charger kit, available for many phone models, includes a charger and a desktop stand that holds your phone while you work. When you need the phone, just reach over and grab it, use it, and then put it back on the stand, which charges the battery while not in use. Very cool and very helpful, and well worth the $50 that it costs.

Chapter 18

Ten Great Wireless Internet Web Sites

In This Chapter

▶ Finding information online

▶ Visiting ten great wireless Internet Web sites

*T*he wireless Internet is always changing, so where can you go to keep up with those changes? You guessed it — the Internet, of course! Many terrific Web sites can help you stay up-to-date about what's new and what's cool in the wireless Internet world. In this chapter, I list my ten favorite wireless Internet sites. Of course, you should keep your eyes open for new sites as well. Just type **wireless Internet** into any search engine and see what you get. These sites can help keep you informed and even entertained.

Unstrung

In the technology world, you need to stay up-to-date. The unstrung site, shown in Figure 18-1 and found at www.unstrung.com, keeps you abreast of all the latest news in the wireless world. This site primarily focuses on the business side of the wireless Internet and wireless Internet gadgets, but it's also a great place to find out what's going on and what may be on the horizon.

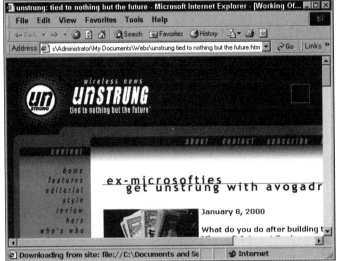

Figure 18-1:
Keep up
with the
business of
the wireless
Internet at
unstrung.
com.

ZDNet

ZDNet is a consumer computing site that contains all kinds of articles and information about virtually every facet of computing. I include it as one of the ten great Web sites because you can search for "wireless Internet" on the site and get all kinds of goodies, including a bunch of downloads for your PDA. You'll find articles and reviews of new services and Web-enabled devices. Before purchasing any Web-enabled device, check out this Web site. Read the reviews and examine competitive products before you part with your hard-earned money. You can visit ZDNet at www.zdnet.com.

WirelessAdvisor.com

WirelessAdvisor.com, shown in Figure 18-2, is a Web site that advises you about all kinds of topics pertaining to the wireless world. You can find lots of information here, such as FAQs (lists of frequently asked questions), discussion boards, articles, and even a wireless glossary. WirelessAdvisor.com has very down-to-earth, practical articles. You can search the site and find what you need and even take part in various polls about wireless technology. Check it out at www.wirelessadvisor.com.

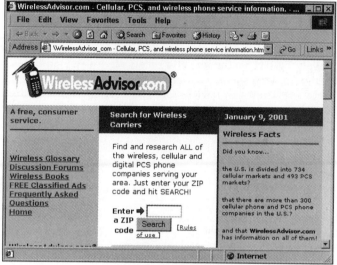

Figure 18-2:
Get advised
at Wireless
Advisor.com.

Internet Wireless Access

Are you interested in the details of the wireless Internet? You can find them at
Internet Wireless Access. This Web site provides all kinds of information about
Wireless Access Protocol (WAP) and related technologies and tools. This site
explains how wireless communications work and how WAP has become the
standard for wireless Internet communications on phones and handheld
devices. So, check out this site for the cool, yet understandable, technical
details. You can find the site at `www.internetwirelessaccess.net.`

Cellular Telecommunications
& Internet Association

Visit Cellular Telecommunications & Internet Association at `www.
wirelessdata.org` to find out all about wireless communications compa-
nies. This site offers clear, concise, unbiased information about various wireless companies and standards. You can find numerous articles here, including
a primer about wireless communications.

Wireless Week

The Wireless Week Web site provides weekly wireless updates. (No, really.) You can even register on the site and receive free e-mail updates and announcements. This site is a super place to keep up with the rapidly changing and growing wireless Internet. You'll find articles and live discussions here, and you can even check the stock market. Check it out at `www.wirelessweek.com`.

The W@P Forum

Web-enabled devices, such as phones, pagers, and PDAs, all rely on the Wireless Application Protocol (WAP). The W@P Forum is a Web site devoted to WAP studies and wireless Internet access information. You can visit this site, find out all kinds of information about WAP, and even find out about conferences that may be happening near you. You may find more details here than you really want, but if you are really interested in understanding how wireless communications work, visit this great Web site. You can find the W@P Forum at `www.wapforum.com`.

The Gadgeteer

Interested in wireless Internet gadgets? Can't wait for the next Web-enabled phone or wireless Internet PDA? Well, look no further, because the Gadgeteer is here! The Gadgeteer Web site, shown in Figure 18-3 and found at `www.the-gadgeteer.com`, is an excellent place to keep up with those cool Web-enabled products — and a whole lot more. You can find all sorts of information and postings about virtually any small device, with plenty of pictures and easy-to-find information. Go surfing!

MSN Computing Central

MSN Computing Central, a part of the MSN network, contains just about everything you may want to know about computers and technology. I include it here because it has some great information about wireless technology and a super discussion board where you can learn all kinds of things and post your own questions or know-how. Just visit `www.computingcentral.com` and search for "wireless Internet" to start the fun.

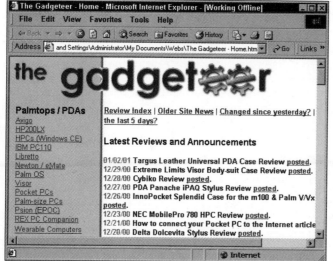

Figure 18-3:
Find the
best and
coolest
gadgets at
The
Gadgeteer.

Wireless.com

Want wireless news? You'll find it at Wireless.com. As shown in Figure 18-4, this site is devoted to bringing you "everything wireless," and you can certainly read all kinds of information about wireless technology developments and the industry here. You'll find many links to other sites and helpful articles for understanding and experiencing the wireless Internet. Check it out at www.wireless.com.

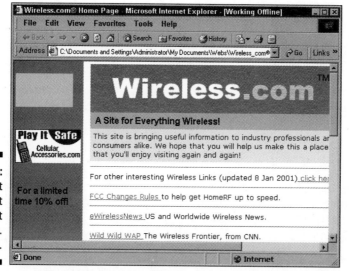

Figure 18-4:
Learn just
about
anything at
Wireless.
com.

Wireless Internet Access Directory

The 5th Wave   By Rich Tennant

"Well, here's what happened—I forgot to put it on my 'To Do' List."

In this directory . . .

*F*rom its humble beginnings with just a few simple, text-only Web sites, the wireless Internet has grown at an amazing rate, and new sites open every day. You can shop, get financial information, read restaurant reviews, check travel information, track weather reports, and find all kinds of good stuff on the wireless Internet. Use this directory as a starting point for finding the information you need.

This directory lists some of the more popular Web sites that you can access from a wireless device. Remember these important points as you use this directory:

- You can access some sites with any wireless device. To access these WAP-compliant sites, simply enter the site's URL in your PDA or your phone's browser.

- To access some sites that I list in this directory, you must use a Palm device and a Palm application called a PQA. Before you can access this type of site, you must download the appropriate PQA from `www.palm.net`. Refer to your Palm documentation for more details. If you're not a Palm user, you can't get the PQA on your device — sorry!

- Wireless Web sites change constantly, so use this directory as a guide, but check your device manufacturer's Web site for updated listings and new information. The wireless World stands still for no one, so know upfront that some information in this directory has changed by the time you read it.

About This Directory

This directory uses *micons* (mini icons) — small graphics that point out some of the special features of a Web site. These micons can give you quick information about the Web sites listed in this directory:

Sites marked with this icon provide entertainment and entertainment-related news and information.

 This micon identifies a site that contains Frequently Asked Questions (FAQs) or related information that can help you.

This micon identifies sites where you can learn more about all kinds of topics.

For news or news-related information, see the sites that I flag with this micon.

Look to these sites for online records and other financial information.

If you see this micon, you know the site has a search engine that can help you find the information or product you want.

This micon identifies a shopping site.

This micon tells you that the site may require you to sign in, or you may need a password to access information.

This micon highlights sites that offer travel information.

Entertainment

The wireless Internet is a great source of help and information, but it's also lots of fun. Check out these entertainment sites; I'm sure something here will suit your fancy or tickle your funny bone. Have fun!

10Best
www.10best.com

Online concierge: 10Best is an online concierge site that can help you find the ten best places to eat or stay and inform you of the top entertainment choices.

AfterDawn.com
www.afterdawn.com

MP3 and DVD news: Keep up with the latest MP3 and DVD news at this site. Find out all kinds of information, including lists of MP3 and DVD software.

AirGuitar Wireless
www.airguitar.net/

Find lyrics to your favorite song: This site is a valuable resource for finding both lyrics and guitar tablature. Airguitar.net also gives you different options for searching out the information you want.

Air Santa Claus
www.airsantaclaus.com

Keep in touch with Santa: Now you can keep in touch with Santa and his elves by using your wireless device. Find out where he is on Christmas Eve as he delivers toys, or send him your wish list.

AllLotto.com - Lottery Results from Across the USA

www.alllotto.com

Discover the winning numbers: Whether you are looking for last night's winning lottery numbers or want to know the winning numbers from a year ago, you can find the information at this site.

Alloy

www.alloy.com

Community and entertainment: This Web site offers all kinds of content, including community, entertainment, and commerce. Alloy primarily targets teens and covers various media products.

Allrecipes.com

www.recipes.com

Find the recipe for that wonderful cake you had: Whether you want a specific recipe, meal planning tips, or help with a cooking dilemma, visit `www.recipes.com`. This site is a must for those who like to cook as well as those who don't and need some guidance.

America Online

www.aol.com

Multifunctional site with a variety of information: This nationally known Web site offers the capability to send and receive e-mail messages. It also provides current news, weather, and stock quotes, as well as entertainment information from such sources as MovieFone.

Astrology.com

www.astrology.com

Learn about your future: Visit Astrology.com to find out your horoscope from the iVillage Astrologer, Kelli Fox. You can also find out the horoscopes and signs of celebrities.

AstrologyIS.com

www.astrologyis.com

Find out what the stars say about your future: Based on the information you supply, AstrologyIS offers predictions about your job, family, and finances.

BaChess

www.banywhere.com

Play a game of chess: Like a good game of chess? Now you can play anytime on your wireless device. This site offers an environment in which you play against other Palm VII users.

BeamMusic

www.beamshop.com

Download music: Check out BeamMusic on your wireless device to view an updated listing of sites for downloading music.

The Internet Beatles Album

www.getback.org

Beatlemania: Beatles fans, visit this site for information about the Fab Four. You can find out details about your favorite Beatle or get an address to join one of their many fan clubs.

Bolt

www.bolt.com

Find some new friends: Interested in making some chat friends or looking for a forum to express your opinions? Visit www.bolt.com. This site also has online polls and quizzes.

BooksBTC

www.booksbtc.com

Electronic books to read: If you like to read, visit BooksBTC. This site enables you to search for a book by author or title. With many features that enable you to customize your online reading experience, this site is truly reader friendly.

BoxerJam

www.boxerjam.com

Have fun playing games: If you're looking for a site where you can play challenging games and puzzles, check out BoxerJam. Created by Julann Griffin, co-creator of Jeopardy, this site is sure to entertain the game player in all of us. And you don't have to pay to play — it's free.

Britannica.com

www.britannica.com

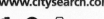

Look for information: If you're having trouble finding information on a specific topic, visit www.britannica.com. Britannica.com has a multitude of resources, including Encyclopedia Britannica, newspapers, magazines, and links to other Web sites.

CitySearch.com

www.citysearch.com

Find out what's happening in any city: Whether you're looking for information in your hometown or looking at cities abroad, visit www.citysearch.com. This site offers a variety of information on events in the city of your choice. CitySearch.com also contains information from www.ticketmaster.com.

City Stages Schedule

Palm PQA

See a play: Using your wireless device, you can access City Stages Schedule to find information on a play.

ClubFONE

www.clubfone.com

Enjoy a night of entertainment: All dressed up, but not sure where to go? Check out ClubFone to find a variety of clubs, nightlife, and music going on in your area. In addition to categorized listings of places and events, the site lists times and dress codes.

Cocktail Wireless
Palm PQA

Know your drinks: Out with your friends and want to know what wine goes with rack of lamb? Click on Cocktail Wireless. Get the answers to all your cocktail questions with no embarrassment.

CollectingChannel.com
www.collectingchannel.com

Attention collectors: This site is a valuable tool whether you're a professional collector or an amateur. You can view information by category or by entering a description in the search box. The site has many other tools and options, including auctions, shopping, and appraisals.

ConvertIT.com
www.convertit.com

Check the rates: Whether you're traveling to Greece or Rhode Island, you can get the local time and the currency conversion rate for the US dollar by visiting www.con-vertit.com. (Okay, I know they accept US currency in Rhode Island.) This site can also help if you need to convert measurements and perform other calculations.

Curses!
Palm PQA

Put the whammy on someone: Visit this site to try the Elizabethan curse generator.

Dodgeball.com
www.dodgeball.com

In New York City: Dodgeball.com is a great way to find the hot spots for kids or kids at heart. You can find all kinds of restaurants, watering holes, and other establishments.

DorCino Interactive Web Casino
www.dorcino.com

Casino-type games: Now you can play casino games while you're stuck in traffic or at the airport, or if you just need a break.

Ebert's Movie Review Archives
Palm PQA

Dig into Roger's vault: Are you a movie buff? Want to find out what Roger Ebert said about a particular show? If so, check out Ebert's Movie Review Archives. If you want information on current reviews, go to www.suntimes.com/ebert.

EMAZING.com
www.emazing.com

Get information you need everyday: Use this site to sign up for daily tips on a variety of topics. The site sends these tips to your e-mail box free of charge.

EventRunner
www.eventrunner.com

Find something fun to do: EventRunner helps you find out what's going on. Get

information on events ranging from concerts to sporting events and much more.

Excite

www.excite.com

Find information and manage your account:
Excite is a popular search engine and per-
sonal information management tool. Use
Excite's mobile features to manage your
Excite e-mail, calendar, news, and other
related information.

Fandango

www.fandango.com

See what's playing: Find out what's playing
at any Cinemark theatre at any time. You
can also purchase tickets online.

Forward Day By Day

www.forwardmovement.org/fdd1.html

Get inspired: Need a daily dose of inspira-
tion? Visit this site daily for inspirational
messages.

The Funnies

www.leerogers.com/funnies

Online funnies: If you're having a rough day
and need to laugh, check out this site with
your wireless device. Read jokes and
search by category or keyword.

FUNNY.com

www.funny.com

Read a good joke: To read a good joke
or share one of your own, visit `www.
funny.com`.

The Gallup Organization

www.gallup.com

Know which way the wind is blowin': The
Gallup Organization's site lists results of
polls on various topics, such as lifestyle,
elections, and business.

Go2

www.go2online.com

Find what you need: Go2 provides a complete directory and locator system for
portable devices. Find all kinds of information and search for topics with this tool.

GodsWord

www.christiancomconcepts.com

Various Bible verses: If you are having some
struggles in your life or just need some
divine guidance, check out this site. You
can read various Bible verses and perform
text searches.

GroupLotto

www.grouplotto.com

Try your luck: Are you one of the millions
of people who like to play the lottery? If so,
visit GroupLotto.

Guy Rules

www.guyrules.com

Male behavior: This entertainment site offers humorous observations about male social behavior.

Hollywood.com

www.hollywood.com

Find out what's playing: Hollywood.com provides movie and entertainment information for theaters nationwide. This site gives you not only movie times and locations, but also movie reviews, trivia games, and entertainment news.

Horoscope

Palm PQA

See your future: Want to check your horoscope? Want to have some fun? Visit this site using your wireless device.

Indiqu Mobile Entertainment Network

www.indiqu.com

Entertainment and games: This site provides entertainment programming for mobile consumers, including various channels and services for consumers and game players. You'll also find news, community information, and sports.

InfoCub

www.wplus.com/infocub

Know before you go: Don't leave a movie disappointed because it wasn't what you

expected. Review it before you go, using your wireless device.

InfoSpace

www.infospace.com

Find a person or a place: InfoSpace.com helps you locate persons, places, or things via its numerous directories.

Iqradio

www.iqradio.com

Find a radio station: Using your wireless Internet device, search for both commercial and noncommercial radio stations.

Joke

www.myhip.com

Get a good laugh: In the mood for a good laugh? Check out the Joke site.

Jokes2Go

Palm PQA

Attention joke tellers: Noted as one of the more popular Internet sites, Jokes2Go is a great resource to get the latest jokes. You may find some of the jokes offensive, so use this site with discretion.

Katrillion.com

www.katrillion.com

Up-to-date entertainment news: Find out what your favorite celebrity is doing, or get the scoop on the entertainment world at Katrillion.com. In addition to news, this site offers information on a variety of other topics along with games and horoscopes.

Keen

www.keen.com

Talk to people: Keen.com is a live answer community where you can talk to people without giving out your phone number. Using the wireless Internet, you can check out Keen.com listings and find another Keen.com member that you want to talk to.

LockOn Movies

Palm PQA

East Texas Movie: Find out what's playing at the movies and read some movie reviews.

Lottery

Palm PQA

Try your luck: Like to play the lottery? Keep track of the winning lottery numbers anytime, day or night, by checking out the Lottery site on the wireless Internet.

Magic 8-Ball Oracle

Phcashman.tripod.com

Ask the 8-Ball Oracle: Check out the Magic 8-Ball Oracle to have some fun while you wrestle with your tough decisions.

Moviefone

www.moviefone.com

Showtime: Check out Moviefone on your wireless device and access theater locations and show times. For no additional charge, you can also buy your tickets online.

MooVRevu

www.pdantic.com

Check out movie reviews: If you want to check what others are saying about a movie before you part with your hard-earned money, visit the MooVRevu.

MSN Mobile

www.devices.msn.com/msnmobile

Access the Everyday Web: MSN members can access their hotmail accounts and check news, sports, and weather at MSN.

MTV.com

www.mtv.com

What's going on in the world of music: MTV.com is a complete source to find out what's in, what's out, and what's going on in the music world.

MysteryNet.com

www.mysterynet.com

Enjoy a good mystery: If you enjoy a good game of mystery, check out MysteryNet.Com. This site offers a variety of interactive games.

nGame

www.ngame.com

Multiplayer games: nGame.com offers multi-player interactive games. This site offers many community features to help people connect and be entertained.

Play for Fun Wireless

Palm PQA

Take a break and have some fun: Play for Fun Wireless has a variety of online games and trivia puzzles, as well as contests and giveaways.

QOD Pilot

www.qod.com

Question of the day: Answer the question of the day and have fun reading questions and answers at this entertainment site.

Random Quote

Palm PQA

Find a quote: Do you like to read quotes? Maybe you're looking for one to use in a speech? Check out this Web site to find a quote. You'll recognize some quotes and their sources; others are more obscure.

RDS Airport

Palm PQA

Watch air traffic control: Check out RDS Airport to see FAA real-time traffic management at the airport you enter (which may be fun and scary, depending on your point of view).

Regal Cinemas Movie Search

www.regalcinemas.com/theatres/wireless
.html

Showtime information: Going to see a movie at a Regal Cinema? Find out show times with ease by using your wireless device.

Rick-T-Land.com-on the Go

www.rick-T-Land.Com

Find your TV show: Check the time and channel for your favorite television show. All stations may not be available, and you may not find daytime schedules.

RomeozuluWX

www.romeozulu.com

Check out aviation weather: Get up-to-date weather information for aviators.

SonicNet.com

www.sonicnet.com

Full-service music network: Use SonicNet.com to access all kinds of music as well as Internet radio.

Soundload's Music Encyclopedia

www.soundload.com

Music enthusiasts: Easily locate information on your favorite album, artist, or song.

Stable Mail
Palm PQA

Horse racing enthusiasts: Now you can get updates and schedules from the world of horse racing. This site also provides e-mail notification of when your horse is scheduled to run.

Stanford Theatre/Palo Alto Weekly
Palm PQA

Current films: Visit this site to find what current films are playing at the Stanford Theatre.

StarCD-Realtime radio song id
www.starcd.com

Listen to radio stations from other cities: If you just heard a song on the radio, and you want to know who sings it or the name of the song, check out this site. You can also listen to radio stations from other metropolitan areas.

Star Trek Voyager Airdates and News
Palm PQA

Attention Trekkies: This site is a must for all you Star Trek Voyager fans. Find out airdate schedules and summaries, along with Star Trek Voyager news and rumors.

Sweet16*com
www.sweet16.com

Attention teen girls: Visit online at Sweet16.com to find out what's in style and what's not. This site also offers many interactive features, such as message boards and trivia.

Theme Park Insider
www.themeparkinsider.com

Find out how your favorite theme park rates: If you want to know how your favorite theme park rates, check out Theme Park Insider. This site also provides top ten lists of favorite and most hated attractions. You can also find out which hotels and restaurants rank among the top five places to stay and eat.

TheSouthSide.com
www.thesouthside.com

Southside humor: Find favorite e-mail humor at this site, which contains a browseable e-mail humor archive.

Ticketmaster.com
www.ticketmaster.com

Get tickets to tonight's game: Check out Ticketmaster.com to get ticket information on sporting events, concerts, and other entertainment venues. You can also purchase your tickets online.

Tu Horoscopo

www.tuhoroscopo.com.mx/

Se Habla Española: Tu Horoscopo is a Spanish language site. This site provides daily horoscope information and entertainment.

VH1.com

www.vh1.com

Music fans: VH1.com is an informative music site that targets folks in the 25-plus age range. This site offers reviews, live radio, and the latest music news, and much more.

Women.com

www.women.com

Women's issues and concerns: Regardless of your age, race, creed, or color, all women will surely find helpful information and advice at Women.com. This site offers a wide range of information concerning women, but at the time of this directory's printing, is only available on the OmniSky service.

The X-Files Airdates

Palm PQA

X-Files enthusiasts: A great site for all you X-Files fans. Get the lowdown on upcoming episodes.

Yahoo!

Mobile.yahoo.com/wireless/home

Get your Yahoo! information: Use the wireless Internet to access your MyYahoo! Email, calendar, address book, news, sports, and all kinds of other information.

Financial Sites

Internet financial sites have become very popular during the last several years. You can manage your money, pay your bills, play the stock market, and manage your investments online. Here are some popular online financial sites that you can access via the wireless Internet.

Ajbrowser

www.ajaxo.com

Wireless stock trading: Ajbrowser offers members the ability to trade stock with investors using a wireless device.

AcctMinder

www.accountminder.com

Managing your money: AcctMinder makes managing your money easy and convenient. This site provides tools to manage your banking and credit card information along with other financial services.

Ameritrade

www.ameritrade.com

Flat-rate commissions for online brokerage services: Ameritrade provides free investment research tools, as well as management tools. Ameritrade's flat-rate commissions make online investing easy and affordable for anyone who wants to make an online investment.

ATM finder

Palm PQA

Find a money machine: ATM finder is a wireless Internet service that helps you locate the ATM nearest to you.

Bank of America HomeBanking

www.bankamerica.com

California-based accounts: California-based customers of Bank of America Home Banking can now access their accounts using their wireless device, anytime, anywhere. You can monitor checking and savings account balances and find out what transactions have happened on the account in the past 90 days.

Beyond The Bull

www.beyondthebull.com

Stock market news: Beyond The Bull provides up-to-date financial news and stock market information.

BigCharts

www.bigcharts.com

Investment site: Get the latest headlines, charts, and intraday quotes at BigCharts.

Bloomberg

www.bloomberg.com

Worldwide leader in financial news and stock quotes: Want to know what the stock market did today? Want to know what's going on in the business world? To get the latest information on the day's news and financial information, visit www.bloomberg.com.

CBS MarketWatch.com

www.cbsmarketwatch.com

For breaking stories on the stock market: Want to know what's going on in today's market? This site features up-to-the minute information on today's financial headlines.

CharlesSchwab

www.charlesschwab.com

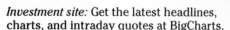

Online investment services: Charles Schwab & Co., Inc., provides clients with a full range of investment services, 24-hour professional support, complete Internet access, multilingual and international services, and numerous branch offices.

Charts2Go

www.prophetfinance.com/charts/
charts2go.asp

Keep track of your favorite stocks: To track your favorite stocks or find out what's going on in the stock market, visit Charts2Go using your wireless device. Charts2Go offers five different chart types and tools for comparing different stocks.

Claritybank.com

www.claritybank.com

Easy access to your financial information: Clarity Bank offers a wide array of online services, including account balance information, bill payment, and transfer of funds, to name just a few.

CNBC.com

Palm PQA

Intraday coverage of stock markets: Check out CNBC.com using your wireless device to review intraday coverage of what's going on with the major stock markets, primary industries, and major companies.

Concord EFS

www.concordefs.com

Stock price information: Concord EFS offers current stock price information and e-mail newsletters.

Countrywide Home Loans

www.countrywide.com

Check today's interest rate: Countrywide Home Loan offers many online lending services. Check today's interest rates or find a local Countrywide team near you.

CSFBdirect Anywhere

www.cbsdirect.com

More than just online investments: CSFBdirect Anywhere offers more than just the ability to do online investments. Get up-to-the-minute news, quotes, and account information.

Currency Calculator

Palm PQA

Up-to-date currency information: Whether you are looking for information on currency fluctuations, or you need the conversion rate from one currency to another, use your wireless device and go to Currency Calculator.

ePriority Wireless

www.epriority.com

Secure, confidential financial information: Get confidential financial information securely with ePriority. You get free wireless e-mail capabilities bundled with security features for safe interaction and data management.

eSignal

www.esignal.com

Find out what's going on in today's market: eSignal is Data Broadcasting Corporation's provider of financial news and data to traders and investors. This site also provides real-time stock quotes.

E*TRADE

www.etrade.com

Manage your personal finances and investments: If you are looking for an online personal financial services provider that offers many different services, check out E*TRADE. E*TRADE is known for providing anytime, anywhere, any-device access to financial information and transactions. E*TRADE also provides its clients superior customer service and investing and research features.

Fairwinds Credit Union

www.fairwinds.org

Find branch locations: Use your wireless device to obtain information about Fairwinds Credit Union. You can locate branches, obtain current rates, or find the nearest ATM.

Fidelity Investments InstantBroker

www.fidelity.com

Investment management and other services: Check out Fidelity Investments for financial services, such as investment management, brokerage and shareholder services for individuals and institutions, and retirement planning.

Finance Wireless

www.rovenet.com/download.htm

Tools to manage your finances: This site is geared toward women, but anyone can find useful tips and information. You can access various tools to help you make decisions concerning your finances and investments.

FIRST CALL Wireless

www.firstcall.com

Real-time earnings: Get the latest earnings and U.S. research information at this site. If you are a First Call Notes or Earnings subscriber, you can access this site from your wireless device at no charge.

fnCentral mobile

www.fnCentral.com/palm.html

Personal finance organizer: This site enables you to add information to your portfolio or just review it using your wireless device.

FRT2go

www.freerealtime.com

Registered members get real-time stock quotes: If you are a registered member of Free RealTime.com, you can now get free, unlimited, real-time stock quotes anytime, anywhere, from your wireless device.

GetWhispers

www.getwhispers.com

Delayed stock quotes: Interested in delayed stock quotes or accessing whisper numbers? Check this site using your wireless device.

golden1.com Wireless!

www.golden1.com

Find ATM and office locations: Now you can locate a Golden 1 Credit Union or office location from your wireless device. You can also access current rates and get current credit union information.

Harris Bank Wireless

www.harriswireless.com

Secure access to Harris Bank: Access your account easily and securely using your wireless device. You can also find other information such as news and sports.

Interact.com

www.interact.com

Access your Interact account: Interact sells a large line of management software, and now you can access your account through your wireless device. Subscribers can find all kinds of information, including travel and news services.

Island BookViewer

www.island.com/bookviewer

View the Island Limit Book: View the Island Limit Book on your wireless device. See the shares available and prices as well as systemwide statistics.

JB Oxford

www.jboxford.com

Speed and ease: The JB Oxford wireless site offers quick and easy features that enable you to use many online investment options. You can view your account, obtain real-time quotes, place stock and option orders, and more.

Lind Anywhere Futures Trading

www.lind-waldock.com

Wireless trading: Lind-Waldock & Company brings you quick, easy wireless trading. Place orders and monitor your account with your wireless device.

MarketWatch.com

www.marketwatch.com

Real-time financial news: Use your wireless device to get comprehensive news and data in a real-time format. Keep up with your relevant financial data and use related tools and services.

MasterCard

www.mastercard.com

Find a MasterCard or Cirrus cash machine: Use your wireless device to find a MasterCard or Cirrus cash machine quickly and easily.

myTrack

www.mytrack.com

View your stock monitor lists: myTrack offers a free myTrack account with services that enable you to view positions, make trades, or check the status of your order. myTrack also offers real-time quotes.

ORTCOnline

www.ortconline.com

View orders: Old Republic Title Company customers can now use the wireless Internet to view the status of orders they have placed.

Paymaster Direct Home Branching

www.paymaster.org

HAEFCU (Hughes Aircraft Employees Federal Credit Union) members: If you are a HAEFCU member, you can now view your account online using your wireless device. This site also enables you to review account history, transfer funds between your accounts, and access other banking options.

PlugnPay Unplugged

www.paymaster.org

Merchants can authorize credit card payments: Online merchants can use this service to authorize credit card payments quickly and easy — and now on the wireless Internet. Merchants must register with PlugnPlay before they can use this service.

Pocket Authorize.Net

www.authorizenet.com

Manage secure wireless transactions: Pocket Authorize.Net enables you to perform secure wireless transactions. Access your Pocket Authorize.Net account via your wireless device.

Progressive Wireless Internet Manager

www.progressive.com

Progressive Insurance on the wireless Internet: Visit Progressive Insurance, now on the wireless Internet. Find a local agent, pay your bill, get information on your account, and obtain all kinds of other information with your wireless device

Prudential

www.prudential.com

Online financial services: You can now access the popular Prudential site and electronic services via your wireless device. Find all kinds of financial information here.

Silicon Investor

www.siliconinvestor.com

Financial discussion community: Now you can participate in Silicon Investor's popular discussion boards and discussion community on your wireless device. Create your own wireless watchlists and keep up to date.

Stock100

www.stock100.com

Check out stock price forecasts: Read forecasts and investment information and even see online trading forms at this site.

StockBoss Interactive

www.softwinc.com

Real-time wireless investments: Use this Palm application to get real-time wireless access to stocks and investment information. Manage your account and get price quotes immediately and easily.

TD Waterhouse Wireless

www.tdwaterhouse.com

Various brokerage services: TD Waterhouse offers a wide range of services, including online stock quotes, banking, and mutual funds.

Texans Credit Union

www.texasncu.org/vb1.html

Online banking: Are you a Texans Credit Union Member? If so, this site is a must. As a member, you can access your banking account information, anytime, anywhere.

Titleserv

www.titleserv.com

View the status of your order: If you are a Titleserv title insurance customer, you can obtain the status of your order. This site also provides calculations for New York State insurance premiums.

USAB

www.usabancshares.com

Real-time banking: Apply for an account, get real-time balances, pay bills, get CD rates, and obtain all kinds of other banking information quickly and easily with USAB.

Visa ATM

www.visa.com

Visa or Plus ATM locations: Need to locate a Visa or Plus ATM? Visit this Web site and simply enter such information as street address, ZIP code, or even the phone number. This site then gives you a list of the three closest ATMs to that location.

WealthHound

www.wealthhound.com

Wireless stock quotes: Get wireless stock quotes quickly and in a real-time format using WealthHound.

News and Sports Sites

The wireless Internet is great for accessing news and sports of all kinds. This section highlights many outstanding wireless sites for getting the latest news and sports results.

2wayNews.com
Palm PQA

Sports scores: This site prides itself on giving you up-to-date sports scores and information, while using the least possible number of bytes on your wireless device.

ABCNews.com

www.abcnews.com

24-hour news source: ABC News.com is accessible from your wireless Internet device. This site provides coverage of local, national, and international news, as well as news on entertainment, sports, and much more.

ABQJournal.com

www.abqjournal.com

Sports and news: ABQJournal, otherwise known as the Albuquerque Journal, gives you all the latest on business, news, and sports. You can also get dining and movie information for sites throughout New Mexico.

ADDS Aviation Weather

Palm PQA

Airport weather conditions: Going to the airport? Check out ADDS Aviation Weather to get up-to-date, thorough weather information for any U.S. airport.

Afronet.com

www.afronet.com

Get African-American news: This site offers news and business information about African-American markets plus numerous community features.

air Heart-Consumer

www2.kumc.edu/wichita/heartdoc

Heart news: Doing research or just needing some information on heart health and disease? Using your wireless device, you can access air Heart-Consumer and review the headlines or see what studies are being conducted.

Baseball Birthdays

www.taohouse.com/baseball

Attention baseball fans: Are you a sports trivia fan? Want to know the birthday of a particular player or whether he's currently playing or not? Check out this site.

Baseball Encyclopedia

Palm PQA

Baseball history: Want to know who won the World Series in 1915? You can find the answer to that question and many more concerning the history of baseball by visiting the Baseball Encyclopedia Web clipping on your wireless device.

Baseball Live

Wireless.sportsline.com

World of baseball: Baseball Live offers play-by-play, lineups, and everything else you want to know about your team. This site is a must for keeping track of what's going on in the world of baseball.

Basketball Live

wireless.sportsline.com

Basketball enthusiasts: Get up-to-the-minute basketball scores, anytime, anywhere.

Bike-Zone.com

www.bike-zone.com/palm/main.htm

Latest cycling news: Visit Bike-Zone.com for a multitude of cycling-related information. Get race schedules, U.S. cycling news, European news, as well as mountain bike news, all from your wireless device, at Bike-Zone.com.

Biojump.com

www.biojump.com

Medical news: Biojump.com is available on your wireless device so that you can obtain medical news and information at anytime.

BiotechWatch News and Milestones

www.biotechwatch.com

Clinical trial information and more: Interested in knowing what's going on in the world of biotechnology? Check out BiotechWatch News and Milestones for the latest information on clinical trials, information on publicly traded biotechnology companies, and more.

Book4golf.com

www.book4golf.com

Book your next golf game: Book4golf.com offers information on golf courses throughout the country. You can locate your desired golf course, inquire about tee-times, and make online reservations.

CQUAD

www.cquad.com

Philadelphia cycling information: Find out what's going on in cycling news. In addition to the news, get race results, events, and more. You can also access the Ride Finder.

College Football Live

wireless.sportsline.com

College football fans: Visit College Football Live for all the latest information from the college football arena.

CNET News

www.cnet.com

Find computer information: CNET is one of the more popular sources of computing information on the Internet. Using CNET News, you can stay abreast of technology news, prices, computer reviews, and all kinds of related computing information.

CNN.com

www.cnn.com

Breaking news and current events: For 24-hour-a-day news, go to CNN.com This online news site has up-to-the-moment information on breaking stories.

Dennis Miller Demystified

www.dmdmyst.com

Dennis Miller and Monday Night Football: After you hear Dennis Miller's MNF commentary, read it from your wireless device so you can figure out what he's ranting about.

eGolfScore Wireless

www.egolfscore.com

Online score keeping: Keep your golf scores online. This service also enables you to broadcast your golf scores to your family and friends in real-time.

Earthquake

www.pdagroove.com

Keep informed: This site can be a valuable tool in the event of an earthquake. This site brings you earthquake status information from the U.S. Geological Survey.

ESPN.com

www.espn.com

Latest sports information: To find out the latest on your favorite sports team, use your wireless Internet device and visit ESPN.com.

Excite Mobile

www.excite.com

Excite news: Get Excite news, sports, financial, and all kinds of information at the Excite Start page, now available on your wireless device.

FinalFour.net

Palm PQA

NCAA news: If you're an NCAA basketball fan, you'll want to visit this site with your wireless device. Stay up-to-date with the scores, breaking news, and stats of your favorite NCAA team.

Football Live

wireless.sportsline.com

Stats and scores: Find out the stats of your favorite NFL team by checking out Football Live. You also get real-time scores and box scores.

FoxSports.com

www.foxsports.com

Get the latest sport scores: Who won last night's game? Who's going to the Super Bowl? For all you sports fans out there, check out FoxSports.com to get the latest news, highlights, and scores.

FSU Weather

www.met.fsu.edu/wireless.html

Florida State University: FSU Weather offers up-to-date weather forecasts and information.

GE PressRoom

Palm PQA

GE News: The GE Press Room keeps you informed about what's going on. The news is available 24 hours a day and is always up-to-date.

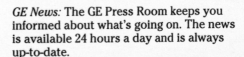

GO.com

www.go.com

News and information: Get your Go.com content wirelessly, including news, sports, weather, and all kinds of useful and fun information.

GolfServ's Wireless GolfGuide

www.golfserv.com

Find out about the golf front: Do you like to keep up with the latest information from the golf scene? Check out GolfGuide to stay on top of the world of golf.

Hurricane!

www.solar.ifa.hawaii.edu/Tropical/

Hurricane information: Get the latest information on hurricanes and other tropical storms at this site, including current locations of storms as well as wind speeds and other important details of the weather conditions. This site is not designed for emergency decision-making concerning weather.

InfoBrand Weather Center

www.infobrand.com

Updated forecasts: Regardless of where you are or where you're going, get current weather conditions at InfoBrand Weather Center. Get current weather forecasts that are updated hourly and use the Almanac feature to find out about weather events from the past.

Intranet Design Magazine Unwired

Idm.internet.com

Intranet design on the wireless Web: The Intranet Design Magazine is now available on the wireless Internet. Great for Intranet designers and administrators who are on the move.

IWIN

Palm PQA

Weather information: Check out IWIN to get interactive weather information from the National Weather Service.

Joe Bryant's CheatSheets.net

www.cheatsheets.net

Fantasy football fans: Fantasy football players can get projections and rankings for your teams, as well as information on the draft picks and a Draft kit.

Link2Semi.com

www.link2semi.com

Semiconductor information: Looking for up-to-date information about semiconductor news? Check out Link2Semi.com.

LinksTime.com

www.linkstime.com

Golfing information and reservations: This site enables you to search for information about your favorite golf course or courses that you'd like to visit. You can also make, cancel, or review your reservations.

Linux Today

www.linuxtoday.com

News and information about Linux: Keep up with the latest news and developments about the Linux operating system. Quick and easy information — now on the wireless Internet.

Mobile PalmCentral.com

www.handango.com

Keep up with your Palm device: Get all the news, information, and latest updates for your Palm operating system. A must-have site for the wireless Palm user.

Mobilicious.com

chasers.mobilicious.com

News about the mobile world: Access this site to get all kinds of information about mobile devices and developments. This is a great place to keep up-to-date with the constantly growing and changing mobile market.

nPorta

www.nporta.com

Managed information: Use the nPorta site to get business news and industry news, as well as sports and weather, in a targeted, managed format. Get the information you need, quickly and easily.

NWS Corpus Christi

www.srh.noaa.gov/crp

Corpus Christi weather: Using your wireless device, get up-to-date information from the National Weather Service for Corpus Christi and surrounding areas.

Ski Reports

Palm PAQ

Check the conditions first: Looking for a great day out on the slopes? Before you go, check the current conditions using your wireless device.

New York Times Digital

www.newyorktimes.com

24-hour a day news coverage: This site offers the latest breaking news, as well as sports and entertainment information. With its 3,000-plus journalists worldwide, *The New York Times* is trusted as one of the more accurate, up-to-the-minute news authorities.

NewsJunkie

Palm PQA

Find out what's happening: Get news and information from a variety of sources, including MSNBC and the BBC.

NOAA Xpress

Palm PQA

News and more: To keep up with news, check out NOAA Xpress from your wireless device. This site also provides other information, such as coastal water temperatures and more.

Palm Organizer News

www.palminfocenter.com

Palm organizer info: Keep up with developments for the Palm operating system by visiting the Palm Organizer news site.

PDAlive.com

www.pdalive.com

PDA news: Get the latest developments in the PDA world. This site includes headlines, forum postings, and much more.

Tim Nicholson's Palm Zone

Palm PQA

PDA info: Keep up-to-date with PDA news and developments.

PDAntic.com

www.pdantic.com

PDA updates: The world of the PDA is always changing, and you can keep up with news and updates at this PDA site.

PDA Buyers Guide

www.pdabuyersguide.com

Keep up-to-date with the PDA world: Keep up with news and late-breaking developments about PDAs at this site.

Pen Computing News

Palm PQA

Handheld computing news: Keep up with the latest news and developments in the handheld computing world. You'll find all kinds of helpful information at this site.

PGA.com

www.pga.com

Golf enthusiasts: This site features the latest golf news and scores nationwide. This site provides a way for golfers from abroad to connect with each other.

RealCities.com Wireless

www.realcities.com

Anytime anywhere news: Find news for any number of cities throughout the U.S. by using your wireless device. You can also find out what's going on in international news, sports, politics, business, and more.

Salon.com

Palm PQA

News: Salon.com offers today's news and technology headlines.

Seattle Weather

Palm PQA

Weather information: Using your wireless device, you can check the weather in the Seattle, WA area.

Silicon Philly

www.siliconphilly.com

Technology news and information: Keep up-to-date with the latest computing news from Silicon Valley.

SportsDrill

www.datadrill.com/examples_wireless.html

Sports news and more: Visit SportsDrill on your wireless device to find your team's scores and statistics, including thorough, current information on Major League Baseball.

SportsFeed.com

www.sportsfeed.com

For in-depth sports coverage: SportsFeed gives you in-depth coverage of the latest sports news, scores, and much more.

SportsXL Amateur Sports News

Palm PQA

Fans of amateur sports: Check out SportsXL Amateur Sports News for the latest on your favorite amateur sports teams and individuals. You can also check out schedules and player rosters.

STATS Inc

www.stats.com

MLB stats: Do you like to keep up with MLB stats? If so, check out this site for statistics and more.

Swell.com

www.swell.com

Surfs up: Swell.com is your online resource for surfing enthusiasts. It offers updates, news, entertainment, and other items related to the sport of surfing.

Techdirt

www.techdirt.com

Real information about technology: Get to the real technology news and reviews at the Techdirt site. This site is for those who want to know the real information about the latest technological developments.

TeeMaster.com

www.temaster.com/PalmVII.asp

Secure your tee time online: Find information on golf courses throughout the country. You can also securely book your tee time online from your wireless device.

Teetimes.com

www.teetimes.com

Reserve your next golf game: This site offers convenience by enabling you to book your next tee time via your wireless device.

TheStreet.com

www.thestreet.com

Financial news: Get financial news and other information at TheStreet.com.

TNL.net

www.tnl.net

Internet newsletter: Use the TNL.net wireless site to access the popular Internet newsletter.

Truckline Wireless

www.truckline.com

Trucking news and information: Visit the Truckline Wireless site to get information and news about the transportation industry.

Unisys To Go

www.unisys.com

Track news and stock quotes: Use the Unisys To Go site to track news, stocks, or even sports . Easy to use and full of information.

USA Today

www.usatoday.com

Rated the number-one online news site: USA Today provides up-to-the-minute news coverage on a wide range of topics.

USTA Boys' Tennis

Palm PQA

Tennis fans: Visit this site to get news on the National Tennis Championships. You can also see player profiles.

Universal Weather and Aviation

www.universalweather.com/wireless

Aviation and weather: This site explores aviation and the weather. Find out about flight plans, fuel prices, and local weather before your next flight.

Venturewire

www.venturewire.com

A must news source: This site is a must for those in the world of finance and investments. The site is devoted to private companies and venture capital.

WAPsight.com

www.wapsight.com

Get information on the wireless Internet: Keep up-to-date with the wireless Internet and the developments of the mobile Web.

WPVI-ABC TV6

www.abclocal.go.com/wpvi

Delaware Valley news: Keep up-to-date with the news in the Delaware Valley area at this site.

WRAL-Raleigh, NC

Palm PQA

News for Raleigh, NC: Now you don't have to be near a television to see what's going on in news for Raleigh, NC. This site gives you weather, sports, news, and traffic information, all from your wireless device.

Wall Street Journal

www.wsj.com

Keep informed about the market: The Wall Street Journal is noted as the world's authority on business news. Now you can find out the latest information and news on your wireless device at the *Journal's* Web site. Of course, you must be a subscriber to get full use of the site.

Washingtonpost.com

www.washingtonpost.com

Keep up with political news: The Washingtonpost.com informs you not only of the latest political news, but also local weather and traffic information.

WeatherNet

www.aws.com

Real-time weather news: Visit WeatherNet to get real-time weather news for more than 4,000 locations, including information from 103 local television stations.

The Weather Guys

www.weatherguys.com

In-depth weather forecasts: Here, you can check current weather conditions or see the extended forecast for a particular city. You can also stay in tune with forecasts, weather alerts, and warnings.

Weather Radar

Palm PQA

Northeast region weather: Check out the weather conditions in the Northeast by visiting Weather Radar from your wireless device.

The Weather Underground

www.weatherunderground.com

Get up-to-the-minute weather information: The Weather Underground provides real-time weather conditions for both domestic and international weather information. Detailed forecasts as well as severe weather advisories are available.

WirelessDevNet Daily

www.wirelessdevnet.com

Developer information about the wireless Internet: This site for wireless Web developers is a great way to keep up with news and developments.

Wireless GolfNow

www.golfnow.com/wireless/download.asp

Keep up with your golf game: If golf is your game, visit this site. Reserve tee times, purchase golf equipment, and check out weather conditions.

The Weather Channel

www.weather.com

Local and national weather: The Weather Channel provides local and national weather information. To find out the weather conditions in any part of the country, use the site's easy ZIP code and city search options. Get current weather conditions as well as the five-day forecast.

ZDNET To Go

www.zdnet.com

Keep up on technology: ZDNET is a very popular Web location for computer news, technology information, and product reviews.

Reference and Directories

In addition to news and entertainment, your wireless device gives you access to all kinds of reference and directory information on just about any subject. This section of the Wireless Internet Access Directory describes various helpful reference sites.

555 Area Code Finder

Palm PQA

Find an area code: Have you noticed that area codes keep changing? Now you don't have to guess what the new area code is. Using your wireless device, access 555 Area Code Finder. Its database of area codes is updated almost every day.

ABFAnywhere

www.abfs.com/ecommerce/anywhere.asp

Find the status of your shipment: ABF Freight System, Inc, now offers real-time

tracking of your shipment's status via your wireless device.

air Heart-Professional

Palm PQA

Heart information: Visit this site to find out what's going on the field of cardiology.

Amazon

Palm PQA

Rainforest: Check on the Amazon's endangered rainforests from your wireless device.

Antivirus.com

www.antivirus.com

Keep abreast of the newest antivirus developments: From your wireless device, you can find out what viruses are lurking in the world of computers. The information at this site is provide by Trend Micro's Information Center.

Astronomy

Palm PQA

Stargazing: If you're interested in stars and the Milky Way, check out the Astronomy Web clipping on your wireless device.

Atomica

Palm PQA

Get answers: If you have unanswered questions, check out Atomica for information on various topics. You can perform searches by entering a word or topic.

BaAlien

www.banywhere.com/downloads.htm

Get personal statistics: Get personal statistics and keep track of the search for extraterrestrial life by monitoring the Search for Extra-Terrestrial Intelligence (SETI) radio signals.

BaNetMon

www.banywhere.com/downloads.htm

Keep up with the network: Get information about domain name registration searches, ping lookups, and additional information about the actual network of the Internet.

BaPolitical

www.banywhere.com/downloads.html

Political news and searches: Get contact information for senators and members of Congress and send them an e-mail!

BaSatellite

www.banywhere.com/downloads.html

Get satellite position information: Using the Navy's tracking information, see the position of Global Positioning System satellites in our orbit.

BaTime

www.banywhere.com

Get the official time: BaTime gives you the official time of day, using the Department of Defense's official clock.

BeamMP3

Palm PQA

Find MP3 information: For all you MP3 lovers, use this site to find MP3 download sites and great prices on MP3-related products.

BioMedNet Medline

www.biomednet.com

Perform medical searches: Locate medical information by searching over 10 million available records. Includes great searching capabilities.

BioMedNet Molecular Biology Quick Reference

www.biomednet.com

Get molecular biology information: Find information about molecular biology, including genetic charts and related information.

Body1

www.body1.com/palm/palm.cfm

Wellness: Visit this site to get information on the world of health and medical information.

BookMarkManager

Palm PQA

Bookmark site with the Palm: This Web application enables Palm users to more easily manage and bookmark Internet sites.

BrainBuzz

www.brainbuzz.com

Find jobs online: Use the BrainBuzz site to find the hottest job postings and information on IT jobs.

Britannica Traveler

www.britannica.com

Use the encyclopedia — online!: Access the entire Encyclopedia Britannica from your wireless device — a quick and easy way to get the information you need.

Catavault

www.catavault.com

Keep your information private: Store your user name and password information privately and securely on the Internet. Using Catavault, you can easily access and log on to more than 1,400 sites.

Central Carolina Technical College Online

www.sum.tec.sc.us

College information: Need information on Central Carolina Technical College? Check out this Web site to get information on what's new and what's going on at the college. You can also obtain information on the school's online courses and admissions applications.

Chase's Calendar of Events

Palm PQA

Find out what's going on and when: Keep up with all the holidays, historical events, and more. With Chase's Calendar of Events, you can easily keep track of what's going on.

Cyphotilapia Frontosa

Palm PQA

East Africa fishing: Find all kinds of reference information about the great lakes of East Africa. This site includes detailed information, including a photo gallery and live fish cameras.

Earthoid WAPsearch

www.wap88.com

Find it on the wireless Internet: This WAP search engine helps you locate the wireless Internet sites you need. Very cool and very useful!

Edmunds.com Automotive Information

www.edmunds.com

Get auto information while you're on the move: Get automotive reviews, news, prices, ratings, and all kinds of auto-related information at this great reference site.

EkNazar.com

www.eknazar.com

Get info on Dallas's Indian community: Find news and information about the DFW metroplex's Indian community, including DFW events, news, businesses, entertainment, and much more.

eLocal.com

www.elocal.com

Find city information quickly: Find out information on more than 30,000 cities in the United States. Find news, travel information, lodging, and much more!

Emergen2

Palm PQA

First-aid information: Out and about and need first-aid information? Using your wireless device, access this site for a full guide to first aid.

eStogies.com Online Cigar Reference and Pricing

Palm PQA

Needing information on cigars: This site is helpful for cigar enthusiasts and novices. Get easy-to-read, understandable information and descriptions about different cigar types and flavors. You can also get pricing online from eStogies.com cigar shop.

Exereo Unplugged

www.irontechnology.com

Find bars and restaurants: Search for bars and restaurants in New York and even by your own personal profile. Find the information you want quickly and easily.

Fboweb.com

www.fboweb.com

Live aviation information: A great site for pilots — find out about news and flight plans, and even track flights and weather.

FedEx

www.fedex.com

Make sure your package arrived: Need to make sure your package arrived, or simply check its status? Use your wireless device to enter your airbill number at FedEx, and you can get the status of your package.

FireDispatch.com

www.firedispatch.com

San Mateo County, CA: Find out about fire department emergencies in San Mateo County.

FitForAll.com

Palm PQA

Interactive community: Get information to help you make healthy choices, and access tools to help manage your health.

Free Online Dictionary of Computing
Palm PQA

Get help: Reading your computer manual or software package, trying to figure out what an acronym means? Check out the Free Online Dictionary of Computing. This site also provides other helpful information.

Freightgate
www.freightgate.com/

Tracking a package: Track your package using the site's meta-search features.

Frisco Business Web
www.friscobusinessweb.com

Frisco, TX: With this complete guide to businesses in Frisco, TX, you can search for a specific business name. This helpful resource offers easy-to-use search features.

Galaxies
www.galaxies.com

Looking at the stars: Interested in the moon, stars, sky, and planets? Check out the Galaxies Web site to find out what time the sun and moon rise, and more.

Get Zip
Palm PQA

Get a ZIP code: You don't have to search endlessly for a ZIP code you need — just use this handy utility that accesses the United States Postal System servers for the correct ZIP code of any city.

Global Communicator
www.rovenet.com

Get instant translations: Enter information and get it translated easily and quickly into several different languages. Then, use the translation in an e-mail — very cool and very helpful!

GMAC Real Estate
Palm PQA

Find a home for sale: Use this handy Better Homes and Gardens site to find homes for sale in your area.

Go Network People
Palm PQA

Find People: Get access to Go.com's White Pages and find telephone numbers and addresses from 118 million listings for the United States and Canada.

Go Network's Translator To Go
Palm PQA

Translate data easily: Use the Go Network's Translator To Go to translate text, articles, e-mail, and just about anything else into five major languages.

Gutenburg Bible
Palm PQA

Find a scripture passage: Whether you are out and about or sitting at home, you can access the Gutenburg Bible site, which provides search capabilities for the King James Bible.

HealthGrades

www.healthgrades.com/information/mobile

Trying to find a doctor: Finding a doctor can be a not-so-pleasant experience. When selecting a doctor, you must ask many questions to make sure you find the right doctor for you and your family. HealthGrades provides helpful tools for making your selection.

Homes.com

www.homes.com

Selling or buying a home: Whether you're trying to sell your home or purchase a new one, check out Homes.Com for help in locating a qualified agent as well as information on current interest rates.

Gensite

Palm PQA

Find your roots: Find out where you and your ancestors came from. For information on your ancestors, check out www.genealogy.org.

Gist TV Listings

www.gist.com/tv/palmvii.jsp

Find out what's on television tonight: Find the right time and channel so you don't miss your favorite television show.

HealthGate's Medline

Palm PQA

Find medical literature: Search Medline for medical abstracts and information about medical conditions. This site's database contains more than nine million records covering all aspects of medicine.

Homestore.com

www.homestore.com

Find homes for sale: Find more than 1.3 million homes nationwide as well as apartments. Use this site to begin your home search.

In-N-Out Burger Locator

Palm PQA

Find a location: Use this handy utility to find the nearest In-N-Out Burger location by entering your ZIP code.

KraftFoods.com

www.kraftfoods.com

Get some dinner suggestions: Instead of staring in your pantry and refrigerator wondering what's for dinner, get help by visiting KraftFoods.com. This site offers easy-to-follow recipes using ingredients that you probably have on hand.

Lookup

Palm PQA

Find a domain name: Use this utility to check for domain name availability.

Martindale-Hubbell Wireless Lawyer Locator

www.xnow.com

Find a lawyer: If you need to find a lawyer, use the Wireless Lawyer Locator, which checks the Martindale-Hubbell directory to find a lawyer in your area.

MassTimes

Palm PQA

Get to the church on time: The MassTimes site helps you locate Catholic churches and mass times.

MCI WorldCom Telecom Library

Palm PQA

Get telecommunications information: Use this glossary site to find information on telecommunications-related terms and issues.

MedFetch

Palm PQA

Find medical information: Use MedFetch to locate articles and information about medical issues based on article name, author name, journal name, or type of disease.

MediaJobz

www.mediajobz.com

Find employment in the field of media: If you are a media professional looking for a job, this site is for you. Find out what jobs are available in your chosen field.

Medical Dictionary

Palm PQA

Get an explanation of a medical term: If you need help with a medical term, find the answer at the Medical Dictionary site.

Medical Glossary

Palm PQA

Clarify medical jargon: The Medical Glossary site gives you detailed information and definitions of confusing medical terms.

Medical Toolkit for Knee Problems and Treatments

Palm PQA

ACL, MCL, OUCH: Find out about research and treatments for knee problems.

Medical Toolkit for Problems and Treatments of Veins

Palm PQA

Looking for information about vein problems: This helpful site has lots of information about treatments and procedures available for treating problems related to veins. You can also find out what research is being done in this field.

Merriam-Webster

www.m-w.com

Find the right word: Need the correct spelling or definition of a word, or a thesaurus? Now you can access your dictionary or thesaurus online, using your wireless device.

MorseCode

www.tow.com

Read Morse Code: This fun site enables your wireless device to read text in Morse Code. You need iKnapsack from Foundation Systems in order to run the utility.

National Academies

www.nationalacademies.org

Get science information: Find all kinds of information about science, technology, health, and much more at this academic site.

Net Tool Box

Palm PQA

Get network tools: Use this site to run common network management and information tools, such as ping, traceroute, whois, nslookup, and other related tools.

Nissan Car Quote

www.nissan1.com

Car quote: Thinking about buying a Nissan automobile? Get a quick quote from this wireless site.

Nutrient Database

Palm PQA

You don't know what that's made of: Interested in knowing what nutrients your food contains? To find the answers, visit the Nutrient Database Web site.

NY Info Wireless

www.rovenet.com

Find it in New York City: If you're in New York City, check out this site to get all kinds of news and information about events. You can also find your way around the city with this site's help.

PGHQ

www.palmgear.com

Find out about Palm gear: Palm users, find out about Palm gear, software, news, and operations tips and tricks at this site.

Physics ePrint Search

Palm PQA

Discover physics research: Search for information on the primary physics server used for posting research and information.

Pocket Blue Book

www.bluebookprco.com

Blue book members: Use this site to locate other Blue Book members and search from a large database of information.

Powerboats4sale

Palm PQA

Sailing, sailing: Rather than scan your newspaper's classified section, go online to find the boat of your dreams.

Public Radio

Palm PQA

Tune in: Use this site to get a listing of public radio stations.

Radio Talk Shows

www.rovenet.com/download.htm

Blah, blah, blah: No more channel surfing on your radio dial trying to find your favorite radio talk show host. Find any radio talk show you're looking for by using this site.

Reference / Resources

www.rovenet.com/download.htm

Get directories quickly: Find out all kinds of information when you're on the move. You can access all kinds of directories, references, and resources in one central location.

SailBoats4Sale

www.sailboats4sale.com

Set sail: Looking to sell or buy a boat? Visit Sailboats4sale.com. You can see online pictures of the boats for sale, along with a description of each boat and the asking price.

Share-A-Note

www.wintervideo.com/shareanote

Share and read information: Share information and read information posted by others — directly from your wireless device.

ShuttleCAM

www.ruffwork.com

Keep up with the space shuttle: Want to know what's going on with the space shuttle? Check this site for an up-to-date miniature picture of the shuttle at work.

Silicon Alley Events

Palm PQA

Find an event: Use this wireless site to find events in Silicon Alley. You can search for information and view event information that is available.

Spyonit Mobile

www.spyonit.com

Watch information easily: The popular SpyOnIt.com Web site is now available in a mobile edition. Watch news, weather, sports, auctions, and all kinds of information that is delivered to you as it becomes available.

Sun and Moon

Palm PQA

Sundown: Want to know when the sun will rise and set, or information about the sun?

Visit this site for daily information about the sun and moon. The data is provided by the Astronomical Applications Department.

Sushi Wireless
Palm PQA

Locate a sushi bar: If you love sushi, use this site to find and contact a sushi bar near you. You can even order online!

Textprices.com
Palm PQA

Find a book and check prices: Search for books by ISBN number, find a list of sites that have the books you want, and check the prices.

TheHealthChannel.com
Palm PQA

Get current health information: Use TheHealthChannel.com site to find all kinds of health information and related news. You can explore a wide range of health topics by accessing this site.

ThinkersGroup WAP Browser
www.thinkersgroup.com

Browser for the Palm VIIx: Use this browser on a Palm VIIx so that you can access any WAP-enabled Internet site directly from your Palm.

THOMAS Legislative Database
Palm PQA

Find legislative data: Use this wireless site to check the status of legislation. The legislative database is provided by the Library of Congress.

U.S. Trademark Search
Palm PQA

Patent pending: Visit this site to view the Pending Trademark database.

U.S. Time
Palm PQA

Get the correct time: Using your wireless device, you can find out what the official U.S. time is.

Ucook
Palm PQA

Find a recipe: Looking for a recipe, but don't have the time or the energy to plow through your cookbooks? Now you don't have to. Visit Ucook and enter search information to find the recipe you want. This site searches tens of thousands of cookbooks.

UPS Shipping
www.ups.com

Check on your package: If you sent your package via UPS, you can check the status of that package from your wireless device.

Upseek Job Search

www.upseek.com

Get a job: Looking for a job doesn't have to mean hours of searching through the classifieds in your local paper. Upseek Job Search gets you connected with career and corporate sites to find out what jobs are available.

US West Dex

Palm PQA

Find a particular business: Don't get frustrated searching for the phone number or address of a business. US West Dex helps you find the information you need via quick, easy search features.

Verizon SuperPages

www.superpages.com

The Yellow Pages at their best: The Verizon SuperPages site gives you access to a complete resource so you can find just about anything you need. Perform searches by location and view maps and driving directions.

Vicinity BrandFinder

www.vicinity.com

Find what you want: Use Vicinity BrandFinder to locate the product that you need, or even hotels, gas stations, restaurants, and other services. Just enter a search query and a location, and BrandFinder locates what you want.

WeatherClip

Palm PQA

Get aviation weather: Find out about weather, area forecasts, flight plans, and other types of information related to professional and amateur aviation.

Westlaw Wireless

www.westlaw.com/wireless

Retrieve case information: Use your wireless device to get all kinds of information about Westlaw cases. Retrieve case information, a synopsis, and even a full history, including an attorney directory.

Wireless Books

Palm PQA

Download wireless books: Using a Palm handheld device, you can view public domain wireless books.

Shopping

Want to shop while you are stranded at the airport or stuck in traffic? No problem! These wireless Internet Web sites can help you find what you're looking for and buy the product you want quickly and painlessly.

Amazon.com

www.amazon.com

Find all kinds of books, music, electronics, and more: Amazon.com is a very popular online bookstore, but you can find more than books on this site. Find your favorite music, movies, electronics, and even home and garden products. Read product reviews and buy items securely and quickly.

Barnes&Noble.com

www.bn.com

Books and more: Go to Barnes&Noble.com for books, music, and more. This Web site also offers online reviews and information to find a Barnes & Noble near you. Another option available at this site is free eCards. For added convenience, you can also check the status of your account or set up a new account.

BarPoint.com

www.barpoint.com

Comparison-shopping made easy: If you know the universal product code (UPC) of any product, you can use BarPoint.com to search for the product on the Internet, find out which Internet stores sell the product, and easily compare prices. BarPoint.com is the quick and easy way to comparison-shop.

Buy.com

www.buy.com

Shopping via your Web-enabled device: Looking for low prices, a wide selection of products, and friendly customer service? Use your wireless Internet device and check out Buy.com.

DealTime

www.dealtime.com

Simplified online shopping: This site is ideal for those of us who want to get the best

deal for our dollar. When you're shopping and you want to make sure you get the most for your money on a particular item, just go to DealTime on your wireless device.

eCompare

www.ecompare.com

Save time and money when you shop: eCompare enables you to shop and compare prices on a large selection of products. Also, by visiting eCompare, you can get movie locations and show times. You can also find a restaurant or the nearest ATM location.

Edmunds.com

www.edmunds.com

Shop for a new or used car: If you're in the market for a new or used vehicle, check out Edmunds.com. This site gives a variety of information to help you with your car-buying decision, including pricing, warranty, and safety information.

eBay

www.ebay.com

Buy and sell anything: eBay is the popular auction site where you can find all kinds of things. Looking for that old record? Look for it on eBay. What about something weird and strange that you can't find anywhere else? Look for it on eBay. Using your wireless device, you can bid on items, check your bid status, and check your eBay account.

FTD.com

www.ftd.com

Send some flowers: Need to say you're sorry or wish someone a happy birthday? What better way than to send some flowers. FTD.com makes it easy to order flowers or other specialty gifts online.

GiftCertificates.com

www.giftcertificates.com

Give a gift certificate: Not sure what to get someone? Gift certificates make the perfect gift. Visit GiftCertificates.com to view the hundreds of well-known stores, restaurants, and other business that offer gift certificates. The gift certificate is delivered via standard mail or overnight — your choice.

mySimon.com

www.mysimon.com

Comparison shopping: Are you a comparison shopper? If so, visit mySimon.com to compare products and prices and locate the best values.

SalesMountain.com

www.salesmountain.com

Find what's on sale : Sales Mountain enables you to search for sales information by location, item, brand, store, or price. Sales information is updated daily.

ShopNow

www.shopnow.com

Use a wireless wallet: Use ShopNow.com to comparison shop and find items directly from your wireless device. You can even use a wireless wallet that enables you to store personal information securely and buy items easily.

StoreRunner

www.storerunner.com

A great shopping tool: Storerunner is a shopping tool that puts all kinds of brands and merchants right at your fingertips. Storerunner.com makes shopping from your wireless device quick and easy.

Travel Information and Assistance

The wireless Internet enables you to stay connected while you're on the move, so travel information and help sites fit perfectly in your wireless world. You can find just about anything — a great restaurant, a gas station, the status of your flight, and so on. Browse this section to find about travel-related sites on the wireless Internet.

1-800-TAXICAB

www.1800taxicab.com

Get a lift: Using your wireless device, you can access 1-800- TAXICAB free of charge. The service connects you to local taxi companies.

AirInfo Wireless

www.rovenet.com/download.htm

Real-time airport information: Check out this site for information about what's really going on at the airport. You can access information for airports in all major cities.

Alaska Airlines

www2.alaskaairlines.com

Flight information: Alaska Airlines offers flights to cities in the U.S., Canada, and Mexico. Visit www2.alaskaairlines.com to get flight schedules and status and to review your mileage plan.

American Airlines

www.aatimetable.com

Check the status of your American Airlines flight: At this American Airlines site, you can easily find out the status of flights and gate information and view AA Vacation specials.

Biztravel.com

www.biztravel.com

Online travel planning: This site enables you to book air, hotel, and other travel-related services online using your wireless device. You can also check flight status and schedules.

BluWater Bistro

www.bluwaterbistro.com/

Hungry in Seattle: If you live in the Seattle area or you're visiting and looking for somewhere to eat, check out BluWater Bistro on your wireless device. You can find out what's on the menu or the wine list at this site.

BookingZone.com

www.bookingzone.com

Making reservations: Now you can book your golf game or dinner reservations and more, all from the same service on your wireless device. Visit BookingZone.com the next time you need to make almost any kind of reservation.

Boston Harbor Marine Forcast

Palm PQA

Check out the weather conditions: Planning an outing to the harbor? Visit Boston Harbor Marine Forecast before heading out.

ChoiceHotels.com

www.choicehotels.com

Discounted hotel rates: Visit the ChoiceHotels.com site to make reservations on hotels worldwide at a discount. This site also gives you different tools to find hotels. The hotel information is extensive, so you know more about what each hotel offers. You can also use this site to check your existing reservation.

Continental Airlines

www.cotimetable.com

Information on Continental Airlines flights: Easily access Continental Airlines information using your wireless device. You can obtain flight schedules and flight status, specials, and information about your Continental Airlines mileage account.

Delta Airlines

www.delta.com

Keep up with Delta flights: Visit www.delta.com for all the flight information you need. Check gate information, flight itineraries, and other flight information from your wireless device.

Etak Traffic Touch

www.traffictouch.com

Avoid traffic problems: Before you head out to your destination, check on current traffic conditions. Using this site can help you avoid getting stuck in traffic. This site covers major U.S. cities.

Expedia.com

www.expedia.com

Travel plans made easy: Expedia.com offers services to help you book a hotel room, a car, or a flight.

Food & Drink

www.rovenet.com/download.html

Find where to dine: By using your wireless device, you can find the dining hotspots. You can also find out the price ranges of restaurants, wine lists (if available), and more information to help make your dining experience a pleasant one.

Frommer's City to Go

www.frommers.com

Local hot spots: Whether you're in your hometown or visiting some other U.S. city, find the hotspots with this site's listings of the best places to stay, eat, and go sightseeing. For a plethora of entertainment, lodging, and eating information, visit this site.

Gas Finder

Palm PQA

Find a gas station: Running low on gas and not sure how far the nearest gas station is? Gas Finder to the rescue! Access Gas Finder from your wireless device and find out where you can fill up.

GetThere DirectMobile

www.getthere.com

Flight information: For 24-hour flight information check out GetThere DirectMobile. This site gives you detailed information on the status of the flight in question as well as flight schedules.

Kenmore Air Seaplanes

www.kenmoreair.com

Find an adventure: For some fun in the Pacific Northwest, book a scenic airplane ride that takes off from the water, not the land. Use your wireless device to book reservations or check flight schedules.

Limo Wireless

www.rovenet.com/downloads.html

Dependable car service: In need of transportation? Now you can access Limo Wireless from your wireless device and schedule a car to meet your transportation needs. No membership fee is required to use this service.

LIRR Schedule

www.rovenet.com/downloads.htm

Long Island-New York commuters: Get up-to-date train schedule information for the Long Island Railroad.

MapQuest.com

www.mapquest.com

Get driving directions: MapQuest is a popular online site that gives you all kinds of maps and driving instructions. Now you can access these same features using your wireless device.

Nautical Wireless

www.rovenet.com/downloads.html

Attention boaters: Nautical Wireless offers a wealth of information to help you stay aware of the conditions around you.

NextBusTransit Information

www.nextbus.com

Find out when the next bus is coming: Waiting for your bus? Check out NextBus Transit Information using your wireless device and find out whether that bus is on time or running behind schedule. NextBus Transit gives information based on the bus's current location, not the schedule.

NextDoor

Palm PQA

Find a service you need: NextDoor helps you find various useful local services while you're on the move. For example, you can have your house cleaned, get a ride to the airport, find a plumber, and access all kinds of other local services.

Northwest Airlines

www.nwa.com

Northwest Airlines flight and gate information: Before you go to the airport, check out the status of your Northwest Airlines flight, including real-time flight and gate information and current weather conditions. If your flight has been canceled, use the one-touch rebooking option to make new arrangements.

OAG Mobile

www.oag.com

Check your flight schedule: OAG Mobile is a mobile service that enables you to check flight schedules from all worldwide flights. You can also check the status of specific flights directly from your wireless device.

PeakAdventures.net

www.peakadventures.net

Find an adventure: Do you want to have an adventure on your next vacation? Let Peak Adventures Online Tour Finder help you find some excitement.

PocketWineList.com

www.wineloverspage.com/pocketwinelist

Choose a wine: Need help deciding on what kind of wine goes best with steak? Not sure if you should serve a red or a white wine with fish? No more embarrassment. Use your wireless device to get answers to all your wine questions.

The Rep Dining Guide
Palm PQA

Find restaurants : Using your wireless device, you can access this site to locate restaurants or read restaurant reviews. This site is provided by *The Arizona Republic.*

Restaurant Row
Palm PQA

Find a restaurant: Looking for somewhere to eat but not sure what's around? Using your wireless device, check out Restaurant Row for restaurant listings.

Seattle Traffic Viewer
Palm PQA

Seattle traffic: If you're in the Seattle area, use this helpful site to find out what's going on with traffic conditions. You can view them in a graphical format.

Shamach-Kosher Restaurant Database
www.shulfinder.com

Get a Kosher meal: Having trouble locating a Kosher establishment? Now you can get information and locations of Kosher restaurants anywhere by simply accessing this site.

Shecky's Bar, Club & Lounge Guide
www.sheckys.com

New York guide to bars and more: If you're in New York and you want to find the top clubs, lounges, or bars, check out Shecky's on your wireless device and save yourself time and aggravation.

Shul Finder
www.shulfinder.com

Find a synagogue: This site can help you locate the synagogue nearest to you. It also provides a helpful tool to add your synagogue, if it is not already listed.

Starbucks Coffee Store Locator
www.starbucks.com

Grab a cup: On the run and want to find the nearest Starbucks Coffee location? Check out the Starbucks Coffee Store Locator to find the store nearest you.

Sun Country Airlines
www.suncountry.com

Flying Sun Country: Using your wireless device, check out Sun Country Airlines to get flight information.

Taxi Finder
Palm PQA

Call a taxi: Instead of waiting on the corner for a taxi, use your wireless device and access Taxi Finder. Taxi Finder has a searchable listing of more than 1,000 taxi companies throughout the U.S.

TrafficStation

www.trafficstation.com

Find an alternate route: Traffic Station currently covers 31 major metropolitan areas in North America. Check out Traffic Station to find out what's going on in traffic in your area. It also provides a service called Personal TrafficAdvisor that gives you customized traffic reports.

Trailworks

www.trailworks.com

Outdoor enthusiasts: Planning your next vacation in the great outdoors? The TrailWorks site provides information on campgrounds, trails, weather conditions, and much more to assist you in planning your getaway.

Travelape

Palm PQA

Get travel info quickly: Find out information about major vacation destinations. Get the inside scoop and even book hotel rooms!

Traveler SOS

www.travelersos.com

Get help on the road: TravelerSOS can get you all kinds of travel information — from what and where to eat to where to stay.

Travelocity.com

www.travelocity.com

Get help arranging travel plans: Travelocity.com is a leading online travel source. By using this site, you can book air, car rental, and hotel, all with the ease and convenience of using your wireless device. You can also review and book more than 5,000 vacations and cruise packages, or check on flight schedules.

TRIP.com

www.trip.com

Time for a vacation: TRIP.com provides online travel services and information to the wireless Internet community. If you're thinking about taking a trip, check out this site.

United Airlines

www.unitedairlines.com

Flying United: Using your wireless device, you can access United Airlines to purchase tickets and check flight status and availability.

Vicinity Brandfinder

Palm PQA

Find what you need: Vicinity Brandfinder is a very helpful service when you are out and about. It helps you locate restaurants, gas stations, and hotels.

VisitCorvallis!

www.visitcorvallis.com

Corvallis, Oregon visitor information:
Looking for something to do in Corvallis?
Visit this site and get up-to-date events and
other visitor information.

Worldwide Travel Information

www.rovenet.com/downloads.html

Real-time travel assistance: Don't be a
weary traveler. Check out Worldwide
Travel to get real-time flight information,
along with airport status. This site also
provides information on currency conver-
sions and time zone calculations.

Where2Go Public Restroom Locator

www.rovenet.com/downloads.html

Nature calling: Ever been out and about
and needed a public restroom, but you
couldn't find one? Now you can use your
wireless device to locate a public
restroom.

Zagat Restaurant

Palm PQA

Make plans for dinner: Going out for break-
fast, lunch, or dinner, and need assistance
locating a restaurant? Using your wireless
device, access Zagat Restaurant. This site
can help you locate a restaurant by price,
type of cuisine, and location.

Index

• Numbers •

1-800-TAXICAB, D-40
10Best, D-3
2WayNews, 190, D-18–D-19
555 Area Code Finder, D-28

• A •

ABFAnywhere, D-28
ABQJournal, D-19
AcctMinder, 170, D-12
activation
  automatic, 87
  Web site, 87
address books, 16, 83, 91, 94, 149, 164
  PDAs, 84
ADDS Aviation Weather, D-19
Aether Systems, 73, 95
Afronet, D-19
AfterDawn, D-3
air Heart-Consumer, D-19
air Heart-Professional, D-28
Air Santa Claus, D-3, D-4
AirGuitar Wireless, D-3
AirInfo Wireless, D-41
airlines
  Alaska Airlines, D-41
  American Airlines, D-41
  Continental Airlines, D-41
  Delta Airlines, D-42
  Northwest Airlines, D-43
  Sun Country Airlines, D-44
  United Airlines, D-45
Ajbrowser, D-12
Alaska Airlines, D-41
Alcatel, 61
AllLotto, D-4
Alloy, D-4
Allrecipes, D-4
Amazon, D-28, D-38, D-39
America Online. *See* AOL

American Airlines, D-41
Ameritrade, D-13
AMPS (Advanced Mobile Phone Service), 52
analog, 52
antenna, 55, 91–92, 119, 129
  replacement, 212
Antivirus, D-28
AOL, 44–45, 95, 140, D-4
appliance-based computing, 110
applications, 160
ARPAnet, 100
ASCII text file, 207
Astrology.com, D-4
AstrologyIS.com, D-4
Astronomy, D-28
AT&T, 60, 129, 143, 163–164, 202
  Adobe Acrobat, 36
  call forwarding, 35
  call waiting, 35
  caller ID, 35
  detailed billing, 35
  Digital PocketNet, 35–36
  e-mail, 36
  long-distance, 36
  Microsoft Word, 36
  phones, 52
  PocketNet, 35, 36, 129, 133–134
  service provider, 51
  Surf Lounge, 164
  text messages, 35
  three-way calling, 35
  Time Division Multiple Access (TDMA), 52
  voice mail, 35
  Web site, 36
  wired ISP, 36
  wireless carrier, 36
  Wireless customers, 182
ATM Finder, 170, D-13
Atomica, D-28
attachments, 125–126, 128, 207
Audiovox, 61
automatic recognition, 107–108

• B •

BaAlien, D-29
BaChess, D-4
bandwidth, 11
  intensive, 125
BaNetMon, D-29
Bank of America, 168
Bank of America HomeBanking, D-13
BaPolitical, D-29
Barnes&Noble, D-39
BarPoint, D-39
BaSatellite, D-29
Baseball
  Birthdays, D-19
  Encyclopedia, D-19
  Live, D-19
Basketball Live, D-20
BaTime, D-29
batteries, 59
  lithium, 211
Beam
  MP3, D-29
  Music, D-4
Bell South Wireless Data. *See* Cingular
belt clip, 211
Beyond The Bull, 169, 171, D-13
BigCharts, D-13
Bike-Zone, D-20
Biojump, D-20
BioMedNet
  Medicine, D-29
  Molecular Biology Quick Reference, D-29
Biotech Watch News and Milestones, D-20
Biztravel, D-41
Bloomberg, D-13
BluWater Bistro, D-41
Body1, D-29
Bolt, D-5
Book4golf, D-20
BookingZone, D-41
BookMarkManager, D-29
BooksBTC, D-5
Boston Harbor Marine Forecast, D-41
BoxerJam, D-5
BrainBuzz, D-30
Britannica, D-5
  Traveler, D-30

browsing, 153, 158
business
  communication, 2
  e-mail, 43
  electronic, 11
  needs, 21
  news, 19
  Nextel Online, 38
  PDAs, 85
  people, 18–19
  wireless Internet, 11
Buy.com, D-39
bytes, 124

• C •

cables, 125, 135, 148
cache store, 162
calendars, 23, 91, 94, 148
  computer, 145, 150
  corporate network, 19
  electronic, 11, 17, 44, 145–146
  Microsoft Outlook, 44–45
  Palm, 147
  paper, 150
  PDAs, 77, 83–84, 147
  personal, 22
  phone, 150
  quick tips, 149–150
  RIM BlackBerry, 73, 81
  Web-based, 11, 145, 149
  wireless, 145
call
  forwarding, 32, 35, 37–38, 59
  waiting, 32, 35, 37–39
caller ID, 32, 35, 37–39
car computer, 116
Casio, 61
Catavault, D-30
CBS MarketWatch, D-13
CDMA (Code Division Multiple Access), 52–53
CD-ROMs, 81, 116
Central Carolina Technical College Online, D-30
charger
  desktop kit, 211–212
  travel, 211
Charles Schwab, D-13

Charts2Go, D-14
Chase's Calendar of Events, D-30
chat. *See* instant messages
chess, D-4
ChoiceHotels, D-41
Cingular, 165
  call forwarding, 38
  call waiting, 38
  caller ID, 38
  detailed billing, 38
  roaming, 38
  service plans, 38
  three-way calling, 38
  Time Division Multiple Access (TDMA), 52
  voice mail, 38
  Web site, 38
City Stages Schedule, D-5
CitySearch, D-5
Claritybank, D-14
ClipACoupon, 186
ClubFONE, D-5
CNBC, D-14
CNET News, D-20
CNN, D-20
Cocktail Wireless, D-6
CollectingChannel, D-6
College Football Live, D-20
combinations, 113, 115, 203
communication
  business, 2
  natural, 117
communications standard. *See* protocol
Compaq, 89, 95
  Home Internet Appliance, 111
  Internet Explorer, 96
  iPAQ, 90, 95–96, 111
  Microsoft Outlook, 96
  Web site, 96
  Windows CE, 96
computer
  appliance-based, 112
  browser, 89
  calendars, 150
  cars, 116
  desktop, 28, 81, 83, 89–91, 94, 104, 159
  synchronization, 164
Concord EFS, D-14
connection
  wired, 26
  wireless, 27

connection hardware, 26, 199
  cable, 125, 135
  DSL, 125, 135
  satellite, 125, 135
contact, 132
Continental Airlines, D-41
ConvertIT, D-6
cookies, 206–207
Countrywide Home Loans, 171, D-14
coverage maps, 29
CQUAD, D-20
cradle, 159
credit cards, 170, 178, 202
  discounts, 179
  Discover, 168
  MasterCard, 168, 170, D-16
  theft, 179
  Visa, 170
CSFBdirect Anywhere, D-14
Currency Calculator PQA, 171, D-14
Curses!, D-6
customizable user experience, 108–109
Cyphotilapia Frontosa, D-30

● *Ɒ* ●

data manipulation, 108
DealTime, D-39
Delta Airlines, D-42
Dennis Miller Demystified, D-21
Denso, 61–62
desktop charger kit, 212
devices
  choosing, 3
  combination, 113, 115, 203
  exploring, 12
  future, 99, 109–114, 116–119
  handheld, 1, 15, 42
  small, 105
  types of, 12
  Web-enabled, 105
  wireless, 3, 5, 11–12, 16, 27, 105, 109, 134,
    158, 168, 191, 199, 205
digital, 52
Discover, 168
Dodgeball, D-6
DorCino Interactive Web Casino, D-6
downloads, 207

DSL, 125, 135
Dummies
  Answer Network, 155
  HTML code, 156
  hyperlinks, 156
  Technology Catalog, 155
  Web site, 155–156
DVD, D-3

• E •

ear piece, 114
Earthlink, 36
Earthoid WAPsearch, D-30
Earthquake, D-21
eBay, D-39
Ebert's Movie Review Archives, D-6
eCompare, D-39
Edmunds.com, D-39
  Automotive Information, D-30
eGolfScore Wireless, D-21
EkNazar, D-31
electronic
  address books, 83
  books, D-5
  business, 11
  calendars, 11, 16, 44, 145–146
eLocal, D-31
e-mail, 1, 2, 4, 9–11, 13, 16, 18, 21–23, 31, 42,
    47, 93, 107–108, 118, 132, 134, 137, 139,
    142, 144, 163–164
  antenna, 129
  attachments, 125–126, 128, 200, 205, 207
  basics of, 123–124, 126
  business, 43
  connectivity, 128, 130
  corporate, 17, 19, 73, 94, 199–200
  Earthlink, 36
  etiquette, 131
  external, 43
  formatting, 207
  forwarding, 44
  internal, 43
  Internet, 69
  MindSpring, 36
  PDAs, 44, 82
  portable, 43
  RCN, 36

  receiving, 130, 132
  sending, 129–130
  understanding, 124, 125, 127, 128
  Web, 44, 135
  wireless, 69, 123, 127, 128, 129, 130, 131, 132
EMAZING, D-6
Emergen2, D-31
encryption, 94, 168, 178, 202
  code, 178
  definition of, 178
Enhanced Data Rates for Global Evolution
    (EDGE), 53
ePriority Wireless, D-14
Ericsson, 62
eSignal, D-15
ESPN, D-21
eStories.com Online Cigar Reference and
    Pricing, D-31
Etak Traffic Touch, D-42
eTrade, D-15
Eudora, 135, 137, 144, 164
EventRunner, D-6
Excite, D-7
  Mobile, D-21
Exereo Unplugged, D-31
Expedia, D-42
expense tracking, 85

• F •

Fairwinds Credit Union, D-15
Fandango, D-7
Fboweb, D-31
FedEx, D-31
Fidelty Investments InstantBroker, D-15
figures
  appliance-based computing, 112
  car computer, 116
  combination devices, 62, 113–115
  electronic calendar, 146–147
  e-mail, 125, 127–128, 130, 136–137
  external e-mail, 43
  future devices, 116–119
  HP Jornada, 97
  HTML code, 101–102, 156
  hyperlinks, 156, 158
  icon-based screen, 58
  internal e-mail, 43

Internet phone keyboard, 56
Internet phone screen, 57
ISPs (Internet Service Providers), 45
Motorola pager, 74–75
MyMotivator homepage, 88–89, 194
mySimon, 181
pagers, 70
Palm PDA, 147, 159, 161
PDA address book, 84
PDA cradle, 82
PDA datebook, 84
PDA screen, 80
PDA To Do list, 86
PDAs, 79, 90, 133, 160
QWERTY keyboard, 79
RIM Blackberry, 73, 93
stylus-based PDA, 80
Web site, 134, 160, 186, 188–192, 194,
    214–215, 217
Web-enabled pager, 15
Web-enabled phone, 14, 62–64, 163
wired Internet connection, 26
wireless Internet connection, 27, 127–128,
    130, 163
wireless PDA, 17
wireless tower, 70
FinalFour.net, D-21
Finance Wireless, D-15
financial
    management, 20, 167, 169, 171
    news, 19, 47
    transactions, 167
    Web sites, 11, 22
fine print, 33–34
FireDispatch, D-31
First Call Wireless, D-15
FitForAll, D-31
flight information, 19
fnCentral Mobile, D-15
FoneSync Pro, 148, 164
    Web sites, 149, 164
Food & Drink, D-42
Football Live, D-21
Forward Day By Day, D-7
FoxSports, D-21
Free Online Dictionary of Computing, D-32
Freightgate, D-32
Frisco Business Web, D-32
Frommer's City to Go, D-42

FRT2go, D-15
FSU Weather, D-21
FTD, D-40
Funnies, The, D-7
FUNNY, D-7

• *G* •

Galaxies, D-32
Gallup Organization, The, D-7
Gas Finder, D-42
GE PressRoom, D-21
General Packet Radio Service (GPRS), 53
Gensite, D-33
Get Zip, D-32
GetThere DirectMobile, D-42
GetWhispers, D-16
GiftCertificates.com, D-40
Gist TV Listings, D-33
Global Communicator, D-32
GMAC Real Estate, D-32
Go, 135, D-22
Go Network
    People, D-32
    Translator To Go, D-32
Go2, D-7
GodsWord, D-7
golden1.com Wireless, D-16
GolfServ's Wireless GolfGuide, D-22
Graffiti software, 92
graphics, 205
GroupLotto, D-7
GroupWise, 73
GSM (Global System for Mobile
    Communications), 52–53
Gutenburg Bible, D-32
Guy Rules, D-8

• *H* •

handheld devices. *See* PDAs
handle, 140
Handspring, 16
handwriting recognition. *See* Graffiti software
hardware, 26–27
Harris Bank, 168, D-16
HDML (Handheld Devices Markup
    Language), 53

headset, 210
HealthChannel, The, D-37
HealthGate's Medicine, D-33
HealthGrades, D-33
Hollywood.com, D-8
home page, 154, 162
homedeck, 164
Homes.com, D-33
Homestore.com, D-33
Horoscope, D-8
Hotmail, 44, 135, 149
HP Jornada 540 Series
  features, 97
  USB (Universal Serial Bus), 96
  Web site, 97
  Windows CE, 96
HTML (Hypertext Markup Language), 53, 100,
    102–103, 153
  code, 101, 155–156
  commands, 155
  hyperlink, 155
HTTP (Hypertext Transfer Protocol), 53, 100,
    102, 153
Hungry Minds, Inc., 172
Hurricane, D-22
hyperlink, 102, 154–157
  Dummies, 156

intuitive, 72, 80
  simple, 106
Internet
  ARPAnet, 100
  connectivity, 92
  exploring, 9
  future of, 107–109
  having fun, 195
  history of, 100–101, 103
  Multimedia, 208
  returns, 179, 181–182
  satellite, 26
  shipping, 179–181
  shopping, 20, 173–177, 179–186, 209
  sports, 188–190
  wired connection, 26
  wireless, 118, 139, 143, 153, 167, 169
  wireless connection, 27
Internet Beatles Album, The, D-5
Internet Explorer, 14, 96, 153, 206
Intranet Design Magazine Unwired, D-22
Investing Online For Dummies,
    3rd Edition, 172
Iqradio, D-8
IRC (Internet Relay Chat), 140
Island BookViewer, D-16
ISP (Internet Service Provider), 25–27, 32, 36,
    44–45, 100–109, 124–127, 135, 140, 157
IWIN, D-22

• I •

icons, 6, 157. *See also* micons
In-N-Out Burger Locator, D-33
index page, 154
Indiqu Mobile Entertainment, D-8
infoBrand
  My Weather Center, 190–191
InfoBrand Weather Center, D-22
InfoCub, D-8
InfoSpace, D-8
instant messages, 12, 15, 45–47, 68–70, 71–72,
    139–144
  definition of, 139–140
  e-mail, 141
  understanding, 142
Interact.com, D-16
interactivity, 109
interface, 56, 114
  human, 111
  icon-based, 58

• J •

JB Oxford, D-16
Joe Bryant's CheatSheets, D-22
Joke, D-8
Jokes2Go, D-8

• K •

Katrillion, D-8, D-9
Keen, D-9
Kenmore Air Seaplanes, D-42
keyboard, 112
  alphabet, 114
  easy-to-use, 72
  onscreen, 78, 80, 97
  QWERTY, 67, 78

keypad
  alphanumeric, 56
  interface, 13
  numeric, 114
  PDAs, 78
  phone, 56, 163
KraftFoods, D-33
Kyocera, 63
  Smartphone, 115

• *L* •

laptop, 10, 42–43
launch pages, 88
legislation, telecommunications, 29
Limo Wireless, D-42
Lind Anywhere Futures Trading, D-16
link. *See* hyperlink
Link2Semi, D-22
LinksTime, D-22
Linux Today, D-23
LIRR Schedule, D-43
LockOn Movies, D-9
Lookup, D-33
Lottery, D-9
lottery, D-4
Lotus
  Domino, 39, 44, 73, 94, 134, 199
  Notes, 73, 134
lyrics, D-3

• *M* •

Macintosh computers, 32, 103
Magic 8-Ball Oracle, D-9
MapQuest, D-43
MarketWatch, D-16
Martindale-Hubbell Wireless Lawyer Locator,
    D-34
MassTimes, D-34
MasterCard, 168, 170, D-16
MCI WorldCom Telecom Library, D-34
MedFetch, D-34
Media Player, 106
MediaJobz, D-34
Medical
  Dictionary, D-34
  Glossary, D-34
  Toolkit for Problems and Treatments of
      Veins, D-34

memos, 85
Merriam-Webster, 193–194, D-35
messages
  definition of, 72
  direct, 12
  guaranteed delivery, 71
  instant, 12, 15, 45–47, 68–72, 139–144
  paging, 32, 139
  phone, 139
  short text, 12
  text, 32, 35, 59
  two-way, 39
  wireless, 45
micons, D-3
  entertainment, D-3
  FAQs, D-3
  financial information, D-3
  news information, D-3
  search engine, D-3
  secured information, D-3
  shopping, D-3
  travel information, D-3
microbrowser, 162
microphone, 114
Microsoft
  Exchange, 94, 96, 134, 199
  Outlook, 73, 96, 132, 134, 135–136, 145–146,
      148, 164
MindSpring, 36
mini-keyboard, 16
Mitsubishi, 63
Mobile PalmCentral, D-23
Mobilicious, D-23
modem, 52, 96, 103
  cable, 26
  DSL, 26
  wireless, 27, 34
monitor, 112
monthly fees, 30
MooVRevu, D-9
MorseCode, D-35
Motorola, 64
  PageWriter 2000X, 75
  PICs (Personal Interactive Communicators),
      72–73
  Talkabout T900 2way, 74
  Timeport P930, 75
  Timeport P935 2way, 74
  Web site, 73

Moviefone, D-9
MSN, 44–45, 126, 140, 157
  Messenger, 45
  Mobile, 39, D-9
MTV, D-9
multiple-function products, 110
MyMotivator, 88–89, 194
mySimon.com, 157–159, 161, 177, 181, D-40
MysteryNet, D-9
myTrack, D-17

• N •

National Academies, D-35
National Science Foundation, 100
Nautical Wireless, D-43
NeoPoint, 64
  2000, 162
  NP1000, 58
Net Tool Box, D-35
Netscape, 14, 135, 140, 149, 153, 205–206
New York Times Digital, D-23
news information, 10, 11, 22, 47, 187
  business, 19
  financial, 19
  receiving, 187
NewsJunkie, D-23
NextBusTransit Information, D-43
NextDoor, D-43
Nextel Online, 38, 143
  browsing, 39
  cellular phone, 39
  connectivity kit, 39
  e-mail, 39
  Lotus Domino, 39
  Microsoft Exchange, 39
  MSN Mobile, 39
  two-way messaging, 39
  Web sites, 39
  wireless service, 44
nGame, D-10
Nissan Car Quote, D-35
NOAA Xpress, D-23, D-24
Nokia, 65
Northwest Airlines, D-43
nPorta, D-23
Nutrient Database, D-35
NWS Corpus Christi, D-23
NY Info Wireless, D-35

• O •

OAG Mobile, D-43
online concierge, D-3
Openwave
  Company, 15
  Mobile Browser, 162, 164
  Systems, 148
ORTCOnline, D-17
overlisting, 149

• P •

pagers, 12
  catalog of, 72
  choosing, 71
  e-mail, 67–68
  features of, 68–69
  guaranteed message delivery, 71
  high-resolution screen, 67
  Motorola Personal Interactive
    Communicators, 73–75
  one-way, 68, 70
  RIM BlackBerry 950, 72, 73
  scroll buttons, 67
  service plans, 67, 69
  service provider, 72
  two-way, 68, 70, 71, 73
  understanding, 67, 68
  Web-enabled, 1, 3, 5, 12–13, 15–17, 27–28, 46,
    48, 67–69, 72, 112, 139–140, 142–144, 200
Palm, 115, 161
  address book, 91
  calendars, 44, 81, 91, 147
  CD, 158
  e-mail, 91–92, 135
  features, 91
  Free Memory Bar, 161
  Graffiti character set, 78
  hyperlinks, 157
  ISPs, 44, 94
  m500, 44, 91
  m505, 44, 91
  Mobile PalmCentral, D-23
  Organizer News, D-24
  organizers, 16
  OS, 79–81
  Palm.net, 28, 44, 92, 134–135, 158,
    201–202, D-2

PGHQ website, D-35
Query Apps (PQAs), 158
VIIx, 23, 44, 83, 91, 129, 157–159, 201–202
Web site, 81
wireless Internet models, 28, 91
wireless plans, 92
Palm PQA
  2WayNews, D-19
  555 Area Code Finder, D-28
  ADDS Aviation Weather, D-19
  air Heart-Professional, D-28
  Amazon, D-28
  Astronomy, D-28
  ATM Finder, D-13
  Atomica, D-28
  Baseball Encyclopedia, D-19
  BeamMP3, D-29
  BookMarkManager, D-29
  Boston Harbor Marine Forecast, D-41
  Chase's Calendar of Events, D-30
  City Stages Schedule, D-5
  CNBC, D-14
  Cocktail Wireless, D-6
  Currency Calculator, D-14
  Curses!, D-6
  Cyphotilapia Frontosa, D-30
  Ebert's Movie Review Archives, D-6
  Emergen2, D-31
  eStories.com Online Cigar Reference and
    Pricing, D-31
  FinalFour.net, D-21
  Free Online Dictionary of Computing, D-32
  Freightgate, D-32
  Gas Finder, D-42
  GE PressRoom, D-21
  Get Zip, D-32
  GMAC Real Estate, D-32
  Go Network People, D-32
  Go Network's Translator To Go, D-32
  Gutenburg Bible, D-32
  HealthChannel, The, D-37
  HealthGate's Medicine, D-33
  Horoscope, D-8
  In-N-Out Burger Locator, D-33
  IWIN, D-22
  Jokes2Go, D-8
  LockOn Movies, D-9
  Lookup, D-33
  Lottery, D-9
  MassTimes, D-34
  MCI WorldCom Telecom Library, D-34
  MedFetch, D-34
  Medical Dictionary, D-34
  Medical Glossary, D-34
  Medical Toolkit for Problems and
    Treatments of Veins, D-34
  Net Tool Box, D-35
  NewsJunkie, D-23
  NextDoor, D-43
  NOAA Xpress, D-23, D-24
  Nutrient Database, D-35
  Pen Computing News, D-24
  Physics ePrint Search, D-35
  Play for Fun Wireless, D-10
  Powerboats4sale, D-36
  Public Radio, D-36
  Random Quote, D-10
  RDS Airport, D-10
  Rep Dining Guide, The, D-44
  Restaurant Row, D-44
  Salon.com, D-24
  Seattle Traffic Viewer, D-44
  Seattle Weather, D-24
  Silicon Alley Events, D-36
  Ski Resorts, D-23
  Stable Mail, D-11
  Stanford Theatre/Palo Alto Weekly, D-11
  Star Trek Voyager Airdates and News, D-11
  Sun and Moon, D-36–D-37
  Sushi Wireless, D-37
  Taxi Finder, D-44–D-45
  Textprices, D-37
  THOMAS Legislative Database, D-37
  Tim Nicholson's Palm Zone, D-24
  Travelape, D-45
  U.S. Time, D-37
  U.S. Trademark Search, D-37
  Ucook, D-37
  US West Dex, D-38
  USTA Boys' Tennis, D-26
  Vicinity BrandFinder, D-45
  Weather Radar, D-27
  WeatherClip, D-38
  Wireless Books, D-38
  WRAL-Raleigh, NC, D-26
  X-Files Airdates, The, D-12
  Zagat Restaurant, D-46
Paymaster Direct Home Branching, D-17

PDAlive, D-24
PDAntic, D-24
PDAs, 3, 15–16, 28, 34, 44–45, 68, 73, 110, 132,
    190, 201, 207
  address books, 16, 84
  Alive, D-24
  applications, 81
  attachments, 18, 90
  business, 85
  Buyers Guide, D-24
  cables, 148
  calendars, 16, 77, 83–84, 147–148
  catalog, 91–92
  choosing, 77
  Compaq iPAQ, 95
  connectivitiy, 87
  cradles, 148, 82
  definition of, 77
  desktop computer, 81
  e-mail, 44, 77, 82, 86, 89–90, 148
  expense tracking, 85
  hard drive, 16
  Internet access, 77, 86
  intuitive interface, 80
  keypad, 78
  kilobyte basis, 87
  launch pages, 88
  memory, 16
  memos, 85
  Microsoft Outlook, 82
  mini-keyboard, 16
  modem, 39
  onscreen keyboard, 78, 80
  operating system, 79–81
  primary types, 78
  processor, 16
  QWERTY keyboard, 79
  RIM BlackBerry, 93–95
  secure information, 86
  storing data, 132–133
  stylus, 78–80
  surfing, 158, 162
  synchronization cradle, 159, 164
  to do list, 86
  touch-sensitive screen, 16
  transmitter, 87
  understanding, 78, 82–83
  Web-enabled, 5, 12–13, 17, 27, 46, 112,
      127–128, 133, 139–140, 143, 158, 173,
      203, D-2
  Windows CE, 81
  wireless, 17, 23, 116
PeakAdventures, D-43
Pen Computing News, D-24
personal communicators. *See* pagers,
    Web-enabled
personal information management services,
    149
PGA.com, D-24
PGHQ, D-35
Philips, 65
  Xenium GSM, 117
Phone.com, 53
phones
  accessories, 59, 209–212
  Alcatel, 61
  analog, 52–53
  antenna, 55
  Audiovox, 61
  batteries, 59
  calendars, 150
  call forwarding, 59
  case, 55, 60, 211
  Casio, 61
  cellular, 13, 16, 19, 39, 42, 68–69, 109
  choosing, 59
  clamshell design, 55
  comfort, 54–55, 60
  companies, 27
  Denso, 61–62
  dialing, 13
  digital, 53
  dual-band, 53
  durability, 55
  e-mail, 59
  Ericsson, 62
  features, 59
  flip design, 55
  GSM, 143
  holding, 54
  interface, 56
  Internet features, 54
  jacks, 43
  keypad, 56, 163
  Kyocera, 63
  manufacturers, 60–61
  minutes, 30
  Mitsubishi, 63
  mobile, 117
  models, 212

Motorola, 64
Motorola StarTAC, 55
NeoPoint, 64
Nokia, 65
Philips, 65
programmable features, 59
ring options, 59
ring vibration, 59
Samsung, 65
Sanyo, 65
screen, 57–59
service provider, 29
shapes, 55
Siemens, 65
single-band, 53
size, 55, 59
storing data, 129, 133
surfing, 162
synchronization, 164
technology, 52, 53
text messaging, 59
Time Division Multiple Access (TDMA), 53
voice recognition, 59
WAP, 60
Web-enabled, 1, 3, 5, 11–15, 17, 23, 27–29, 34, 37, 44, 47–48, 51, 53–54, 60, 112, 127–128, 133, 139–140, 142–144, 148, 158, 162–165, 173, 199, 203, 206, D-2
wireless, 34, 46, 211
Physics ePrint Search, D-35
Play for Fun Wireless, D-10
PlugnPay Unplugged, D-17
Pocket Authorize.Net, D-17
Pocket Blue Book, D-35
PocketWineList, D-43
port
serial, 82
USB, 82
portable information, 42
portals, 11
personal, 36
Powerboats4sale, D-36
PQAs, 159, D-2, D-5–D-6, D-8–D-14, D-18–D-19, D-21–D-38, D-42–D-46
Compaq iPAQ, 96
HP Jornada 540 Series, 96–97
Progressive Wireless Internet Manager, D-17
protocol, 13, 124, 140
network, 100

POP3 mail, 44
Prudential, 169, D-17
Public Radio, D-36

• Q •

QOD Pilot, D-10
QWERTY keyboard, 67, 78–79, 93

• R •

Radio Talk Shows, D-36
Random Quote, D-10
RCN, 36
RDS Airport, D-10
RealCities.com Wireless, D-24
RealPlayer, 106
recipes, D-4
Reference/Resources, D-36
Regal Cinemas Movie Search, D-10
removable faceplate, 209
Rep Dining Guide, The, D-44
Restaurant Row, D-44
Rick-T-Land.com-on the Go, D-10
RIM (Research In Motion)
AOL, 95
Compaq, 95
Java, 95. *See also* RIM BlackBerry
RIM BlackBerry, 16, 78, 80, 93, 96, 134, 148, 199
950, 72–73, 93
957, 72, 93
address book, 94
Aether Systems, 95
Ask@OracleMobile, 94
calendars, 44, 73, 81, 94, 148
corporate e-mail, 94
Enterprise edition, 94
Go.Web, 95
Internet edition, 94
intuitive interface, 72
ISPs, 94
keyboard, 72
Lotus Domino, 44, 73
Microsoft Exchange, 44, 73
pager, 44
PDA, 44
PocketGenie, 95

RIM BlackBerry *(continued)*
 QWERTY keyboard, 93
 Web site, 73, 95
ring
 options, 59
 vibrations, 59
roaming, 37, 38
RomeozuluWX, D-10
Rovenet, 171
Rush MP3, 117

• S •

SailBoats4Sale, D-36
SalesMountain, D-40
Salon.com, D-24
Samsung, 65
Santa Claus, D-3
Sanyo, 65
satellite, 26, 125, 135
 mini-satellite dish, 26
screen, 114
 graphics, 58
 high-resolution, 67
 icons, 58
 monochrome, 205
 size, 59
Seattle Traffic Viewer, D-44
Seattle Weather, D-24
secure information, 86, 162
server, 112
service plans, 51, 129, 199, 201
 AT&T, 35–36
 call forwarding, 32
 call waiting, 32
 caller ID, 32
 cancellation, 33
 Cingular, 38
 e-mail, 34, 37
 evaluating, 30–31
 flat rate, 31–32, 37
 free usage, 30–31
 higher monthly minute, 31
 Internet, 37
 long-distance coverage, 31, 33
 low minute, 30
 minutes, 31
 monthly rates, 69, 96
 Nextel, 38–39

pagers, 67
paging messages, 32
promotional, 31, 34
Sprint PCS, 37
text messages, 32
unused minutes, 34
URLs, 34
usage, 71
Verizon, 37–38
voice mail, 32, 37
VoiceStream, 39
wireless, 33
service provider
 AT&T, 29
 Cingular, 29
 pagers, 72
 PDAs, 87
 phones, 29
 Sprint, 29
 Verizon, 29
Shamach-Kosher Restaurant Database, D-44
Share-A-Note, D-36
Shecky's Bar, Club & Lounge Guide, D-44
ShopNow, D-40
SHTTP (Secure HTTP), 168
Shul Finder, D-44
ShuttleCAM, D-36
Siemens, 65
Silicon
 Philly, D-25
Silicon Alley Events, D-36
Silicon Investor, D-17
Sindell, Kathleen, 172
Ski Resorts, D-23
SMS (Short Message Service), 143
SMTP (Simple Mail Transfer Protocol), 124
SonicNet, D-10
Soundload's Music Encyclopedia, D-10
space savers, 110
spam, 144
SportsDrill, D-25
SportsFeed, D-25
SportsXL Amateur Sports News, D-25
Sprint PCS, 60, 129, 143
 call forwarding, 37
 call waiting, 37
 caller ID, 37
 Code Division Multiple Access (CDMA), 52
 e-mail, 37
 flat rate plan, 37

Internet, 37
numeric paging, 37
phones, 52
service provider, 51
three-way calling, 37
voice mail, 37
Web site, 37
Spyonit Mobile, D-36
Stable Mail, D-11
Stanford Theatre/Palo Alto Weekly, D-11
Star Trek Voyager Airdates and News, D-11
Starbuck's Coffee Store Locator, D-44
StarCD-Realtime radio song id, D-11
STATS Inc, D-25
stock
  market, 11–12, 20, 23
  quotes, 10
  Web sites, 108, 167
Stock100, D-18
StockBoss Interactive, D-18
StoreRunner, D-40
stylus, 79, 80, 93, 159
  definition of, 78
Sun and Moon, D-36, D-37
Sun Country Airlines, D-44
sun glasses, 119
surfing, 1, 157, 158, 162, 205
Sushi Wireless, D-37
Sweet16*com, D-11
Swell.com, D-25
synchronization, 148
  cradle, 159
  phones, 164

● T ●

Taxi Finder, D-44, D-45
TCP/IP (Transmission Control Protocol and
    Internet Protocol), 100, 102, 178
TD Waterhouse Wireless, D-18
TDES (Triple Data Encryption Standard), 94
TDwaterhouse.com, 169
Techdirt, D-25
TeeMaster, D-25
Teetimes, D-25
telecommunications legislation, 29
Texans Credit Union, D-18
Texas Credit Union, 168
Textprices, D-37
Theme Park Insider, D-11

TheSouthSide, D-11
TheStreet.com, D-25
ThinkersGroup WAP Browser, D-37
THOMAS Legislative Database, D-37
Ticketmaster, D-11
Tim Nicholson's Palm Zone, D-24
Time Division Multiple Access (TDMA), 52
Titleserv, D-18
TNL.net, D-26
touch-sensitive screen, 16
TrafficStation, D-45
Trailworks, D-45
transmission, analog, 52
transmitter, 87
travel
  help, 191–193
travel charger, 210–211
Travelape, D-45
Traveler SOS, D-45
Travelocity, D-45
TRIP.com, D-45
Truckline Wireless, D-26
Tu Horoscopo, D-12

● U ●

U.S. Advanced Research Projects Agency, 100
U.S. Congress, 29
U.S. Time, D-37
U.S. Trademark Search, D-37
Ucook, D-37
Unisys To Go, D-26
United Airlines, D-45
Universal Weather and Aviation, D-26
UP.Browser, 15, 16, 53, 60
UPS Shipping, D-37
Upseek Job Search, D-38
URLs, 34, 157
US West Dex, D-38
USA Today, D-26
USAB, 168, D-18
USB (Universal Serial Bus), 96
USTA Boys' Tennis, D-26

● V ●

Venturewire, D-26
Verizon, 60, 143
  call waiting, 37
  caller ID, 37

Verizon *(continued)*
  CDMA (Code Division Multiple Access), 52
  roaming, 37
  service provider, 51
  SuperPages, D-38
  Web sites, 37, 38
VH1, D-12
Vicinity BrandFinder, D-38, D-45
Visa, 168, 170
Visa ATM, D-18
VisitCorvallis, D-46
voice
  mail, 23, 32, 35, 37–39
  recognition, 59
VoiceStream
  call waiting, 39
  caller ID, 39
  detailed billing, 39
  InfoStream, 39
  paging, 39
  text messaging, 39
  voice mail, 39
  Web sites, 39
  Wireless Enotes, 39

• W •

Wall Street Journal, The, D-27
WAP (Web Application Protocol), 13, 21, 53,
    60, 102–103, 135, 162, 168, 170
  compliant sites, D-2
  ThinkersGroup WAP Browser, D-37
  WAPsight.com, D-26
WAPsight.com, D-26
Washingtonpost.com, D-27
WCDMA (Wideband Code Division Multiple
    Access), 53
WealthHound, D-18
Weather Channel, The, D-27–D-28
Weather Guys, The, D-27
Weather Radar, D-27
Weather Underground, The, D-27
WeatherClip, D-38
WeatherNet, D-27
Web
  addressing, 154
  applications, 160
  browser, 14, 15, 153, 157–158, 206

  calendars, 149
  clippings, 88
  e-mail, 44
  microbrowser, 14
  pages, 10
  portals, 11
  surfing, 157, 206
  wireless, 157
Web sites
  1-800-TAXICAB, D-40
  10Best, D-3
  2WayNews, 190, D-18
  ABC News, 46, 48, 187
  ABF Anywhere, D-28
  ABQJournal, D-19
  AcctMinder, 170, D-12
  Afronet, D-19
  AfterDawn, D-3
  air Heart–Consumer, D-19
  Air Santa Claus, D-3–D-4
  AirGuitar Wireless, D-3
  AirInfo Wireless, D-41
  Ajbrowser, D-12
  Alaska Airlines, D-41
  AllLotto, D-4
  Alloy, D-4
  Allrecipes, D-4
  Amazon, D-38–D-39
  American Airlines, D-41
  Ameritrade, 20, 171, D-13
  Antivirus, D-28
  AOL, D-4
  Astrology.com, D-4
  AstrologyIS.com, D-4
  AT&T, 36
  BaAlien, D-29
  BaChess, D-4
  BaNetMon, D-29
  Bank of America HomeBanking, D-13
  BaPolitical, D-29
  Barnes&Noble, D-39
  BarPoint, D-39
  BaSatellite, D-29
  Baseball Birthdays, D-19
  Baseball Live, D-19
  Basketball Live, D-20
  BaTime, D-29
  BeamMusic, D-4
  Beyond The Bull, 169, 171, D-13

BigCharts, D-13
Bike-Zone, D-20
Biojump, D-20
BioMedNet Medicine, D-29
BioMedNet Molecular Biology Quick
     Reference, D-29
Biztravel, D-41
Bloomberg, 169, D-13
BluWater Bistro, D-41
Body1, D-29
Bolt, D-5
Book4golf, D-20
BookingZone, D-41
BooksBTC, D-5
BoxerJam, D-5
BrainBuzz, D-30
Britannica, D-5
Britannica Traveler, D-30
Buy.com, D-39
cartoons, 21
Catavault, D-30
CBS Market Watch, 12, 169, 171, D-13
Cellular Telecommunications & Internet
     Association, 215
Central Carolina Technical College Online,
     D-30
Charles Schwab, 12, 46, 169, D-13
Charts2Go, D-14
chess, D-4
ChoiceHotels, D-41
Cingular, 38
CitySearch, D-5
Claritybank, D-14
ClipACoupon, 186
ClubFONE, D-5
CNBC, 169
CNET News, D-20
CNN, 12, 46, 187, D-20
CollectingChannel, D-6
College Football Live, D-20
Compaq iPAQ, 96
Concord EFS, D-14
Continental Airlines, D-41
ConvertIT, D-6
Countrywide Home Loans, 171, D-14
CQUAD, D-20
CSFBdirect Anywhere, D-14
DealTime, D-39
Delta Airlines, D-42
Dennis Miller Demystified, D-21

Dodgeball, D-6
DorCino Interactive Web Casino, D-6
driving directions, 47, 192
DVD, D-3
Earthoid WAPsearch, D-30
Earthquake, D-21
eBay, D-39
eCompare, D-39
Edmunds.com, D-39
Edmunds.com Automotive Information,
     D-30
eGolfScore Wireless, D-21
EkNazar, D-31
electronic books, D-5
eLocal, D-31
EMAZING, D-6
entertainment, D-2–D-12
ePriority Wireless, D-14
eSignal, D-15
ESPN, D-21
Etak Traffic Touch, D-42
eTrade, 20, 169, D-15
EventRunner, D-6
Excite, D-7
Excite Mobile, D-21
Exereo Unplugged, D-31
Expedia, D-42
Fairwinds Credit Union, D-15
Fandango, D-7
Fboweb, D-31
FedEx, D-31
Fidelity, 20
Fidelity Investments InstantBroker, D-15
Finance Wireless, D-15
financial, 12, 20, 22, D-12–D-18
FireDispatch, D-31
First Call Wireless, D-15
FitForAll, D-31
flight information, 19, 47
fnCentral Mobile, D-15
FoneSync, 149, 164
Food & Drink, D-42
Football Live, D-21
For Dummies, 154–156
Forward Day By Day, D-7
FoxSports, D-21
Frisco Business Web, D-32
Frommer's City to Go, D-42
FRT2go, D-15

Web sites *(continued)*
FSU Weather, D-21
FTD, D-40
Funnies, The, D-7
FUNNY, D-7
Gadgeteer, The, 216
Galaxies, D-32
Gallup Organization, The, D-7
games, 11
Gensite, D-33
GetThere DirectMobile, D-42
GetWhispers, D-16
GiftCertificates.com, D-40
Gist TV Listings, D-33
Global Communicator, D-32
Go, D-22
Go2, D-7
GodsWord, D-7
golden1.com Wireless, D-16
GolfServ's Wireless GolfGuide, D-22
Google, 157
GroupLotto, D-7
Guy Rules, D-8
Harris Bank Wireless, D-16
HealthGrades, D-33
Hollywood.com, D-8
Homes.com, D-33
Homestore.com, D-33
HP Jornada, 97
Hungry Minds, 5
Hurricane, D-22
Indiqu Mobile Entertainment, D-8
InfoBrank Weather Center, D-22
InfoCub, D-8
InfoSpace, D-8
instant messaging, 47
Interact.com, D-16
interest rates, 171
Internet Beatles Album, The, D-5
Internet phone reviews, 60
Internet Wireless Access, 215
Intranet Design Magazine Unwired, D-22
Iqradio, D-8
Island BookViewer, D-16
JB Oxford, D-16
Joe Bryant's CheatSheets, D-22
Joke, D-8
Katrillion, D-8, D-9
Keen, D-9
Kenmore Air Seaplanes, D-42

KraftFoods, D-33
Limo Wireless, D-42
Lind Anywhere Futures Trading, D-16
Link2Semi, D-22
LinksTime, D-22
Linux Today, D-23
LIRR Schedule, D-43
lottery, D-4
lyrics, D-3
Magic 8-Ball Oracle, D-9
MapQuest, D-43
maps, 12, 19–20, 46, 192
MarketWatch, D-16
Martindale-Hubbell Wireless Lawyer
    Locator, D-34
MasterCard, 170, D-16
MediaJobz, D-34
Merriam-Webster, D-35
Mobile PalmCentral, D-23
Mobilicious, D-23
MoovVRevu, D-9
MorseCode, D-35
Motorola, 73
Moviefone, D-9
MSN Computing Central, 216
MSN Mobile, D-9
MTV, D-9
MyMotivator, 88–89, 194
mySimon, 157–159, 161, 177, 181, D-40
MysteryNet, D-9
myTrack, D-17
National Academies, D-35
Nautical Wireless, D-43
New York Times Digital, D-23
news information, 4, 11–12, 20, 46, 187, D-3,
    D-18–D-28
NextBus Transit Information, D-43
Nextel Online, 39
nGame, D-10
Nissan Car Quote, D-35
Northwest Airlines, D-43
nPorta, D-23
NWS Corpus Christi, D-23
NY Info Wireless, D-35
OAG Mobile, D-43
Openwave Mobile Browser, 162
ORTCOnline, D-17
Palm, 82
Palm Organizer News, D-24
Paymaster Direct Home Branching, D-17

PDA Buyers Guide, D-24
PDAlive, D-24
PDAntic, D-24
PeakAdventures, D-43
PGA.com, D-24
PGHQ, D-35
PlugnPay Unplugged, D-17
Pocket Authorize.Net, D-17
Pocket Blue Book, D-35
PocketWineList, D-43
popular culture, 21, 23, 48
Progressive Wireless Internet Manager, D-17
Prudential, 169, D-17
QOD Pilot, D-10
Radio Talk Shows, D-36
RealCities.com Wireless, D-24
recipes, D-4
references and dictionaries, D-28–D-38
References/Resources, D-36
Regal Cinemas Movie Search, D-10
restaurant reviews, 47
Rick-T-Land.com-on the Go, D-10
RIM BlackBerry, 73, 95
RomeozuluWX, D-10
Rovenet, 171
SailBoats4Sale, D-36
SalesMountain, D-40
Santa Claus, D-3
search engines, 11
Shamach-Kosher Restaurant Database, D-44
Share-A-Note, D-36
Shecky's Bar, Club & Lounge Guide, D-44
ShopNow, D-40
shopping, 11, 20, 22, 47, 54, 108, 182,
    D-38–D-40
Shul Finder, D-44
ShuttleCAM, D-36
Silicon Investor, D-17
Silicon Philly, D-25
SonicNet, D-10
Soundload's Music Encyclopedia, D-10
sports, 12, 20, 22, 47, 188–189, D-18–D-28
SportsDrill, D-25
SportsFeed, D-25
SportsXL Amateur Sports News, D-25
Sprint PCS, 37, 143
Spyonit Mobile, D-36
Starbuck's Coffee Store Locator, D-44
StarCD-Realtime radio song id, D-11
STATS Inc, D-25

Stock100, D-18
StockBoss Interactive, D-18
stocks, 108
StoreRunner, D-40
Sun Country Airlines, D-44
Sweet16*com, D-11
Swell.com, D-25
TD Waterhouse Wireless, D-18
Tdwireless, 169
Techdirt, D-25
TeeMaster, D-25
Teetimes, D-25
Texans Credit Union, D-18
Theme Park Insider, D-11
TheSouthSide, D-11
TheStreet.com, D-25
ThinkersGroup WAP Browser, D-37
Ticketmaster, D-11
Titleserv, D-18
TNL.net, D-26
TrafficStation, D-45
Trailworks, D-45
travel, 4, 12, 19–20, 22, 46, 187, 191–192,
    D-40–D-46
Traveler SOS, D-45
Travelocity, D-45
TRIP.com, D-45
Truckline Wireless, D-26
Tu Horoscopo, D-12
Unisys To Go, D-26
United Airlines, D-45
Universal Weather and Aviation, D-26
Unstrung, 213
UPS Shipping, D-37
Upseek Job Search, D-38
USA Today, D-26
USAB, D-18
Venturewire, D-26
Verizon, 37, 38
Verizon SuperPages, D-38
VH1, D-12
Vicinity BrandFinder, D-38
Visa, 170
Visa ATM, D-18
VisitCorvallis, D-46
VoiceStream, 39
W@P Forum, The, 216
Wall Street, 20
Wall Street Journal,The, D-27
WAP, 13, 20

Web sites *(continued)*
  WAP-enabled, 163
  WAPsight.com, D-26
  Washingtonpost.com, D-27
  weather, 4, 11, 22, 47, 108, 187, 190, 191
  Weather Channel, The, D-27, D-28
  Weather Guys, The, D-27
  Weather Underground, The, D-27
  WeatherNet, D-27
  Westlaw Wireless, D-38
  Where2Go Public Restroom Locator, D-46
  wireless, D-2
  Wireless GolfNow, D-27
  Wireless Week, 216
  Wireless.com, 217
  WirelessAdvisor, 214
  WirelessDevNet Daily, D-27
  Women.com, D-12
  Worldwide Travel Information, D-46
  WPVI-ABC TV6, D-26
  Yahoo, D-12
  ZDNet, 214
  ZDNET To Go, D-28
Westlaw Wireless, D-38
Where2Go Public Restroom Locator, D-46
Windows
  CE, 79, 81, 96
  Media Player, 106
wireless
  calendars, 145
  connectivity, 17, 25
  devices, 3, 5, 11–12, 16, 27, 158, 168, 191,
      199, 205
    handheld, 11
  FAQs, 199–203

Internet, 143, 153, 167, 169
  business, 11
  definition of, 9, 10
limitations, 205–208
messaging, 45
phones, 211
plans, 92
service providers, 60
tower, 70
voice plans, 30
Web sites, 213–217
Wireless Books, D-38
Wireless GolfNow, D-27
WirelessDevNet Daily, D-27
WML (Wireless Markup Language), 53
Women.com, D-12
Worldwide Travel Information, D-46
WPVI-ABC TV6, D-26
WRAL-Raleigh, NC, D-26

• X •

X-Files Airdates, The, D-12
XML (Extensible Markup Language), 108

• Y •

Yahoo, 44, 135, 140, 149, D-12

• Z •

Zagat Restaurant, D-46
ZDNET To Go, D-28

Notes

Dummies Books™
Bestsellers on Every Topic!

GENERAL INTEREST TITLES

BUSINESS & PERSONAL FINANCE

Accounting For Dummies®	John A. Tracy, CPA	0-7645-5014-4	$19.99 US/$27.99 CAN
Business Plans For Dummies®	Paul Tiffany, Ph.D. & Steven D. Peterson, Ph.D.	1-56884-868-4	$19.99 US/$27.99 CAN
Business Writing For Dummies®	Sheryl Lindsell-Roberts	0-7645-5134-5	$16.99 US/$27.99 CAN
Consulting For Dummies®	Bob Nelson & Peter Economy	0-7645-5034-9	$19.99 US/$27.99 CAN
Customer Service For Dummies®, 2nd Edition	Karen Leland & Keith Bailey	0-7645-5209-0	$19.99 US/$27.99 CAN
Franchising For Dummies®	Dave Thomas & Michael Seid	0-7645-5160-4	$19.99 US/$27.99 CAN
Getting Results For Dummies®	Mark H. McCormack	0-7645-5205-8	$19.99 US/$27.99 CAN
Home Buying For Dummies®	Eric Tyson, MBA & Ray Brown	1-56884-385-2	$16.99 US/$24.99 CAN
House Selling For Dummies®	Eric Tyson, MBA & Ray Brown	0-7645-5038-1	$16.99 US/$24.99 CAN
Human Resources Kit For Dummies®	Max Messmer	0-7645-5131-0	$19.99 US/$27.99 CAN
Investing For Dummies®, 2nd Edition	Eric Tyson, MBA	0-7645-5162-0	$19.99 US/$27.99 CAN
Law For Dummies®	John Ventura	1-56884-860-9	$19.99 US/$27.99 CAN
Leadership For Dummies®	Marshall Loeb & Steven Kindel	0-7645-5176-0	$19.99 US/$27.99 CAN
Managing For Dummies®	Bob Nelson & Peter Economy	1-56884-858-7	$19.99 US/$27.99 CAN
Marketing For Dummies®	Alexander Hiam	1-56884-699-1	$19.99 US/$27.99 CAN
Mutual Funds For Dummies®, 2nd Edition	Eric Tyson, MBA	0-7645-5112-4	$19.99 US/$27.99 CAN
Negotiating For Dummies®	Michael C. Donaldson & Mimi Donaldson	1-56884-867-6	$19.99 US/$27.99 CAN
Personal Finance For Dummies®, 3rd Edition	Eric Tyson, MBA	0-7645-5231-7	$19.99 US/$27.99 CAN
Personal Finance For Dummies® For Canadians, 2nd Edition	Eric Tyson, MBA & Tony Martin	0-7645-5123-X	$19.99 US/$27.99 CAN
Public Speaking For Dummies®	Malcolm Kushner	0-7645-5159-0	$16.99 US/$24.99 CAN
Sales Closing For Dummies®	Tom Hopkins	0-7645-5063-2	$14.99 US/$21.99 CAN
Sales Prospecting For Dummies®	Tom Hopkins	0-7645-5066-7	$14.99 US/$21.99 CAN
Selling For Dummies®	Tom Hopkins	1-56884-389-5	$16.99 US/$24.99 CAN
Small Business For Dummies®	Eric Tyson, MBA & Jim Schell	0-7645-5094-2	$19.99 US/$27.99 CAN
Small Business Kit For Dummies®	Richard D. Harroch	0-7645-5093-4	$24.99 US/$34.99 CAN
Taxes 2001 For Dummies®	Eric Tyson & David J. Silverman	0-7645-5306-2	$15.99 US/$23.99 CAN
Time Management For Dummies®, 2nd Edition	Jeffrey J. Mayer	0-7645-5145-0	$19.99 US/$27.99 CAN
Writing Business Letters For Dummies®	Sheryl Lindsell-Roberts	0-7645-5207-4	$16.99 US/$24.99 CAN

TECHNOLOGY TITLES

INTERNET/ONLINE

America Online® For Dummies®, 6th Edition	John Kaufeld	0-7645-0670-6	$19.99 US/$27.99 CAN
Banking Online Dummies®	Paul Murphy	0-7645-0458-4	$24.99 US/$34.99 CAN
eBay™ For Dummies®, 2nd Edition	Marcia Collier, Roland Woerner, & Stephanie Becker	0-7645-0761-3	$19.99 US/$27.99 CAN
E-Mail For Dummies®, 2nd Edition	John R. Levine, Carol Baroudi, & Arnold Reinhold	0-7645-0131-3	$24.99 US/$34.99 CAN
Genealogy Online For Dummies®, 2nd Edition	Matthew L. Helm & April Leah Helm	0-7645-0543-2	$24.99 US/$34.99 CAN
Internet Directory For Dummies®, 3rd Edition	Brad Hill	0-7645-0558-2	$24.99 US/$34.99 CAN
Internet Auctions For Dummies®	Greg Holden	0-7645-0578-9	$24.99 US/$34.99 CAN
Internet Explorer 5.5 For Windows® For Dummies®	Doug Lowe	0-7645-0738-9	$19.99 US/$28.99 CAN
Researching Online For Dummies®, 2nd Edition	Mary Ellen Bates & Reva Basch	0-7645-0546-7	$24.99 US/$34.99 CAN
Job Searching Online For Dummies®	Pam Dixon	0-7645-0673-0	$24.99 US/$34.99 CAN
Investing Online For Dummies®, 3rd Edition	Kathleen Sindell, Ph.D.	0-7645-0725-7	$24.99 US/$34.99 CAN
Travel Planning Online For Dummies®, 2nd Edition	Noah Vadnai	0-7645-0438-X	$24.99 US/$34.99 CAN
Internet Searching For Dummies®	Brad Hill	0-7645-0478-9	$24.99 US/$34.99 CAN
Yahoo!® For Dummies®, 2nd Edition	Brad Hill	0-7645-0762-1	$19.99 US/$27.99 CAN
The Internet For Dummies®, 7th Edition	John R. Levine, Carol Baroudi, & Arnold Reinhold	0-7645-0674-9	$19.99 US/$27.99 CAN

OPERATING SYSTEMS

DOS For Dummies®, 3rd Edition	Dan Gookin	0-7645-0361-8	$19.99 US/$27.99 CAN
GNOME For Linux® For Dummies®	David B. Busch	0-7645-0650-1	$24.99 US/$37.99 CAN
LINUX® For Dummies®, 2nd Edition	John Hall, Craig Witherspoon, & Coletta Witherspoon	0-7645-0421-5	$24.99 US/$34.99 CAN
Mac® OS 9 For Dummies®	Bob LeVitus	0-7645-0652-8	$19.99 US/$28.99 CAN
Red Hat® Linux® For Dummies®	Jon "maddog" Hall, Paul Sery	0-7645-0663-3	$24.99 US/$37.99 CAN
Small Business Windows® 98 For Dummies®	Stephen Nelson	0-7645-0425-8	$24.99 US/$34.99 CAN
UNIX® For Dummies®, 4th Edition	John R. Levine & Margaret Levine Young	0-7645-0419-3	$19.99 US/$27.99 CAN
Windows® 95 For Dummies®, 2nd Edition	Andy Rathbone	0-7645-0180-1	$19.99 US/$27.99 CAN
Windows® 98 For Dummies®	Andy Rathbone	0-7645-0261-1	$19.99 US/$27.99 CAN
Windows® 2000 For Dummies®	Andy Rathbone	0-7645-0641-2	$19.99 US/$27.99 CAN
Windows® 2000 Server For Dummies®	Ed Tittel	0-7645-0341-3	$24.99 US/$37.99 CAN
Windows® ME Millennium Edition For Dummies®	Andy Rathbone	0-7645-0735-4	$19.99 US/$27.99 CAN

Dummies Books™
Bestsellers on Every Topic!

GENERAL INTEREST TITLES

FOOD & BEVERAGE/ENTERTAINING

Bartending For Dummies®	Ray Foley	0-7645-5051-9	$14.99 US/$21.99 CAN
Cooking For Dummies®, 2nd Edition	Bryan Miller & Marie Rama	0-7645-5250-3	$19.99 US/$27.99 CAN
Entertaining For Dummies®	Suzanne Williamson with Linda Smith	0-7645-5027-6	$19.99 US/$27.99 CAN
Gourmet Cooking For Dummies®	Charlie Trotter	0-7645-5029-2	$19.99 US/$27.99 CAN
Grilling For Dummies®	Marie Rama & John Mariani	0-7645-5076-4	$19.99 US/$27.99 CAN
Italian Cooking For Dummies®	Cesare Casella & Jack Bishop	0-7645-5098-5	$19.99 US/$27.99 CAN
Mexican Cooking For Dummies®	Mary Sue Miliken & Susan Feniger	0-7645-5169-8	$19.99 US/$27.99 CAN
Quick & Healthy Cooking For Dummies®	Lynn Fischer	0-7645-5214-7	$19.99 US/$27.99 CAN
Wine For Dummies®, 2nd Edition	Ed McCarthy & Mary Ewing-Mulligan	0-7645-5114-0	$19.99 US/$27.99 CAN
Chinese Cooking For Dummies®	Martin Yan	0-7645-5247-3	$19.99 US/$27.99 CAN
Etiquette For Dummies®	Sue Fox	0-7645-5170-1	$19.99 US/$27.99 CAN

SPORTS

Baseball For Dummies®, 2nd Edition	Joe Morgan with Richard Lally	0-7645-5234-1	$19.99 US/$27.99 CAN
Golf For Dummies®, 2nd Edition	Gary McCord	0-7645-5146-9	$19.99 US/$27.99 CAN
Fly Fishing For Dummies®	Peter Kaminsky	0-7645-5073-X	$19.99 US/$27.99 CAN
Football For Dummies®	Howie Long with John Czarnecki	0-7645-5054-3	$19.99 US/$27.99 CAN
Hockey For Dummies®	John Davidson with John Steinbreder	0-7645-5045-4	$19.99 US/$27.99 CAN
NASCAR For Dummies®	Mark Martin	0-7645-5219-8	$19.99 US/$27.99 CAN
Tennis For Dummies®	Patrick McEnroe with Peter Bodo	0-7645-5087-X	$19.99 US/$27.99 CAN
Soccer For Dummies®	U.S. Soccer Federation & Michael Lewiss	0-7645-5229-5	$19.99 US/$27.99 CAN

HOME & GARDEN

Annuals For Dummies®	Bill Marken & NGA	0-7645-5056-X	$16.99 US/$24.99 CAN
Container Gardening For Dummies®	Bill Marken & NGA	0-7645-5057-8	$16.99 US/$24.99 CAN
Decks & Patios For Dummies®	Robert J. Beckstrom & NGA	0-7645-5075-6	$16.99 US/$24.99 CAN
Flowering Bulbs For Dummies®	Judy Glattstein & NGA	0-7645-5103-5	$16.99 US/$24.99 CAN
Gardening For Dummies®, 2nd Edition	Michael MacCaskey & NGA	0-7645-5130-2	$16.99 US/$24.99 CAN
Herb Gardening For Dummies®	NGA	0-7645-5200-7	$16.99 US/$24.99 CAN
Home Improvement For Dummies®	Gene & Katie Hamilton & the Editors of HouseNet, Inc.	0-7645-5005-5	$19.99 US/$26.99 CAN
Houseplants For Dummies®	Larry Hodgson & NGA	0-7645-5102-7	$16.99 US/$24.99 CAN
Painting and Wallpapering For Dummies®	Gene Hamilton	0-7645-5150-7	$16.99 US/$24.99 CAN
Perennials For Dummies®	Marcia Tatroe & NGA	0-7645-5030-6	$16.99 US/$24.99 CAN
Roses For Dummies®, 2nd Edition	Lance Walheim	0-7645-5202-3	$16.99 US/$24.99 CAN
Trees and Shrubs For Dummies®	Ann Whitman & NGA	0-7645-5203-1	$16.99 US/$24.99 CAN
Vegetable Gardening For Dummies®	Charlie Nardozzi & NGA	0-7645-5129-9	$16.99 US/$24.99 CAN
Home Cooking For Dummies®	Patricia Hart McMillan & Katharine Kaye McMillan	0-7645-5107-8	$19.99 US/$27.99 CAN

TECHNOLOGY TITLES

WEB DESIGN & PUBLISHING

Active Server Pages For Dummies®, 2nd Edition	Bill Hatfield	0-7645-0603-X	$24.99 US/$37.99 CAN
Cold Fusion 4 For Dummies®	Alexis Gutzman	0-7645-0604-8	$24.99 US/$37.99 CAN
Creating Web Pages For Dummies®, 5th Edition	Bud Smith & Arthur Bebak	0-7645-0733-8	$24.99 US/$34.99 CAN
Dreamweaver™ 3 For Dummies®	Janine Warner & Paul Vachier	0-7645-0669-2	$24.99 US/$34.99 CAN
FrontPage® 2000 For Dummies®	Asha Dornfest	0-7645-0423-1	$24.99 US/$34.99 CAN
HTML 4 For Dummies®, 3rd Edition	Ed Tittel & Natanya Dits	0-7645-0572-6	$24.99 US/$34.99 CAN
Java™ For Dummies®, 3rd Edition	Aaron E. Walsh	0-7645-0417-7	$24.99 US/$34.99 CAN
PageMill™ 2 For Dummies®	Deke McClelland & John San Filippo	0-7645-0028-7	$24.99 US/$34.99 CAN
XML™ For Dummies®	Ed Tittel	0-7645-0692-7	$24.99 US/$37.99 CAN
Javascript For Dummies®, 3rd Edition	Emily Vander Veer	0-7645-0633-1	$24.99 US/$37.99 CAN

DESKTOP PUBLISHING GRAPHICS/MULTIMEDIA

Adobe® In Design™ For Dummies®	Deke McClelland	0-7645-0599-8	$19.99 US/$27.99 CAN
CorelDRAW™ 9 For Dummies®	Deke McClelland	0-7645-0523-8	$19.99 US/$27.99 CAN
Desktop Publishing and Design For Dummies®	Roger C. Parker	1-56884-234-1	$19.99 US/$27.99 CAN
Digital Photography For Dummies®, 3rd Edition	Julie Adair King	0-7645-0646-3	$24.99 US/$37.99 CAN
Microsoft® Publisher 98 For Dummies®	Jim McCarter	0-7645-0395-2	$19.99 US/$27.99 CAN
Visio 2000 For Dummies®	Debbie Walkowski	0-7645-0635-8	$19.99 US/$27.99 CAN
Microsoft® Publisher 2000 For Dummies®	Jim McCarter	0-7645-0525-4	$19.99 US/$27.99 CAN
Windows® Movie Maker For Dummies®	Keith Underdahl	0-7645-0749-1	$19.99 US/$27.99 CAN

Dummies Books™
Bestsellers on Every Topic!

GENERAL INTEREST TITLES

EDUCATION & TEST PREPARATION

The ACT For Dummies®	Suzee Vlk	1-56884-387-9	$14.99 US/$21.99 CAN
College Financial Aid For Dummies®	Dr. Herm Davis & Joyce Lain Kennedy	0-7645-5049-7	$19.99 US/$27.99 CAN
College Planning For Dummies®, 2nd Edition	Pat Ordovensky	0-7645-5048-9	$19.99 US/$27.99 CAN
Everyday Math For Dummies®	Charles Seiter, Ph.D.	1-56884-248-1	$14.99 US/$21.99 CAN
The GMAT® For Dummies®, 3rd Edition	Suzee Vlk	0-7645-5082-9	$16.99 US/$24.99 CAN
The GRE® For Dummies®, 3rd Edition	Suzee Vlk	0-7645-5083-7	$16.99 US/$24.99 CAN
Politics For Dummies®	Ann DeLaney	1-56884-381-X	$19.99 US/$27.99 CAN
The SAT I For Dummies®, 3rd Edition	Suzee Vlk	0-7645-5044-6	$14.99 US/$21.99 CAN

AUTOMOTIVE

Auto Repair For Dummies®	Deanna Sclar	0-7645-5089-6	$19.99 US/$27.99 CAN
Buying A Car For Dummies®	Deanna Sclar	0-7645-5091-8	$16.99 US/$24.99 CAN

LIFESTYLE/SELF-HELP

Dating For Dummies®	Dr. Joy Browne	0-7645-5072-1	$19.99 US/$27.99 CAN
Making Marriage Work For Dummies®	Steven Simring, M.D. & Sue Klavans Simring, D.S.W	0-7645-5173-6	$19.99 US/$27.99 CAN
Parenting For Dummies®	Sandra H. Gookin	1-56884-383-6	$16.99 US/$24.99 CAN
Success For Dummies®	Zig Ziglar	0-7645-5061-6	$19.99 US/$27.99 CAN
Weddings For Dummies®	Marcy Blum & Laura Fisher Kaiser	0-7645-5055-1	$19.99 US/$27.99 CAN

TECHNOLOGY TITLES

SUITES

Microsoft® Office 2000 For Windows® For Dummies®	Wallace Wang & Roger C. Parker	0-7645-0452-5	$19.99 US/$27.99 CAN
Microsoft® Office 2000 For Windows® For Dummies® Quick Reference	Doug Lowe & Bjoern Hartsfvang	0-7645-0453-3	$12.99 US/$17.99 CAN
Microsoft® Office 97 For Windows® For Dummies®	Wallace Wang & Roger C. Parker	0-7645-0050-3	$19.99 US/$27.99 CAN
Microsoft® Office 97 For Windows® For Dummies® Quick Reference	Doug Lowe	0-7645-0062-7	$12.99 US/$17.99 CAN
Microsoft® Office 98 For Macs® For Dummies®	Tom Negrino	0-7645-0229-8	$19.99 US/$27.99 CAN
Microsoft® Office X For Macs® For Dummies®	Tom Negrino	0-7645-0702-8	$19.95 US/$27.99 CAN

WORD PROCESSING

Word 2000 For Windows® For Dummies® Quick Reference	Peter Weverka	0-7645-0449-5	$12.99 US/$19.99 CAN
Corel® WordPerfect® 8 For Windows® For Dummies®	Margaret Levine Young, David Kay & Jordan Young	0-7645-0186-0	$19.99 US/$27.99 CAN
Word 2000 For Windows® For Dummies®	Dan Gookin	0-7645-0448-7	$19.99 US/$27.99 CAN
Word For Windows® 95 For Dummies®	Dan Gookin	1-56884-932-X	$19.99 US/$27.99 CAN
Word 97 For Windows® For Dummies®	Dan Gookin	0-7645-0052-X	$19.99 US/$27.99 CAN
WordPerfect® 9 For Windows® For Dummies®	Margaret Levine Young	0-7645-0427-4	$19.99 US/$27.99 CAN
WordPerfect® 7 For Windows® 95 For Dummies®	Margaret Levine Young & David Kay	1-56884-949-4	$19.99 US/$27.99 CAN

SPREADSHEET/FINANCE/PROJECT MANAGEMENT

Excel For Windows® 95 For Dummies®	Greg Harvey	1-56884-930-3	$19.99 US/$27.99 CAN
Excel 2000 For Windows® For Dummies®	Greg Harvey	0-7645-0446-0	$19.99 US/$27.99 CAN
Excel 2000 For Windows® For Dummies® Quick Reference	John Walkenbach	0-7645-0447-9	$12.99 US/$17.99 CAN
Microsoft® Money 99 For Dummies®	Peter Weverka	0-7645-0433-9	$19.99 US/$27.99 CAN
Microsoft® Project 98 For Dummies®	Martin Doucette	0-7645-0321-9	$24.99 US/$34.99 CAN
Microsoft® Project 2000 For Dummies®	Martin Doucette	0-7645-0517-3	$24.99 US/$37.99 CAN
Microsoft® Money 2000 For Dummies®	Peter Weverka	0-7645-0579-3	$19.99 US/$27.99 CAN
MORE Excel 97 For Windows® For Dummies®	Greg Harvey	0-7645-0138-0	$22.99 US/$32.99 CAN
Quicken® 2000 For Dummies®	Stephen L . Nelson	0-7645-0607-2	$19.99 US/$27.99 CAN
Quicken® 2001 For Dummies®	Stephen L . Nelson	0-7645-0759-1	$19.99 US/$27.99 CAN
Quickbooks® 2000 For Dummies®	Stephen L . Nelson	0-7645-0665-x	$19.99 US/$27.99 CAN

Dummies Books™
Bestsellers on Every Topic!

GENERAL INTEREST TITLES

CAREERS

Cover Letters For Dummies®, 2nd Edition	Joyce Lain Kennedy	0-7645-5224-4	$12.99 US/$17.99 CAN
Cool Careers For Dummies®	Marty Nemko, Paul Edwards, & Sarah Edwards	0-7645-5095-0	$16.99 US/$24.99 CAN
Job Hunting For Dummies®, 2nd Edition	Max Messmer	0-7645-5163-9	$19.99 US/$26.99 CAN
Job Interviews For Dummies®, 2nd Edition	Joyce Lain Kennedy	0-7645-5225-2	$12.99 US/$17.99 CAN
Resumes For Dummies®, 2nd Edition	Joyce Lain Kennedy	0-7645-5113-2	$12.99 US/$17.99 CAN

FITNESS

Fitness Walking For Dummies®	Liz Neporent	0-7645-5192-2	$19.99 US/$27.99 CAN
Fitness For Dummies®, 2nd Edition	Suzanne Schlosberg & Liz Neporent	0-7645-5167-1	$19.99 US/$27.99 CAN
Nutrition For Dummies®, 2nd Edition	Carol Ann Rinzler	0-7645-5180-9	$19.99 US/$27.99 CAN
Running For Dummies®	Florence "Flo-Jo" Griffith Joyner & John Hanc	0-7645-5096-9	$19.99 US/$27.99 CAN

FOREIGN LANGUAGE

Spanish For Dummies®	Susana Wald	0-7645-5194-9	$24.99 US/$34.99 CAN
French For Dummies®	Dodi-Kartrin Schmidt & Michelle W. Willams	0-7645-5193-0	$24.99 US/$34.99 CAN

TECHNOLOGY TITLES

DATABASE

Access 2000 For Windows® For Dummies®	John Kaufeld	0-7645-0444-4	$19.99 US/$27.99 CAN
Access 97 For Windows® For Dummies®	John Kaufeld	0-7645-0048-1	$19.99 US/$27.99 CAN
Access 2000 For Windows For Dummies® Quick Reference	Alison Barrons	0-7645-0445-2	$12.99 US/$17.99 CAN
Approach® 97 For Windows® For Dummies®	Deborah S. Ray & Eric J. Ray	0-7645-0001-5	$19.99 US/$27.99 CAN
Crystal Reports 8 For Dummies®	Douglas J. Wolf	0-7645-0642-0	$24.99 US/$34.99 CAN
Data Warehousing For Dummies®	Alan R. Simon	0-7645-0170-4	$24.99 US/$34.99 CAN
FileMaker® Pro 4 For Dummies®	Tom Maremaa	0-7645-0210-7	$19.99 US/$27.99 CAN

NETWORKING/GROUPWARE

ATM For Dummies®	Cathy Gadecki & Christine Heckart	0-7645-0065-1	$24.99 US/$34.99 CAN
Client/Server Computing For Dummies®, 3rd Edition	Doug Lowe	0-7645-0476-2	$24.99 US/$34.99 CAN
DSL For Dummies®, 2nd Edition	David Angell	0-7645-0715-X	$24.99 US/$35.99 CAN
Lotus Notes® Release 4 For Dummies®	Stephen Londergan & Pat Freeland	1-56884-934-6	$19.99 US/$27.99 CAN
Microsoft® Outlook® 98 For Windows® For Dummies®	Bill Dyszel	0-7645-0393-6	$19.99 US/$28.99 CAN
Microsoft® Outlook® 2000 For Windows® For Dummies®	Bill Dyszel	0-7645-0471-1	$19.99 US/$27.99 CAN
Migrating to Windows® 2000 For Dummies®	Leonard Sterns	0-7645-0459-2	$24.99 US/$37.99 CAN
Networking For Dummies®, 4th Edition	Doug Lowe	0-7645-0498-3	$19.99 US/$27.99 CAN
Networking Home PCs For Dummies®	Kathy Ivens	0-7645-0491-6	$24.99 US/$35.99 CAN
Upgrading & Fixing Networks For Dummies®, 2nd Edition	Bill Camarda	0-7645-0542-4	$29.99 US/$42.99 CAN
TCP/IP For Dummies®, 4th Edition	Candace Leiden & Marshall Wilensky	0-7645-0726-5	$24.99 US/$35.99 CAN
Windows NT® Networking For Dummies®	Ed Tittel, Mary Madden, & Earl Follis	0-7645-0015-5	$24.99 US/$34.99 CAN

PROGRAMMING

Active Server Pages For Dummies®, 2nd Edition	Bill Hatfield	0-7645-0065-1	$24.99 US/$34.99 CAN
Beginning Programming For Dummies®	Wally Wang	0-7645-0596-0	$19.99 US/$29.99 CAN
C++ For Dummies® Quick Reference, 2nd Edition	Namir Shammas	0-7645-0390-1	$14.99 US/$21.99 CAN
Java™ Programming For Dummies®, 3rd Edition	David & Donald Koosis	0-7645-0388-X	$29.99 US/$42.99 CAN
JBuilder™ For Dummies®	Barry A. Burd	0-7645-0567-X	$24.99 US/$34.99 CAN
VBA For Dummies®, 2nd Edition	Steve Cummings	0-7645-0078-3	$24.99 US/$37.99 CAN
Windows® 2000 Programming For Dummies®	Richard Simon	0-7645-0469-X	$24.99 US/$37.99 CAN
XML For Dummies®, 2nd Edition	Ed Tittel	0-7645-0692-7	$24.99 US/$37.99 CAN

Dummies Books™
Bestsellers on Every Topic!

GENERAL INTEREST TITLES

THE ARTS

Art For Dummies®	Thomas Hoving	0-7645-5104-3	$24.99 US/$34.99 CAN
Blues For Dummies®	Lonnie Brooks, Cub Koda, & Wayne Baker Brooks	0-7645-5080-2	$24.99 US/$34.99 CAN
Classical Music For Dummies®	David Pogue & Scott Speck	0-7645-5009-8	$24.99 US/$34.99 CAN
Guitar For Dummies®	Mark Phillips & Jon Chappell of Cherry Lane Music	0-7645-5106-X	$24.99 US/$34.99 CAN
Jazz For Dummies®	Dirk Sutro	0-7645-5081-0	$24.99 US/$34.99 CAN
Opera For Dummies®	David Pogue & Scott Speck	0-7645-5010-1	$24.99 US/$34.99 CAN
Piano For Dummies®	Blake Neely of Cherry Lane Music	0-7645-5105-1	$24.99 US/$34.99 CAN
Shakespeare For Dummies®	John Doyle & Ray Lischner	0-7645-5135-3	$19.99 US/$27.99 CAN

HEALTH

Allergies and Asthma For Dummies®	William Berger, M.D.	0-7645-5218-X	$19.99 US/$27.99 CAN
Alternative Medicine For Dummies®	James Dillard, M.D., D.C., C.A.C., & Terra Ziporyn, Ph.D.	0-7645-5109-4	$19.99 US/$27.99 CAN
Beauty Secrets For Dummies®	Stephanie Seymour	0-7645-5078-0	$19.99 US/$27.99 CAN
Diabetes For Dummies®	Alan L. Rubin, M.D.	0-7645-5154-X	$19.99 US/$27.99 CAN
Dieting For Dummies®	The American Dietetic Society with Jane Kirby, R.D.	0-7645-5126-4	$19.99 US/$27.99 CAN
Family Health For Dummies®	Charles Inlander & Karla Morales	0-7645-5121-3	$19.99 US/$27.99 CAN
First Aid For Dummies®	Charles B. Inlander & The People's Medical Society	0-7645-5213-9	$19.99 US/$27.99 CAN
Fitness For Dummies®, 2nd Edition	Suzanne Schlosberg & Liz Neporent, M.A.	0-7645-5167-1	$19.99 US/$27.99 CAN
Healing Foods For Dummies®	Molly Siple, M.S. R.D.	0-7645-5198-1	$19.99 US/$27.99 CAN
Healthy Aging For Dummies®	Walter Bortz, M.D.	0-7645-5233-3	$19.99 US/$27.99 CAN
Men's Health For Dummies®	Charles Inlander	0-7645-5120-5	$19.99 US/$27.99 CAN
Nutrition For Dummies®, 2nd Edition	Carol Ann Rinzler	0-7645-5180-9	$19.99 US/$27.99 CAN
Pregnancy For Dummies®	Joanne Stone, M.D., Keith Eddleman, M.D., & Mary Murray	0-7645-5074-8	$19.99 US/$27.99 CAN
Sex For Dummies®	Dr. Ruth K. Westheimer	1-56884-384-4	$16.99 US/$24.99 CAN
Stress Management For Dummies®	Allen Elkin, Ph.D.	0-7645-5144-2	$19.99 US/$27.99 CAN
The Healthy Heart For Dummies®	James M. Ripple, M.D.	0-7645-5166-3	$19.99 US/$27.99 CAN
Weight Training For Dummies®	Liz Neporent, M.A. & Suzanne Schlosberg	0-7645-5036-5	$19.99 US/$27.99 CAN
Women's Health For Dummies®	Pamela Maraldo, Ph.D., R.N., & The People's Medical Society	0-7645-5119-1	$19.99 US/$27.99 CAN

TECHNOLOGY TITLES

MACINTOSH

Macs® For Dummies®, 7ᵗʰ Edition	David Pogue	0-7645-0703-6	$19.99 US/$27.99 CAN
The iBook™ For Dummies®	David Pogue	0-7645-0647-1	$19.99 US/$27.99 CAN
The iMac For Dummies®, 2nd Edition	David Pogue	0-7645-0648-X	$19.99 US/$27.99 CAN
The iMac For Dummies® Quick Reference	Jenifer Watson	0-7645-0648-X	$12.99 US/$19.99 CAN

PC/GENERAL COMPUTING

Building A PC For Dummies®, 2nd Edition	Mark Chambers	0-7645-0571-8	$24.99 US/$34.99 CAN
Buying a Computer For Dummies®	Dan Gookin	0-7645-0632-3	$19.99 US/$27.99 CAN
Illustrated Computer Dictionary For Dummies®, 4th Edition	Dan Gookin & Sandra Hardin Gookin	0-7645-0732-X	$19.99 US/$27.99 CAN
Palm Computing® For Dummies®	Bill Dyszel	0-7645-0581-5	$24.99 US/$34.99 CAN
PCs For Dummies®, 7th Edition	Dan Gookin	0-7645-0594-7	$19.99 US/$27.99 CAN
Small Business Computing For Dummies®	Brian Underdahl	0-7645-0287-5	$24.99 US/$34.99 CAN
Smart Homes For Dummies®	Danny Briere	0-7645-0527-0	$19.99 US/$27.99 CAN
Upgrading & Fixing PCs For Dummies®, 5th Edition	Andy Rathbone	0-7645-0719-2	$19.99 US/$27.99 CAN
Handspring Visor For Dummies®	Joe Hubko	0-7645-0724-9	$19.99 US/$27.99 CAN

FOR DUMMIES
BOOK REGISTRATION

Register This Book and Win!

We want to hear from you!

Visit **dummies.com** to register this book and tell us how you liked it!

✔ Get entered in our monthly prize giveaway.

✔ Give us feedback about this book — tell us what you like best, what you like least, or maybe what you'd like to ask the author and us to change!

✔ Let us know any other *For Dummies* topics that interest you.

Your feedback helps us determine what books to publish, tells us what coverage to add as we revise our books, and lets us know whether we're meeting your needs as a *For Dummies* reader. You're our most valuable resource, and what you have to say is important to us!

Not on the Web yet? It's easy to get started with *Dummies 101: The Internet For Windows 98* or *The Internet For Dummies* at local retailers everywhere.

Or let us know what you think by sending us a letter at the following address:

For Dummies Book Registration
Dummies Press
10475 Crosspoint Blvd.
Indianapolis, IN 46256

...FOR DUMMIES™

BESTSELLING
BOOK SERIES